Collins

German

Phrase Book & Dictionary

Other languages in the *Collins Phrase Book & Dictionary* series:

FRENCH
GREEK
ITALIAN
JAPANESE
PORTUGUESE
SPANISH

These titles are also published in a Language pack containing 60-minute CD and phrase book

HarperCollins*Publishers*
Westerhill Road,
Bishopbriggs, Glasgow G64 2QT

www.collins.co.uk

First published 2005

Reprint 10 9 8 7 6 5 4 3 2 1 0

© HarperCollins*Publishers* 2004

ISBN 0 00-717978-2

Typeset by Davidson Pre-Press Graphics Ltd, Glasgow

Printed in Italy by Amadeus Srl

Introduction

Your *Collins Phrase Book & Dictionary* is a handy, quick-reference guide that will help you make the most of your stay abroad. Its clear layout will save you valuable time when you need that crucial word or phrase. There are four main sections in this book:

Everyday Germany – photoguide

Packed full of photos, this section allows you to see all the practical visual information that will help with using cash machines, driving on motorways, reading signs, etc.

Phrases

Practical topics are arranged thematically with an opening section Key talk containing vital phrases that should stand you in good stead in most situations.

Phrases are short, useful and each one has a pronunciation guide so that there is no problem saying them.

Eating out

This section contains phrases for ordering food and drink (and special requirements) plus a photoguide showing different eating places, menus and practical information to help choose the best options. The menu reader allows you to work out what to choose.

Dictionary

The practical 5000-word English-German and German-English Dictionary means that you won't be stuck for words.

And finally, there is a short Grammar section explaining how the language works.

So, just flick through the pages to find the information you need. Why not start with a look at Pronouncing German on page 6. From there on the going is easy with your *Collins Phrase Book & Dictionary*.

Useful websites

Currency Converters
www.x-rates.com

Foreign Office Advice
www.fco.gov.uk/travel/
countryadvice.asp

Passport Office
www.ukpa.gov.uk

Health advice
www.thetraveldoctor.com
www.doh.gov.uk/traveladvice

Pets
www.defra.gov.uk/animalh/
quarantine

Weather
www.bbc.co.uk/weather

Transport
www.bahn.de (German railway)
www.eurostar.com (Channel Tunnel)
www.lufthansa.co.uk (German airline)
www.germanwings.com (German budget airline)
www.dfdsseaways.co.uk (ferry)
www.poferries.com (ferry)
www.superfast.com (ferry)

Driving
www.drivingabroad.co.uk
www.tank.rast.de (German motorway service stations, with route planner)

Tourism/Sightseeing
www.germany-tourism.de (tourist board)
www.germany-info.org

www.bayern.by (guide to Bavaria)
www.berlin-tourist-information.com
www.hamburg-tourism.de
www.koeln.de (Cologne)
www.muenchen.de (Munich)
www.unesco-welterbe.de (Unesco world heritage sites in Germany)
www.k-d.com (Rhine cruises)
Austrian National Tourist Office:
www.austria-tourism.at
Switzerland Tourism:
www.myswitzerland.com

Accommodation
www.hrs.com (hotel reservation service)
www.bed-and-breakfast.de
www.djh.de (youth hostels)
www.landtourismus.de (farm holidays)

Internet Cafés
www.cybercafes.com

Culture & Activities
www.oktoberfest.de
www.germany-christmas-market.org.uk (about German Christmas markets)
www.smb.spk-berlin.de (site of the 16 national museums in Berlin)
www.deutsches-museum.de (museum of technology and science in Munich)
www.gastroscout.com (restaurant guide for Germany, Austria and Switzerland)
www.germanwine.de

Contents

Pronouncing German

We've tried to make the pronunciation under the phrases as clear as possible. We've split up words to make them easy to read, but don't pause too long between the syllables. German is not all that hard to pronounce and once you get the hang of unfamiliar letters or letter combinations, you should find yourself reading straight from the German.

You'll notice some differences in the way the language is written. The most obvious is that all nouns begin with capital letters. There is also a letter which doesn't exist in English – ß – which is like **ss**.

Most letters are pronounced in much the same way as their English equivalents. However, when they appear at the end of a word **b** *is pronounced like* **p**, **d** *like* **t**, *and* **g** *like* **k**; *and* **v** *is pronounced like* **f**. **S** *is pronounced like* **sh** *in* **shock** *before* **p** *and* **t** *when they are at the beginning of a word, and when it is combined with* **ch**.

The umlaut ¨ often appears over German vowels and makes a difference to the pronunciation. Two sounds, **ö** *and* **ü**, *are rather different from anything in English. We show* **ö** *as* **ur'** *because the nearest sound to it is in English words like 'hurt', but don't roll the* **r**! *The sound of* **ü** *can be made if you purse your lips and try to say* **ee**. *We give this sound as* **oo** *in the pronuciation.*

A final **e** *is always pronounced, and sounds like* **a** *in* sof**a** *or* **e** *in* Porsch**e**. *So German 'bitte' sounds like English 'bitter' (but without the r).*

The syllable to be stressed is the one in **heavy type**.

Here are a few other rules to be aware of:

German	sounds like	example	pronunciation
au	*ow*	**Auto**	*owto*
äu	*oy*	**Säule**	*zoy-le*
ch	*kh*	**ich**	*ikh*
ei	*'eye'*	**ein**	*ine*
		zwei	*tsvy*
ie	*ee*	**sie**	*zee*
eu	*oy*	**neun**	*noyn*

Everyday Germany

OPEN

Small shops tend to close between 12.30 and 2.30pm, but stay open later till about 6pm, Mon-Fri. Most close on Sat afternoon and all day Sun. There is no Sunday shopping in Germany.

CLOSED

Geschlossen
von 13.00 bis 14.30 Uhr

from   to   hour

OPENING HOURS

Geschäftszeiten:

		Uhr
Montag:	9.00 - 12.30	Uhr
Dienstag:	9.00 - 12.30	Uhr
Mittwoch:		Uhr
Donnerstag:	8.30-12.30	14.30-18.00 Uhr
Freitag:	8.30-12.30	14.30-18.00 Uhr
Samstag:	8.30-12.30	Uhr

ENTRANCE

EINGANG

NO EXIT
Kein means 'no'.

KEIN AUSGANG

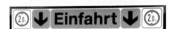

ENTRANCE (for vehicle)

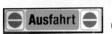

EXIT (for vehicle)

Fahrt comes from *fahren* ('to drive'), so *Einfahrt* and *Ausfahrt* are used on road signs. *Gang* comes from *gehen* ('to walk'), so you see *Eingang* and *Ausgang* on signs for pedestrians.

Kasse→

PAY HERE
Kasse means 'till/check out'.

PLEASE

bitte

The word for 'forbidden' or 'prohibited' is *verboten*.

PUSH

Drücken

PULL

Ziehen

Deutsche means German. Germany is *Deutschland*.

Zutritt
verboten

NO ADMITTANCE

Symbol for the euro. Germany is in the eurozone. The euro replaced the former *Deutschmark*.

Prices are generally written with a comma. This is 3 euro and 70 cents per kilo. Germany is metric so weights are in kilos.

Most banks can be identified by the word *Bank* or *Sparkasse*. Among the big banks in Germany are *Sparkasse*, *Deutsche Bank* and *Dresdner Bank*.

Geldwechsel and *Reise Bank* are both bureau de change.

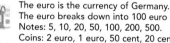

OPENING TIMES
These may vary from bank to bank. Generally they resemble office hours rather than shop hours, i.e. from about 9am to 4pm (Mon-Fri). Most banks open longer on Thursdays (until 5.30pm). All are closed on Sat and Sun.

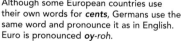
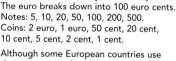

The euro is the currency of Germany. The euro breaks down into 100 euro cents. Notes: 5, 10, 20, 50, 100, 200, 500. Coins: 2 euro, 1 euro, 50 cent, 20 cent, 10 cent, 5 cent, 2 cent, 1 cent.

Although some European countries use their own words for *cents*, Germans use the same word and pronounce it as in English. Euro is pronounced *oy-roh*.

Euro notes are the same throughout Europe. The backs of coins carry different designs from each of the member European countries.

Cash machines operate as at home.

Abbruch = cancel

Korrektur = error

Bestätigung = proceed

Geldautomat

CASHPOINT (ATM)

PLEASE SELECT

Bitte wählen Sie

PAY WITH

zahlbar mit

RECEIPT

HIRSCH APOTHEKE

PHARMACY
Sign for the pharmacy. If you know roughly what is wrong, speak to a pharmacist. They can help with advising treatment. Note that in Germany, supermarkets do not sell medicines.

Automat gibt Rückgeld

CHANGE GIVEN

NO SMOKING ZONE
Smoking is not allowed in public buildings except in areas where ashtrays are provided. Only some restaurants have a dedicated non-smoking area.

There is usually one pharmacy open for emergencies (*Notdienst*).

HOSPITAL You have to ring a local number for an ambulance (displayed in phone boxes), but if you need it urgently, you can ring the fire brigade on 112.

 NOTAUFNAHME

The Accident & Emergency department is called the *Notaufnahme*.

Everyday Germany

zu vermieten TO RENT

ACCOMMODATION

Gasthof

A *Gasthof* is usually a pub or winebar that has rooms.

A *Hotel garni* is a small hotel offering bed and breakfast prices.

HOTEL
—— GARNI ——
☎ 06326 / 708 - 0

PENSION

A *Pension* is like a guesthouse.

Tourist offices can help with accommodation.

ZIMMER

ROOMS/VACANCIES

Empfang

RECEPTION

Germans are very recycling-conscious and you must use the correct bin for rubbish.

brown = biodegradable
blue = paper
black = general waste
yellow = packaging carrying recycling symbol (see below)

DER GRÜNE PUNKT

Ferien unter'm Rohrdach

Ferienhaus   Zimmer
frei   belegt

ACCOMMODATION

Ferienhaus
frei

Ferienhaus is a self-catering holiday house. *Frei* shows that there is availability.

Zimmer
belegt

The word *belegt* means that it is full up (no vacancies).

Postboxes are yellow. Post office opening hours are 8am to 6pm Monday to Friday and 8am to 2pm on Saturday.

verboten

PROHIBITED

Außer Betrieb

OUT OF ORDER

TOILETTEN
RESTROOMS

TOILETS

WC

There aren't very many public toilets around in Germany. Wherever you go, you will be expected to pay or at least leave a tip for the attendants. Check out shopping centres for toilets and some department stores will have them. In bigger cities, make for public buildings such as the railway station if you are looking for a toilet. You can also follow the city signpost system. In most petrol stations you will have to ask the attendant for the key to the toilet.

DAMEN

LADIES

HERREN

GENTS

Ladies and mens toilets are generally shown with a pictogram.

Trinkwasser

DRINKING WATER
The word for water is
Wasser (*vas-ser*).

heiß

HOT

kalt

COLD

besetzt

ENGAGED

frei

VACANT

11

TAGE	DAYS		MONATE	MONTHS
Montag *mon*-tahk	Monday		Januar *yan*-ooar	January
Dienstag *deens*-tahk	Tuesday		Februar *feb*-rooar	February
Mittwoch *mit*-vokh	Wednesday		März *mehrts*	March
Donnerstag *donn*ers-tahk	Thursday		April ap-*reel*	April
Freitag *fry*-tahk	Friday		Mai *mye*	May
Samstag *zams*-tahk	Saturday		Juni *yoo*-nee	June
Sonntag *zon*-tahk	Sunday		Juli *yoo*-lee	July
			August ow-*goost*	August
			September sep-*tem*ber	September
			Oktober ok-*to*ber	October
			November no-*vem*ber	November
			Dezember dayt-*sem*ber	December

Abbreviations for days of the week on a duty pharmacy sign.

WEEKLY MARKET

Tue, Fri, Sat 7am–2pm

TIMETABLE

TODAY   **TOMORROW**

Fahrkarten

TICKETS
(for public transport)

KARTEN HIER ERHÄLTLICH!

BUY TICKETS HERE!

Karten is the general word for 'tickets'.

Busfahrkarten

BUS TICKETS

ReiseZentrum

You can buy tickets and get information here.

TRAVEL CENTRE

Ankunft

ARRIVALS
abbreviated to *an*

DEPARTURES
abbreviated to *ab*

Abfahrt

VALIDATE HERE

You have to validate any ticket you buy for public transport in a validating machine. These are found at the entrance of buses, train platforms and metro stations. Simply insert your ticket in the slot for punching.

CHOOSE YOUR TICKET TYPE

Zuschlag supplement

2. Wählen Sie bitte Ihre Fahrkarte

Einzelfahrt	Tageskarte	Sammelkarte	Zuschlag
zum sofortigen Fahrtantritt	gültig ab Kauf bis Betriebsschluß	vor Fahrtantritt entwerten	(pro Person) zusätzlich zur Fahrkarte
Taste drücken	Taste drücken	Taste drücken	Taste drücken

Einzelfahrt single ticket

Tageskarte day ticket

Sammelkarte multiple tickets
(must validate for each journey)

YOU ARE HERE

TOWN HALL

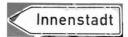

TOWN CENTRE

RECHTS

RIGHT

The numbers under the sign tell you the house numbers you can find.

OLD PART OF TOWN

LINKS

LEFT

CATHEDRAL

Pedestrian city signs

Street signs are usually blue and white. They often have additional info about the person or event the street was named after.

RAILWAY STATION

Distances are in kilometres. Yellow roadsigns are for out of town destinations.

NORTH

Nord

WEST
West

EAST
Ost

Süd

SOUTH

Most German cities operate an integrated transport system which means that all the different kinds of transport are part of one network and you can use any of them with your ticket. You buy your ticket in advance and validate it in the machine when you get on board the bus or tram. With the *U-Bahn* and *S-Bahn* you validate your ticket on entering the station or platform. You can find ticket machines at some bus stops. The word for stop is *Haltestelle* (hence the *H*).

TO THE TRAINS

← zu den Zügen

METRO

Lines are colour-coded and numbered.

Richtung

Richtung means direction

U-Bahn is the underground system.
S-Bahn is the suburban train system.

Hauptbahnhof   **MAIN STATION**

DEPARTURE BOARD

Zeit	Zuglauf	Ziel	Gleis	Hinweis
10 56	S1			
10 57	ICE		FRANKFURT HÖCHST	20
11 02	RB		HAMBURG-ALTONA	
11 03	IR		HANAU	
			DÜSSELDORF	

10 54 Departure **Abfahrt** Départ

GLEIS
2

PLATFORM

time   via   destination   platform   further info

ROAD SIGNS

Motorway signs are blue and numbered.

Secondary roads signposted in yellow and local destinations in white.

A green sign with E and a number indicates that it is a European route.

DIVERSION

Petrol stations sell parking disks. It works in 30-minute blocks: always rotate the arrow so it points to the next half hour or hour from your start time.

You can park for 2 hours (**2 Std.**). **Std** is an abbreviation for **Stunden** (hours). Restriction applies weekdays 9am to 6pm.

SPEED RESTRICTIONS

built up area   50 km/h
ordinary roads   100 km/h
motorway   no restriction, but 130km/h is recommended and some sections will have speed restrictions.

Where you see this sign you must give way to the priority road. Drivers on the priority road must indicate when turning. Drivers on the top secondary road must yield to drivers on the bottom, as they are on their right. The yellow diamond indicates a priority road.

mit Parkschein means its a pay and display zone.

A multi-storey car park is called a **Parkhaus**. Note the roof over the P.

Motorway signs are in blue. 66 is the number of the motorway.

This symbol indicates the exit number.

Ausfahrt EXIT

If you break down on the motorway, put on your warning lights

and place your warning triangle about 100 m behind the car. An arrow on the distance indicator will show you which way the nearest phone is.
It is never more than 1 km away. The police will arrange for a recovery vehicle to come to you.

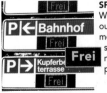

SPACES Watch out, *Frei* means spaces not free parking!

Unlike German motorways, Austrian and Swiss motorways are not free.

Autobahn

MOTORWAY

Austrian motorway toll sticker for sale (valid for 10 days, 2 months or one year).
In Switzerland you buy a sticker that is valid for one year.

WATER AIR

PETROL

Benzin PETROL

bleifrei UNLEADED

Diesel DIESEL

Netto is a supermarket chain

Fleischer is a butcher's

Bäcker is a baker's

Shop hours are generally 8am to 6pm Monday to Friday and 8am to 4pm on Saturday. There is no Sunday opening (except in tourist areas where shops selling holiday items may be open). Petrol stations selling snacks, bread, drinks, etc, are open on Sundays. Baker's can also open on Sunday mornings.

PAY HERE

PLEASE LEAVE YOUR BAG IN THE CAR

REDUCTIONS

At supermarkets you aren't allowed to take any bags (except handbags) in with you. If you need plastic carriers, you have to pay for them.

Lassen Sie bitte Ihre Taschen im Auto

In most supermarkets you have to use a coin (usually 1 euro) or a special plastic coin to release the trolley.

WEEKLY MARKET
Tue, Fri, Sat from 7am to 2pm. These times vary from town to town, but most of them have a market on Saturday.

Untergeschoss
BASEMENT `UG`

Erdgeschoss
GROUND FLOOR `EG`

1. Obergeschoss
FIRST FLOOR `1.OG`

BREAD

You can find many varieties of bread in Germany.
Schwarzbrot = very dark bread
Vollkornbrot = wholemeal bread
Weißbrot = white bread

ORGANIC

Health food shops selling many organic products are called ***Reformhaus***.

NUTRITION LABELS

kjoules	Kilojoule (kJ)	111
calories	Kilokalorien (kcal)	26
protein	Eiweiß	0,7g
carbohydrates	Kohlenhydrate	5,6g
fat	Fett	0,1g

MILK

Vollfettmilch FULL FAT MILK

Halbfettmilch SEMI-SKIMMED MILK

Magermilch SKIMMED MILK

GLUTEN-FREE

Glutenfreies Produkt

FRUIT/VEGETABLES

OBST / GEMÜSE
Karin Ohler

nur means 'only'; *ab* means 'from' and ***Stück*** means 'each'.

Auch für Mikrowelle

Suitable to microwave.

Postboxes are yellow. Collection times are marked. A red dot indicates a Sunday collection.
It should also list the nearest postbox (**nächster Briefkasten**) with collection times.

BRIEFEINWURF

LETTERBOX

German post office logo. The word for post office is **die Post**.

There are internet cafés in most cities. The most common service providers are T-Online and AOL. German websites end in **.de** for **Deutschland**.

Most payphones take phonecards. Ones that take coins are becoming rare.

Familie Grün
Berliner Str. 23
65205 Wiesbaden
Deutschland

Addressing an envelope:

Str. = abbrev for **Straße** street
postcode town
Germany.

International dialling codes

UK 00 44	Australia 00 61
USA/Canada 00 1	Germany 00 49
Austria 00 43	Switzerland 00 41

LUFTPOST

AIRMAIL

German phone numbers are given in single digits.

21	882	03	48
zwei, eins	acht, acht, zwei	null, drei	vier, acht

Germans use 'at' as in English.

 www dot is
veh veh
veh poonkt

- Among friends you will hear **hallo!** or **hi!** and **tschüss!** ('bye') but avoid these unless you know the person well.
- In southern Germany and Austria you often hear the greeting **Grüß Gott** for 'hello'.
- In Switzerland you will hear **Grüezi** for **hello** and **Ade** for 'goodbye'.

yes ja *ya*	**no** nein *nine*	**that's fine** das ist gut so *das ist goot zoh*
please bitte *bi-te*	**thank you** danke *dang-ke*	**a pleasure!** bitte! *bi-te*
hello guten Tag *gooten tahk*	**goodbye** auf Wiedersehen *owf veeder-zayn*	**goodnight** gute Nacht *goote nakht*
excuse me Entschuldigung *entshool-digoong*	**sorry** Verzeihung *fer-tsy-oong*	**pardon?** wie bitte? *vee bi-te*

Here is an easy way to ask for something ... just add **bitte**

a... einen... ('der' words) *ine-en...*	**a coffee** einen Kaffee *ine-en kafay*	**2 coffees** zwei Kaffee *tsvy kafay*
a... eine... ('die' words) *ine-e...*	**a bottle** eine Flasche *ine-e fla-she*	**2 bottles** zwei Flaschen *tsvy fla-shen*
a... ein... ('das' words) *ine...*	**a Pils** ein Pils *ine pils*	**2 Pils** zwei Pils *tsvy pils*

a coffee and two Pils, please
einen Kaffee und zwei Pils, bitte
ine-en kafay oont tsvy pils bi-te

Key Talk

- To catch someone's attention use **Entschuldigung!**
  You can use the same word for 'sorry' when bumping into someone, etc.
- **Bitte** means 'please' but **bitte schön** or **bitte sehr** is also used for 'here you are' when passing something to somebody.

I'd like...
ich möchte...
*ikh **mur'kh**-te...*

we'd like...
wir möchten...
*veer **mur'kh**-ten...*

I'd like an ice cream
ich möchte ein Eis
*ikh **mur'kh**-te ine ice*

we'd like to visit Potsdam
wir möchten Potsdam besuchen
*veer **mur'kh**-ten **pots**-dam be**zoo**khen*

do you have ...?
haben Sie...?
***hah**-ben zee...*

do you have any milk?
haben Sie Milch?
***hah**-ben zee milkh*

do you have stamps?
haben Sie Briefmarken?
***hah**-ben zee **breef**-marken*

do you have a map?
haben Sie eine Landkarte?
***hah**-ben zee **ine**-e **lant**-kar-te*

do you have salami?
haben Sie Salami?
hah**-ben zee zala**mee

how much is it?
was kostet das?
*vas **kos**tet das*

how much does ... cost?
was kostet...?
*vas **kos**tet...*

how much is the cheese?
was kostet der Käse?
*vas **kos**tet der **kay**-ze*

how much is the room?
was kostet das Zimmer?
*vas **kos**tet das **tsim**mer*

how much is a kilo?
was kostet ein Kilo?
*vas **kos**tet ine **kee**lo*

how much is it each?
was kostet es pro Stück?
*vas **kos**tet es pro shtook*

● Germans tend to be more formal than the British or Americans and there is also some truth in the cliché that Germans are compulsive law abiders. Jay walking is not very common and littering is subject to very high fines in some cities.
● Germany is very recycling conscious. There are different coloured bins for different types of rubbish.

where is...?
wo ist...?
voh ist...

where are...?
wo sind...?
voh zint...

where is the station?
wo ist der Bahnhof?
*voh ist der **bahn**-hof*

where are the toilets?
wo sind die Toiletten?
*voh zint dee twa-**le**-ten*

is/are there ...?
gibt es ...?
gipt es...

is there a restaurant?
gibt es ein Restaurant?
*gipt es ine restoh-**rong***

where's there a chemist?
wo gibt es eine Apotheke?
*voh gipt es **ine**-e apoh-**tay**-ke*

are there reductions?
gibt es Ermäßigung?
*gipt es er-**may**-sigoong*

is there a golf course?
gibt es einen Golfplatz?
*gipt es **ine**-en **golf**-plats*

there is/are no...
es gibt kein (*das*)/keinen (*der*)/keine (*die & plural*)...
*es gipt **ki**ne/**kine**-en/**kine**-e...*

there is no hot water
es gibt kein heißes Wasser
*es gipt kine **hy**-ses **vas**ser*

there are no towels
es gibt keine Handtücher
*es gipt **kine**-e **hant**-tookher*

I need...
ich brauche...
*ikh **brow**-khe...*

I need help
ich brauche Hilfe
*ikh **brow**-khe **hil**-fe*

I need a receipt
ich brauche eine Quittung
*ikh **brow**-khe **ine**-e **kvi**-toong*

Key Talk

● Politeness and respect are very important to Germans. You always shake hands on meeting (especially for the first time). Normally the older person proffers their hand first.
● Except among friends and young people, the transition from the formal **Sie** to the informal **du** has to be mutually agreed and is often sealed with a toast.

can I...
kann ich...
kan ikh...

can I phone?
kann ich telefonieren?
kan ikh taylay-fo-neeren

can I book a ticket?
kann ich ein Ticket buchen?
kan ikh ine ticket boo-khen

where can I...?
wo kann ich...?
voh kan ikh...

where can I buy tickets?
wo kann ich Karten kaufen?
voh kan ikh kar-ten kowfen

where can I hire a bike?
wo kann ich ein Fahrrad leihen?
voh kan ikh ine fah-rat lye-en

when?
wann?
van

when is breakfast?
wann gibt es Frühstück?
van gipt es froo-shtook

when is lunch?
wann gibt es Mittagessen?
van gipt es mitahk-essen

when does it open?
wann ist geöffnet?
van ist ge-ur'fnet

when does it close?
wann wird geschlossen?
van virt geshlossen

yesterday
gestern
gestern

today
heute
hoy-te

tomorrow
morgen
morgen

this morning
heute morgen
hoy-te morgen

this afternoon
heute nachmittag
hoy-te nakh-mitahk

this evening
heute abend
hoy-te ahbent

is it open?
ist es geöffnet?
ist es ge-ur'fnet

is it closed?
ist es geschlossen?
ist es geshlossen

- Abbreviations for Mr and Mrs are **Hr.** for **Herr** and **Fr.** for **Frau. Fräulein** (Miss) is considered old-fashioned or even discriminatory nowadays. A woman of any age should be addressed as **Frau.**
- **Vorname** means 'first name', **Nachname** means 'surname'.
- Always use a person's title (Dr, Prof, etc), if you know it.

Familie Grün
Berliner Str. 23
65205 Wiesbaden
Deutschland

how are you?
wie geht es Ihnen?
*vee gayt es **ee**-nen*

fine, thanks. And you?
danke, gut. Und Ihnen?
***dang**-ke goot. oont **ee**-nen*

my name is...
mein Name ist...
*mine **nah**-me ist...*

what is your name?
wie ist Ihr Name?
*vee ist eer **nah**-me*

I don't understand
ich verstehe nicht
*ikh fer-**shtay**-e nikht*

do you speak English?
sprechen Sie Englisch?
***shpre**-khen zee **eng**-lish*

the meal was delicious
das Essen war köstlich
*das **es**-sen var **kur's**-tlich*

thanks for everything
danke für alles
***dan**-ke foor **a**-lez*

you have a beautiful house
sie haben ein schönes Haus
*zee **hab**-ben ine **shur'**nez hows*

we must stay in touch
wir müssen in Kontakt bleiben
*weer **moos**-sen een **kon**-takt **bly**ben*

here is my address
hier ist meine Adresse
*heer ist **mine**-e a-**dres**-se*

we'd like to come back
wir würden gerne wieder kommen
*veer **wur'd**-en **gehr**-ne **vee**-der **kom**-men*

Money – changing

- *The euro is the currency of Germany.*
- *Euro is pronounced **oy-roh** and cent as in English.*
- *You can use your cash card to get euros from cash machines if your card supports Maestro or Cirrus services.*
- *Cash machines (ATM) are called **Geldautomat** (**gelt**-owto-maht) in German.*

where can I change money?
wo kann ich Geld wechseln?
*voh kan ikh gelt **vek**-seln*

where is the nearest cash machine?
wo ist der nächste Geldautomat?
*voh ist der **naykh**-ste **gelt**-owto-maht*

where is the bank?
wo ist die Bank?
voh ist dee bank

when does the bank open?
wann macht die Bank auf?
van makht dee bank owf

when does the bank close?
wann macht die Bank zu?
van makht dee bank tsoo

is there a bureau de change?
gibt es einen Geldwechsel?
*gipt es **ine**-nen **gelt**-veksel*

I want to cash these traveller's cheques
ich möchte gern diese Reiseschecks einlösen
*ikh **mu'rkh**-te gern **dee**-ze **ry**-ze-sheks **ine**-lur'-zen*

what's the rate...?
wie ist der Kurs...?
vee ist der koors...

for pounds
für Pfund Sterling
*foor pfoont **ster**-ling*

for dollars
für Dollars
*foor **do**llars*

I want to change £50
ich möchte fünfzig Pfund wechseln
*ikh **mur'kh**-te **foonf**-tsikh pfoont **vek**-seln*

what's the commission?
wie hoch ist die Gebühr?
*vee hohkh ist dee ge-**boohr***

spending – Money

- Banks are usually open Mon–Fri 8.30am to 1pm and from 2pm to 4pm (5.30 on Thursdays).
- Banks are closed on Saturday and Sunday.
- Credit cards are accepted for most purchases, but are not used as widely as in the UK.
- Coins are **Münze**, notes are **Geldschein**.

how much is it?
was kostet das?
*vas **kos**tet das*

where can I pay?
wo kann ich bezahlen?
*voh kan ikh be**tsah**-len*

I want to pay
zahlen, bitte
***tsah**-len **bi**-te*

we want to pay separately
wir möchten einzeln bezahlen
*veer **mur'kh**-ten ine-tseln be**tsah**-len*

can I pay by credit card?
kann ich mit Kreditkarte bezahlen?
*kan ikh mit kre**deet**-kar-te be**tsah**-len*

do you accept traveller's cheques?
nehmen Sie Reiseschecks?
***nay**men zee **ry**-ze-sheks*

how much is it...?	**per person**	**per night**	**per kilo**
was kostet das...?	pro Person	pro Nacht	pro Kilo
*vas **kos**tet das...*	*pro per-**zon***	*pro nakht*	*pro **kee**-lo*

are service and VAT included?
sind Bedienung und Mehrwertsteuer inbegriffen?
*zint be-**dee**noong oont **mayr**-vayrt-shtoy-er **in**-be-griffen*

I need a receipt
ich brauche eine Quittung
*ikh **brow**-khe **ine**-e **kvi**-toong*

do you require a deposit?
nehmen Sie eine Kaution?
nay**men zee **ine**-e kow-**tsyohn

I've nothing smaller
ich habe es nicht kleiner
*ikh **hah**-be es nikht **kline**-er*

keep the change
stimmt so
shtimt zoh

27

Airport

- Most signs are in German and English and you may not need to speak any German.
- The German national airline is Lufthansa, their website is **www.lufthansa.co.uk**.
- You can find information on Swiss and Austrian airports at **www.europeforvisitors.com/switzaustria/**

to the airport, please
zum Flughafen, bitte
tsoom **flook**-hafen **bi**-te

how can I get into town?
wie komme ich in die Stadt?
vee **kom**me ikh in dee shtat

where do I get the bus to the town centre?
wo fährt der Bus zum Stadtzentrum ab?
voh fayrt der boos tsoom **shtat**-tsentroom ap

how much is it...?
was kostet die Fahrt...?
vas **kos**tet dee fahrt...

to the town centre
ins Stadtzentrum
ins **shtat**-tsentroom

to the airport
zum Flughafen
tsoom **flook**-hafen

where do I check in for...?
wo ist der Check-in für...?
voh ist der **check**-in foor...

which gate for the flight to...?
welches Gate hat der Flug nach...?
vel-khes gate hat der flook nakh...

boarding will take place at gate number...
Sie steigen von Gate Nummer ... ein
zee **shty**-gen fon gate noomer ... ine

go immediately to gate number...
gehen Sie sofort zu Gate Nummer...
gayen zee zo-**fort** tsoo gate noomer...

your flight is delayed
Ihr Flug hat Verspätung
eer flook hat fer-**shpay**-toong

Customs & Passports

- There is no restriction by quantity or value, on goods purchased by travellers in another EU country provided they are for their own personal use (this covers gifts). Check guidelines on **www.hmce.gov.uk**.
- EU citizens with nothing to declare can use the blue customs channels.

I have nothing to declare
ich habe nichts zu verzollen
*ikh **hah**-be nikhts tsoo fer-**tsoll**en*

here is...	**my passport**	**my green card**
hier ist...	mein Pass	meine grüne Versicherungskarte
heer ist...	*mine pass*	***mine**-e **groo**-ne fer-**zikh**-e-roongz-kar-te*

do I have to pay duty on this?
muss ich das verzollen?
*moos ikh das fer-**tsoll**en*

it's for my own personal use
es ist für meinen persönlichen Gebrauch
*es ist foor **mine**-en per-**zur'n**-likhen ge-**browkh***

we're on our way to...
wir sind auf der Durchreise nach...
*veer zint owf der **doorkh**-ry-ze nakh...*

the children are on this passport
die Kinder stehen in diesem Pass
*dee **kin**der **shtay**-en in **dee**-zem pass*

I'm...	**British** (m/f)	**Australian** (m/f)
Ich bin...	Brite/Britin	Australier/Australierin
ikh bin...	***bree**-te/**bree**-tin*	*ow**strah**lee-er/ow**strah**lee-er-in*

I have a visa
ich habe ein Visum
*ikh **hah**-be ine **vee**zoom*

Asking the Way – questions

- Remember to use the polite form **Sie** when addressing people.
- You can catch people's attention with **Entschuldigung!**
- Even if people don't approach you on their own initiative, don't be afraid to ask for help. Many Germans speak English and, once over any initial reserve, are very helpful.

excuse me, please
entschuldigen Sie, bitte
ent**shool**-digen zee **bi**-te

where is...?
wo ist...?
voh ist...

where is the nearest...?
wo ist der/die/das nächste...?
voh ist der/dee/das **naykh**-ste...

where are the toilets?
wo sind die Toiletten?
voh zint dee twa-**le**-ten

how do I get to...?
wie komme ich...?

vee **kom**me ikh...?

to the station
zum Bahnhof
   (der/das nouns)
tsoom **bahn**-hohf

to Bonn
nach Bonn
   (with places)
nakh bon

is this the right way to...?
bin ich hier richtig zum/zur/nach...?
bin ikh heer **rikh**tikh tsoom/tsoor/nakh...

to the castle
zur Burg (die nouns)
tsoor boork

is it far to the...?
ist es weit zum/zur/nach...?
ist es vite tsoom/tsoor/nakh...

is the beach far?
ist es weit zum Strand?
ist es vite tsoom strant

can I walk there?
kann ich dahin laufen?
kan ikh da**hin low**fen

is there a bus that goes there?
fährt ein Bus dahin?
fayrt ine boos da**hin**

I'm looking for...
ich suche...
ikh **zoo**khe...

we're looking for...
wir suchen...
veer **zoo**khen...

we're lost (on foot)
wir haben uns verlaufen
veer **hah**-ben oons fer-**low**fen

we're lost (in car)
wir haben uns verfahren
veer **hah**-ben oons fer-**fah**ren

answers – Asking the Way

- It's no use being able to ask the way if you're not going to understand the reply. We've tried to anticipate the likely answers, so listen carefully for these key phrases.
- As in all places, policemen, taxi drivers and bus drivers are good people to ask directions from.
- You can get free maps from tourist offices.

keep going straight ahead
gehen Sie immer geradeaus weiter
gay-en zee immer ge-rah-de-ows vye-ter

you have to turn round
kehren Sie um
kehr-ren zee oom

turn...
biegen Sie...
bee-gen zee...

right
rechts ab
rekhts ap

left
links ab
links ap

you go... *(on foot)*
gehen Sie...
gay-en zee...

towards...
in Richtung...
in rikh-toong...

as far as...
bis zu...
bis tsoo...

you go... *(driving)*
fahren Sie...
fah-ren zee...

right
nach rechts
nakh rekhts

left
nach links
nakh links

take...
nehmen Sie...
nay-men zee...

the first road on the right
die erste Straße rechts
dee ers-te shtrah-se rekhts

the second road on the left
die zweite Straße links
dee tsvye-te shtrah-se links

the road to...
die Straße nach...
dee shtrah-se nakh...

follow the signs for...
folgen Sie den Schildern nach...
fol-gen zee den shil-dern nakh...

Bus

● Bus and tram tickets can be purchased from ticket machines, tobacconists or sometimes from the bus driver.
● Multi-journey tickets (**Mehrfahrtenkarte**) and day tickets (**Tageskarte**) are also available.
● Central bus stations (**Busbahnhof**) are usually located near the main railway station (**Hauptbahnhof**).

where is the bus station?
wo ist der Busbahnhof?
*voh ist der **boos**-bahn-hohf*

where is the tram stop?
wo ist die Straßenbahnhaltestelle?
*voh ist dee **shtrah**senbahn-**hal**-te-shtel-le*

I want to go...
ich möchte...
*ikh **mur'kh**-te...*

to the station
zum Bahnhof (m)
*tsoom **bahn**-hohf*

to the museum
zum Museum (nt)
*zum moo-**zay**-oom*

to the art gallery
zur Kunsthalle (f)
*tsoor **koonst**-hal-le*

to Bonn
nach Bonn
nakh bon

does this bus go to... ?
fährt dieser Bus nach... ?
*fayrt **dee**-ser boos nakh...*

which bus do I take to get there?
mit welchem Bus komme ich dahin?
*mit **vel**-khem boos **kom**me ikh da**hin***

where does the bus go from?
wo fährt der Bus ab?
voh fayrt der boos ap

how often are the buses?
wie oft fahren die Busse?
*vee oft **fah**-ren dee **boo**-se*

when is the last bus?
wann geht der letzte Bus?
*van gayt der **let**-ste boos*

please tell me when to get off
sagen Sie mir bitte, wann ich aussteigen muss
***zah**gen zee meer **bi**-te van ikh **ows**-shtygen moos*

Underground

- **U** is the sign for the metro (**U-Bahn**), **S** is for the suburban trains (**S-Bahn**). Parts of the **U-Bahn** can also be overground.
- In many cities you can get **eine Touristenkarte** (which covers all public transport), or **eine Familienkarte** (2 adults, 2 children). Ask for **spezielle Fahrkarten**.
- **Die Innenstadt** is the inner city.

where is the nearest underground station?
wo ist die nächste U-Bahn-Haltestelle?
*voh ist dee **nay**kh-ste **oo**bahn-**hal**-te-shtel-le*

what special tickets are there?
welche speziellen Fahrkarten gibt es?
***vel**-khe shpe-tsee-**el**-len **fahr**-kar-ten gipt es*

a tourist ticket, please
eine Touristenkarte, bitte
***ine**-e too**ris**ten-karte **bi**-te*

inner zones
die Innenstadt
*dee **in**-nen-shtat*

all zones
alle Zonen
*al-le **tsoh**-nen*

do you have a map of the metro?
gibt es eine Karte mit allen U-Bahn-Linien?
*gipt es **ine**-e **kar**-te mit **al**-len **oo**-bahn-**lee**-nee-en*

I want to go to...
ich möchte zum/zur/nach...
*ikh **mur'kh**-te tsoom/tsoor/nakh...*

can I go by underground?
kann ich mit der U-Bahn fahren?
*kan ikh mit der **oo**bahn **fah**-ren*

do I have to change?
muss ich umsteigen?
*moos ikh **oom**-shtygen*

where?
wo?
voh

which line is it for...?
welche Linie fährt nach...?
***vel**-khe **lee**-nee-e fayrt nakh...*

what is the next stop?
was ist der nächste Halt?
*vas ist der **naykh**-ste halt*

which zones?
welche Zonen?
***vel**-khe **tsoh**-nen*

for the inner city or all zones?
für die Innenstadt oder für alle Zonen?
*foor dee **in**nen-shtat **oh**der foor **al**-le **tsoh**-nen*

Train

- Buy your ticket prior to boarding the train.
- Check if a supplement, **ein Zuschlag**, is required before you board the train. It costs less if you buy it with your ticket. There is usually a surcharge for the InterCity Express (ICE).
- It is usually a good idea to pre-book seats in advance on ICE trains during busy periods.

where is the station?
wo ist der Bahnhof?
*voh ist der **bahn**-hohf*

to the station, please
zum Bahnhof, bitte
*tsoom **bahn**-hohf bi-te*

a single to...
einmal einfach nach...
*ine-mal **ine**-fakh nakh...*

2 singles to...
zweimal einfach nach...
***tsvy**-mal **ine**-fakh nakh...*

a return to...
eine Rückfahrkarte nach...
*ine-e **rook**-fahr-kar-te nakh...*

2 returns to...
zweimal hin und zurück nach...
***tsvy**-mal hin oont tsoo-**rook** nakh...*

a child's return to...
eine Kinderrückfahrkarte nach...
*ine-e kinder-**rook**-fahr-kar-te nakh...*

1st class	**2nd class**	**Smoking**	**Non smoking**
erster Klasse	zweiter Klasse	Raucher	Nichtraucher
***er**-ster **kla**-se*	***tsvy**-ter **kla**-se*	***row**-kher*	***nikht**-row-kher*

do I have to pay a supplement?
muss ich einen Zuschlag zahlen?
*moos ikh **ine**-en **tsoo**shlak **tsah**len*

is my pass valid on this train?
ist mein Pass für diesen Zug gültig?
*ist mine pass foor **dee**zen tsook **gool**tikh*

I want to book...	**a seat**	**a couchette**
ich möchte ... buchen	einen Platz	einen Liegewagenplatz
*ikh **mur'kh-te** ... **boo**-khen*	*ine-en plats*	*ine-en **lee**-ge-vahgen-plats*

Train

2

- In Germany children under 6 always travel free, children between 6 and 14 also travel free if accompanied by parents and are included on their tickets.
- Visit **www.bahn.de** and click on 'int.guests' for lots of information in English including the timetable for Germany and many other countries. There is a booking centre in the UK at **www.bahn.co.uk**.

do you have a timetable?
haben Sie einen Fahrplan?
hah-ben zee ine-en fahr-plahn

do I need to change?
muss ich umsteigen?
moos ikh oom-shty-gen

where?
wo?
voh

which platform does it leave from?
von welchem Bahnsteig fährt er ab?
fon vel-khem bahn-shtike fayrt er ap

does the train to ... leave from here?
fährt hier der Zug nach ... ab?
fayrt heer der tsook nakh ... ap

is this the train for...?
ist das der Zug nach...?
ist das der tsook nakh...

where is the left-luggage?
wo ist die Gepäckaufbewahrung?
voh ist dee gepek-owf-bevahroong

is there a buffet on the train?
hat der Zug einen Speisewagen?
hat der tsook ine-en shpy-ze-vahgen

is this seat free?
ist hier noch frei?
ist heer nokh fry

this is my seat
das ist mein Platz
das ist mine plats

Taxi

- Most German taxis are cream with a yellow sign on the roof.
- In Germany to get a taxi you have to find a taxi rank, **Taxistand**, or phone for one.
- You can often find ads for taxi firms in phoneboxes: you must give your name and the address of the phonebox which is written under the word **Standort**.

to the airport, please
zum Flughafen, bitte
tsoom **flook**-hafen **bi**-te

to the station, please
zum Bahnhof, bitte
tsoom **bahn**-hohf **bi**-te

to this address, please
zu dieser Adresse bitte
tsoo **dee**zer a-**dre**-se **bi**-te

to hotel...
zum Hotel...
tsoom ho**tel**...

how much will it cost?
was wird das kosten?
vas virt das **kos**ten

why is it so much?
warum ist das so teuer?
vah**room** ist das zoh **toy**-er

how much is it to the centre?
was kostet die Fahrt ins Zentrum?
vas **kos**tet dee fahrt ins **tsen**troom

where can I get a taxi?
wo bekomme ich hier ein Taxi?
voh be-**kom**me ikh heer ine **ta**xi

please order me a taxi
bitte bestellen Sie mir ein Taxi
bi-te be-**shte**llen zee meer ine **ta**xi

straightaway
sofort
zo-**fort**

for ...
für ... Uhr
foor ... oor

I need a receipt
ich brauche eine Quittung
ikh **brow**-khe **ine**-e **kvi**-toong

I've nothing smaller
ich habe es nicht kleiner
ikh **hah**-be es nikht **kline**-er

keep the change
stimmt so
shtimt zoh

- The Swiss rail pass allows you reduced travel on the Swiss Lakes. Passes have to be purchased in your own country before arriving in Switzerland.
- A car ferry is an **Autofähre**.
- An outside cabin is **Außenkabine**, an inside cabin is an **Innenkabine**. A single cabin is a **Einzelkabine**.

1 ticket	**2 tickets**	**single**	**round trip**
einmal	zweimal	einfach	eine Rundfahrt
ine-mal	**tsvy**-mal	*ine*-fakh	*ine*-e **roont**-fahrt

is there a tourist ticket?
gibt es eine Touristenkarte?
*gipt es ine-e tooris*ten-kar-te

are there any boat trips?
gibt es Bootsausflüge?
gipt es boats-ows-floo-ge

how long is the trip?
wie lange dauert die Fahrt?
vee lang-e dow-ert dee fahrt

when is the next boat?
wann geht das nächste Schiff?
van gayt das naykh-ste shif

when is the next ferry?
wann geht die nächste Fähre?
van gayt dee naykh-ste fair-re

when is the first boat?
wann geht das erste Schiff?
van gayt das er-ste shif

when is the last boat?
wann geht das letzte Schiff?
van gayt das lets-te shif

where does the boat leave from?
wo fährt das Schiff ab?
voh fairt das shif ap

is there a timetable?
gibt es einen Fahrplan?
gipt es ine-en fahr-plahn

can we hire a boat?
können wir ein Boot mieten?
kur'-nen veer ine boat mee-ten

can we eat on board?
können wir an Bord essen?
kur'-nen veer an board es-sen

Car – driving

● Motorway tax (in sticker form – vignette) is payable in Switzerland and Austria.
  ● The Swiss tax is valid for one year and runs from 1 Dec to 31 Jan. It can be purchased at the border. For Austria there are stickers valid for ten days, two months or a year.
● Always have your car documents and passport with you.

can I park here?
kann ich hier parken?
*kan ikh heer **par**ken*

do I need a parking disk?
brauche ich eine Parkscheibe?
***brow**-khe ikh **ine**-e **park**-shy-be*

where can I park?
wo kann ich parken?
*voh kan ikh **par**-ken*

is there a car park?
gibt es einen Parkplatz?
*gipt es **ine**-en **park**-plats*

where can I get a parking disk?
wo kann ich eine Parkscheibe bekommen?
*voh kan ikh **ine**-e **park**-shy-be be-**kom**men*

how long can I park here?
wie lange kann ich hier parken?
*vee **lang**-e kan ikh heer **par**ken*

we're going to....
wir fahren nach...
*veer **fah**-ren nakh...*

what's the best route?
was ist der beste Weg?
*vas ist der **bes**-te vayk*

how do I get to the motorway?
wie komme ich zur Autobahn?
*vee **kom**-me ikh tsoor **ow**to-bahn*

which exit is it for...
welche Ausfahrt muss ich nach ... nehmen?
*vel-khe **ows**-fahrt muss ikh nakh ... **nay**-men*

is the pass open?
ist der Pass offen?
*ist der pass **of**fen*

do I need snow chains?
brauche ich Schneeketten?
***brow**-khe ikh **shnay**-ketten*

petrol station – Car

- Prices are higher at motorway filling stations in Germany. A cheaper alternative is an **Autohof** (truck-stop) which you find just off the motorway.
- It's against the law to run out of petrol on the **Autobahn**. Fines are on-the-spot and high.
- It is compulsory to carry a first-aid kit and warning triangle.

is there a petrol station near here?
ist hier in der Nähe eine Tankstelle?
*ist heer in der **nay**-e **ine**-e **tank**-shte-le*

fill it up, please
voll tanken, bitte
*fol **tang**-ken **bi**-te*

30 euro worth of unleaded petrol
für dreißig Euro bleifrei bitte
*foor **dry**-sikh **oy**-roh **bly**-fry **bi**-te*

which pump?
welche Säule?
***vel**-khe **zoy**-le*

pump number...
Säule Nummer...
***zoy**-le **noo**mer...*

where is the air line?
wo ist die Druckluft?
*voh ist dee **drook**-looft*

where is the water?
wo ist das Wasser?
*voh ist das **vas**ser*

please check...
bitte überprüfen Sie...
***bi**-te oober-**proof**en zee...*

the oil
das Öl
das ur'l

the tyre pressure
den Reifendruck
*den **ry**fen-drook*

the water
das Wasser
*das **vas**ser*

a token for wash number...
einen Chip für Waschprogramm Nummer...
***ine**-en chip foor **vash**-pro-gram **noo**mer...*

Car – problems/breakdown

- If you break down on the motorway in Germany you can call the roadside services from one of the orange emergency phones. Assistance is free, though any parts must be paid for.
- The police must be called to any accident whether there are injuries or not (dial 110).
- Fire and ambulance can be contacted on 112.

the road patrol, please
die Straßenwacht, bitte
*dee **shtra**sen-vakht **bi**-te*

I'm on my own
ich bin allein
*ikh bin **al**-line*

where is the nearest garage?
wo ist die nächste Werkstatt?
*voh ist dee **naykh**-ste **verk**-shtat*

is it serious?
ist es etwas Ernstes?
*ist es **et**vas **ern**-stes*

when will it be ready?
wann wird es fertig sein?
*van virt es **fer**-tikh zine*

the car won't start
das Auto springt nicht an
*das **ow**to shpringt nikht an*

the engine is overheating
der Motor wird zu heiß
*der **moh**tor virt tsoo hice*

I've broken down
ich habe eine Panne
*ikh **hah**-be **ine**-e **pa**-ne*

I have children in the car
ich habe Kinder dabei
*ikh **hah**-be **kin**der da-**by***

something is wrong with...
es stimmt etwas nicht mit...
*es shtimt **et**vas nikht mit...*

can you repair it?
können Sie es reparieren?
***kur'n**-en zee es raypa-**ree**ren*

how much will it cost?
was wird das kosten?
*vas virt das **kos**ten*

I have a flat tyre
ich habe einen Platten
*ikh **hah**-be **ine**-en **pla**-ten*

the battery is flat
meine Batterie ist leer
***mine**-e ba-te**ree** ist layr*

can you put in a new windscreen?
können Sie eine neue Windschutzscheibe einsetzen?
***kur'**-nen zee **ine**-e **noy**-e **vint**shoots-shy-be **ine**-zetsen*

hire – Car

- You can pre-book a car prior to your trip. This means you are guaranteed the car you want.
- To rent a car from most agencies in Germany you need to be at least 21 and have had your licence for at least a year.
- Check the insurance offered. The standard one is just 3rd party. For fully comprehensive you have to pay extra.

I want to hire a car
ich möchte ein Auto mieten
ikh **mur'kh**-te ine **ow**to **mee**ten

for one day
für einen Tag
foor **ine**-en tahk

for ... days
für ... Tage
foor ... **tah**-ge

how much is it?
was kostet es?
vas **kos**tet es

is fully comprehensive insurance included?
ist eine Vollkaskoversicherung inbegriffen?
ist **ine**-e **fol**-kasko-fer-**zikh**eroong **in**-be-griffen

do you have...?
haben Sie...?
hah-ben zee...

a larger car
ein größeres Auto
ine **grur'**-ser-es **ow**to

a smaller car
ein kleineres Auto
ine **kline**-e-res **ow**to

a cheaper car
ein billigeres Auto
ine **bil**-ig-er-es **ow**to

an automatic
eins mit Automatik
ines mit owto-**mah**-tik

what do we do if we break down?
was tun wir bei einem Unfall?
vas toon veer by **ine**-em **oon**fal

what petrol must I use?
was muss ich tanken?
vas mus ikh **tang**-ken

must I return the car here?
muss ich das Auto hierher zurückbringen?
moos ikh das **ow**to **heer**-her tsoo**rook**-bringen

by what time?
bis wann?
bis van

I'd like to leave it in...
ich würde es gern in ... abgeben
ikh **voor**-de es gern in ... **ap**-gayben

please show me the controls
bitte erklären Sie mir die Schalter
bi-te er-**klay**-ren zee meer dee **shal**-ter

where are the documents?
wo sind die Papiere?
voh zint dee pa**pee**re

Shopping – holiday

- Most large shops in Germany are open all day approx. 9am to 6pm Mon to Fri (with the largest ones staying open until 8pm). On Sat they are open until 4pm. Shops shut on Sun and public holidays. Late night shopping on Thurs.
- Christmas markets are great for handicrafts and culinary specialities. The most famous is in Nuremberg.

do you sell...?
verkaufen Sie...?
fer-**kow**fen zee...

stamps
Briefmarken
breef-mar-ken

batteries for this camera
Batterien für diese Kamera
ba-te**ree**-en foor **dee**-ze **ka**mera

where can I buy...?
wo bekomme ich...?
voh be-**kom**me ikh...

stamps
Briefmarken
breef-marken

films
Filme
filme

10 stamps
zehn Briefmarken
tsayn **breef**-marken

for postcards
für Postkarten
foor **post**-kar-ten

to Britain
nach England
nakh **eng**-lant

a colour film
einen Farbfilm
ine-en **farp**-film

a tape for this video camera
ein Videoband für diese Videokamera
ine **vee**day-o-bant foor **dee**-ze **vee**day-o-kamera

I'm looking for a present
ich suche ein Geschenk
ikh **zook**he ine ge**shenk**

have you anything else?
haben Sie noch etwas Anderes?
hah-ben zee nokh **et**vas **an**-de-res

it's a gift
es ist ein Geschenk
es ist ine ge**shenk**

please wrap it up
bitte verpacken Sie es
bi-te fer-**pak**-en zee es

is there a market?
gibt es einen Markt?
gipt es **ine**-en markt

when?
wann?
van

clothes – Shopping

● Department stores such as **Karstadt** offer a wide range of clothes (**Kaufhaus** means department store). You also find familiar chains such as Gap, but there are many smaller and more individualistic shops in German towns.
● You may find clothes sizes more generous in Germany than other European countries.

can I try this on?
kann ich das anprobieren?
*kan ikh das **an**proh-beeren*

where are the changing rooms?
wo sind die Umkleidekabinen?
*voh zint dee **oom**-kly-de-ka-**bee**nen*

it's too big
es ist zu groß
es ist tsoo grohs

have you anything smaller?
haben Sie etwas Kleineres?
***hah**-ben zee **et**vas **kline**-er-es*

it's too small
es ist zu klein
es ist tsoo kline

have you anything larger?
haben Sie etwas Größeres?
***hah**-ben zee **et**vas **grur'**-ser-es*

it's too expensive
es ist zu teuer
*es ist tsoo **toy**-er*

have you anything cheaper?
haben Sie etwas Billigeres?
***hah**-ben zee **et**vas **bil**-ig-er-es*

I'm just looking
ich schaue mich nur um
*ikh **show**-e mikh noor oom*

I'll take this one
ich nehme das hier
*ikh **nay**-me das heer*

I take size...
ich habe Größe...
*ikh **hah**-be **grur'**-se...*

I take size ... shoe
ich habe Schuhgröße...
*ikh **hah**-be **shoo**-grur'-se...*

what size are you?
welche Größe haben Sie?
***vel**-khe **grur'**-se **hah**-ben zee*

does it fit?
passt es?
past es

Shopping – food

- *Supermarkets are generally open from 8am to 8pm Mon-Fri, and from 8am to 4pm on Sat (closed Sun and public holidays).*
- *When supermarkets are closed you can still get essentials at some petrol stations.*
- *You need a coin (usually a euro) to release a trolley.*
- *You pay for plastic bags at the checkout.*

where can I buy...?
wo kann ich ... kaufen?
*voh kan ikh ... **kow**fen*

bread	**fruit**	**milk**
Brot	Obst	Milch
broht	*ohbst*	*milkh*

where is the baker's?
wo ist die Bäckerei?
*voh ist dee be-ke-**rye***

where is the supermarket?
wo ist der Supermarkt?
*voh ist der **su**per-markt*

where is the market?
wo ist der Markt?
voh ist der markt

when is the market?
wann ist Markt?
van ist markt

it's my turn next
ich bin dran
ikh bin dran

that's enough
das reicht
das rykht

a litre of ...
einen Liter...
***ine**-en **lee**ter...*

milk
Milch
milkh

water
Wasser
***vas**ser*

beer
Bier
beer

a bottle of...
eine Flasche...
***ine**-e **fla**-she...*

water
Wasser
***vas**ser*

wine
Wein
vine

sparkling wine
Sekt
sekt

a can of...
eine Dose...
***ine**-e **doh**-ze...*

coke
Cola
***co**la*

beer
Bier
beer

tonic water
Tonic
***to**nic*

a carton of...
einen Karton...
***ine**-en kar-tong...*

orange juice
Orangensaft
*o**ron**jen-saft*

apple juice
Apfelsaft
***ap**fel-saft*

milk
Milch
milkh

food – Shopping

- In most German towns there are weekly markets (**Wochenmarkt**), usually held on Sat (and another week day).
- Supermarkets often have a separate area for drinks and mineral waters (**Getränkemarkt**). Bottles and cans carry a deposit which you get back on returning them.
- Cash/debit card are the commonest ways to pay in supermarkets.

4oz/100 grams of...
hundert Gramm...
*hoon*dert gram...

cheese
Käse
kay-ze

ham
Schinken
shin-ken

half a pound of...
ein halbes Pfund...
ine **hal**-bes pfoont...

liver sausage
Leberwurst
leh-ber-voorst

minced pork
Schweinehack
shvy-nehak

a kilo of...
ein Kilo...
ine **kee**lo...

potatoes
Kartoffeln
kar-**tof**eln

apples
Äpfel
*ep*fel

8 slices of...
acht Scheiben...
akht **shy**-ben...

ham
Schinken
shin-ken

salami
Salami
sa**lam**ee

a portion of...
eine Portion...
ine-e por-tsy**ohn**...

sauerkraut
Sauerkraut
sauerkraut

salad
Salat
za**laht**

a packet of...
ein Päckchen...
ine **pek**-khen...

biscuits
Kekse
kayk-se

pumpernickel bread
Pumpernickel
poomper-nickel

a tin of...
eine Dose...
ine-e **doh**-ze...

tomatoes
Tomaten
to**mah**-ten

stew
Eintopf
ine-topf

a jar of...
ein Glas...
ine glahs...

jam
Marmelade
mar-me**lah**-de

olives
Oliven
o**lee**ven

gherkins
Gurken
goorken

Sightseeing

- Tourist offices organize city walks (**Stadtrundgänge**) and city bus tours (**Stadtrundfahrten**).
- Museums and galleries are open on Sundays, but are usually closed on Mondays.
- In cities with lots of tourist attractions, you can often buy tickets that allow you multiple entry.

where is the tourist office?
wo ist die Touristeninformation?
*voh ist dee too**ris**ten-infor-matsy**ohn***

we want to visit...
wir möchten ... besuchen
*veer **mur'kh**-ten ... be**zoo**khen*

when can we visit...?
wann können wir ... besichtigen?
*van **kur'**-nen veer ... be**zikh**-tigen*

what day does it close?
an welchem Tag ist es zu?
*an **vel**-khem tahk ist es tsoo*

we'd like to go to...
wir möchten nach...
*veer **mur'kh**-ten nakh...*

when does it leave?
wann ist die Abfahrt?
*van ist dee **ap**-fahrt*

how much is the entrance?
was kostet der Eintritt?
*vas **kos**tet der **ine**-trit*

have you any leaflets?
haben Sie Broschüren?
***hah**-ben zee bro-**shoo**ren*

how long is ... open?
wie lange ist ... geöffnet?
*vee **lan**-ge ist ... ge-**ar'f**-net*

are there any excursions?
gibt es Ausflugsfahrten?
*gipt es **ows**-flooks-fahrten*

where does it leave from?
wo ist die Abfahrt?
*voh ist dee **ap**-fahrt*

are there reductions for...?
gibt es Ermäßigung für...?
*gipt es er-**may**-sigoong foor...*

students	**seniors** *(pl)*
Studenten	Rentner
*shtoo-**den**ten*	***rent**ner*

- In the Baltic, a red ball on top of a pole indicates that it is too dangerous to swim. If the ball is halfway down, then it's dangerous for children but ok for adult swimmers.
- In southern Germany there are many outdoor swimming pools (**Freibad**).
- Designated nudist beaches are marked **FKK**.

which is a good beach?
welcher Strand ist gut?
vel-kher shtrahnt ist goot

how do I get there?
wie komme ich dahin?
*vee **komm**e ikh da**hin***

is there a swimming pool near here?
gibt es ein Schwimmbad in der Nähe?
*gipt es ine **shvim**-baht in der **nay**-e*

can we swim in the lake?
können wir im See baden?
*kur'-nen veer im zeh **bah**-den*

is the water clean?
ist das Wasser sauber?
*ist das **vas**ser **zow**-ber*

is the water deep?
ist das Wasser tief?
*ist das **vas**ser teef*

is the water cold?
ist das Wasser kalt?
*ist das **vas**ser kalt*

is it safe for children?
ist es sicher für Kinder?
*ist es **zi**kher foor **kin**der*

are there currents?
gibt es Strömungen?
*gipt es **shtrur'**-moong-en*

where can we...?
wo können wir...?
voh kur'-nen veer...

windsurf
windsurfen
***wint**-surfen*

waterski
Wasserski fahren
***vas**ser-shee **fah**-ren*

can we hire...?
können wir ... mieten?
*kur'-nen veer ... **mee**-ten*

a jetski
einen Jetski
***ine**-en **jet**ski*

a deck chair
einen Liegestuhl
***ine**-en **lee**-ge-shtool*

how do we hire a beach hut?
wie können wir einen Strandkorb mieten?
*vee **kur'**-nen veer **ine**-en **shtrant**-korb **mee**-ten*

Sport

- Most tourist offices will have details of local sports facilities.
- There are many well-marked walks (from gentle strolls to more strenuous Alpine hikes) in southern Germany. Check at local tourist offices for information and guides.
- There are over 200 signposted long-distance cycle routes throughout Germany with special bike lanes in most cities.

where can we...?
wo können wir...?
*voh **kur'**-nen veer...*

play tennis
Tennis spielen
***ten**nis **shpee**len*

play golf
Golf spielen
*golf **shpee**len*

go swimming
baden
***bah**-den*

hire bikes
Fahrräder leihen
***fah**-rehder **lye**-en*

go fishing
angeln
***ang**eln*

go riding
reiten
***ry**-ten*

how much is it...?
was kostet es...?
*vas **kos**tet es...*

per hour
pro Stunde
*pro **shtoon**-de*

per day
pro Tag
pro tahk

how do I book a court?
wie reserviere ich einen Platz?
*vee ray-zer-**vee**-re ikh **ine**-en plats*

can we hire rackets?
kann man Schläger leihen?
*kan man **shlay**-ger **lye**-en*

is there a guide to local walks?
gibt es einen Wanderführer von dieser Gegend?
*gipt es **ine**-en **van**der-foorer fon **dee**zer **gay**gent*

do I need walking boots?
brauche ich Wanderstiefel?
***brow**-khe ikh **van**der-shteefel*

how long is this walk?
wie lange dauert diese Wanderung?
*vee lang **dow**-ert **dee**-ze **van**-de-rung*

Skiing

- Switzerland and Austria offer many opportunities for winter sports.
- Germany has a number of winter sports areas where you can enjoy anything from downhill skiing to snowboarding and cross-country skiing.
- Check out **www.bbc.co.uk/weather** for snow information.

can I hire skis?
kann ich Skier leihen?
*kan ikh **shee**-er **lye**-en*

I'm a beginner
ich bin Anfänger
*ikh bin **an**-fenger*

is it safe to ski today?
ist das Skifahren heute ungefährlich?
*ist das **shee**-fahren **hoy**-te **oon**-gefayrlikh*

is there a map of the ski runs?
gibt es eine Pistenkarte?
*gipt es **ine**-e **pis**ten-kar-te*

how much is a pass?
was kostet ein Pass?
*vas **kos**tet ine pass*

which is an easy run?
welche Abfahrt ist einfach?
***vel**-khe **ap**-fahrt ist **ine**-fakh*

what is the snow like?
wie ist der Schnee?
vee ist der shnay

my skis are...	**too long**	**too short**
meine Skier sind...	zu lang	zu kurz
***mine**-e **shee**-er zint...*	*tsoo lang*	*tsoo koorts*

my bindings are...	**too loose**	**too tight**
meine Bindungen sind...	zu locker	zu fest
***mine**-e **bin**-doong-en zint...*	*tsoo **lo**cker*	*tsoo fest*

where can we go cross-country skiing?
wo können wir Langlauf fahren?
*voh **kur'**-nen veer **lang**-lowf **fah**-ren*

what length skis do you want?
welche Länge brauchen Sie?
***vel**-khe **leng**-e **brow**-khen zee*

what is your shoe size?
welche Schuhgröße haben Sie?
***vel**-khe **shoo**-grur'-se **hah**-ben zee*

Nightlife – popular

- Bars and discos in Germany are open till late. You have to be over 18 years to drink alcohol (and often to get into discos where ID card checks are common).
- Student clubs are open to the public at a slightly higher charge.
- Music festivals include the **Love Parade** in Berlin and the **Sound of Frankfurt**.

what is there to do at night?
was kann man abends machen?
*vas kan man **ah**bents **ma**khen*

which is a good bar?
welche Bar ist gut?
***vel**-khe bar ist goot*

where can we hear live music?
wo gibt es Live-Musik?
*voh gipt es **live**-moo-zeek*

is there a student club?
gibt es hier einen Studentenklub?
*gipt es heer **ine**-en shtoo-**den**ten-klup*

where do local people go at night?
wo gehen die Einheimischen abends hin?
*voh **gay**-en dee **ine**-hime-mee-shen **ah**bents hin*

is it a safe area?
ist die Gegend sicher?
*ist dee **gay**gent **zi**kher*

do you want to dance with me?
möchten Sie mit mir tanzen?
***mur'kh**-ten zee mit meer **tan**tsen*

would you like to go out tomorrow night?
möchten Sie morgen abend mit mir ausgehen?
***mur'kh**-ten zee **mor**gen **ah**bent mit meer **ows**-gay-en*

are there any concerts?
gibt es Konzerte?
*gipt es kon-**tser**te*

which is a good disco?
welche Disko ist gut?
***vel**-khe **dis**co ist goot*

is it expensive?
ist es teuer?
*ist es **toy**-er*

cultural – Nightlife

- A list of cultural events should be available from tourist offices or listed in the local paper.
- Germany has many music theatres with permanent ensembles and orchestras such as the **Gewandhaus Orchestra** in Leipzig and the **Bamberger Symphoniker**.
- Eating and drinking is not allowed in auditoriums.

is there a list of cultural events?
gibt es einen Veranstaltungskalender?
gipt es **ine**-en fehr-**an**shtaltoongs-ka**len**der

are there any festivals?
gibt es hier Festivals?
gipt es heer **fes**tivals

we'd like to go...
wir möchten ... gehen
veer **mur'kh**-ten ... **gay**-en

to the theatre
ins Theater
ins tay-**ah**ter

to the opera
in die Oper
in dee **oh**-per

to the ballet
ins Ballett
ins bahl-**let**

to a concert
in ein Konzert
in ine kon-**tsert**

what's on?
was wird gespielt?
vas virt ge**shpeelt**

do I need to book?
muss ich reservieren?
moos ikh ray-zer-**vee**-ren

how much are the tickets?
was kosten die Karten?
vas **kos**ten dee **kar**-ten

row 3...
Reihe 3...
rye-e dry...

seat number 10
Platz 10
plats tsayn

2 tickets...
zwei Karten...
tsvy **kar**-ten...

for tonight
für heute Abend
foor **hoy**-te **ah**bent

for tomorrow night
für morgen Abend
foor **mor**gen **ah**bent

for 5th August
für den fünften August
foor den **foonf**-ten ow**goost**

when does the performance end?
wann ist die Vorstellung zu Ende?
van ist dee **for**-shtelloong tsoo **en**-de

Hotel

- Tourist information offices will be able to provide a list of all the different kinds of accommodation available.
- **Urlaub auf dem Bauernhof** (holidays on farms) are popular for families.
- A **Hotel garni** is usually a smaller hotel offering bed and breakfast prices.

have you a room for tonight?
haben Sie ein Zimmer für heute Nacht?
hah-ben zee ine **tsim**mer foor **hoy**-te nakht

a single room
ein Einzelzimmer
*ine **ine**-tsel-tsimmer*

a double room
ein Doppelzimmer
*ine **dop**pel-tsimmer*

a family room
ein Familienzimmer
*ine fa**mee**lee-en-tsimmer*

with bath
mit Bad
mit baht

with shower
mit Dusche
*mit **doo**-she*

how much is it per night?
wie viel kostet es pro Nacht?
*vee*feel **kos**tet es pro nakht

is breakfast included?
ist das Frühstück inbegriffen?
*ist das **froo**-shtook **in**-be-griffen*

I booked a room
ich habe ein Zimmer reserviert
ikh hah-be ine **tsim**mer ray-zer-**veert**

my name is...
mein Name ist...
*mine **nah**-me ist...*

I'd like to see the room
ich möchte das Zimmer gern ansehen
*ikh **mur'kh**-te das **tsim**mer gern an-**zay**en*

have you anything cheaper?
haben Sie etwas Billigeres?
hah-ben zee **et**vas **bi**li-ge-res

what time is...?
wann gibt es...?
van gipt es...

breakfast
Frühstück
froo-shtook

dinner
Abendessen
ahbent-essen

the key, please
den Schlüssel, bitte
den **shloo**-sel **bi**-te

room number...
Zimmer (number)...
tsimmer...

are there any messages for me?
sind Nachrichten für mich da?
zint **nahkh**-rikhten foor mikh dah

come in!
herein!
he-**rine**

please come back later
bitte kommen Sie später noch einmal
bi-te **kom**men zee **shpay**ter nokh **ine**-mal

I'd like breakfast in my room
ich möchte gern Frühstück auf meinem Zimmer
ikh **mur'kh**-te gern **froo**-shtook owf **mine**-em **tsim**mer

please bring...
bitte bringen Sie...
bi-te **bring**en zee...

toilet paper
Toilettenpapier
twa-**le**-ten-pa**peer**

soap
Seife
zye-fe

clean towels
saubere Handtücher
zow-be-re **hant**-tookher

a glass
ein Glas
ine glahs

please clean...
bitte machen Sie ... sauber
bi-te **ma**khen zee ... **zow**-ber

my room
mein Zimmer
mine **tsim**mer

the bath
das Bad
das baht

I need an alarm call
ich brauche einen Weckruf
ikh **brow**-khe **ine**-en **vek**-roof

at 7 o'clock
um sieben Uhr
oom **zee**ben oor

is there a laundry service?
gibt es einen Wäschereiservice?
gipt es **ine**-en veshe-**rye**-service

can I borrow an iron?
kann ich ein Bügeleisen haben?
kan ikh ine **boo**gel-ize-en **hah**-ben

I'm leaving tomorrow
ich reise morgen ab
ikh **ry**-ze **mor**gen ap

please prepare the bill
machen Sie bitte die Rechnung fertig
makhen zee **bi**-te dee **rekh**-noong **fer**tikh

Self-catering

● Germany, Austria and Switzerland all use 220 volts. If you plan to take any electrical appliances such as hairdryers, irons or kettles, you should make sure you have an adaptor.
● Holiday flats and cottages are normally rented out on a weekly basis (Sat to Sat) and you are normally expected to clean the property before you leave.

which is the key for this door?
welcher Schlüssel ist für diese Tür?
vel-kher shloo-sel ist foor dee-ze toor

where are the fuses?
wo sind die Sicherungen?
voh zint dee zikh-eroong-en

please show us how this works
bitte zeigen Sie uns, wie das funktioniert
bi-te tsy-gen zee oons vee das foonk-tsyoh-neert

how does ... work?	**the dryer**	**the waterheater**
wie funktioniert...?	der Wäschetrockner	der Wasserboiler
vee foonk-tsyoh-neert...	*der veshe-trok-ner*	*der vasser-boy-ler*

the heating	**the washing machine**	**the cooker**
die Heizung	die Waschmaschine	der Herd
dee hye-tsung	*die vash-mah-shee-ne*	*der hert*

whom do I contact if there are any problems?
wen spreche ich bei Problemen an?
vehn shprekhe ikh by prohblehmen an

we need extra...	**keys**	**cutlery**	**sheets**
wir brauchen extra...	Schlüssel	Besteck	Bettwäsche
veer brow-khen ekstra...	*shloo-sel*	*beshtek*	*bet-veshe*

the gas has run out	**what do I do?**
das Gas ist alle	was muss ich tun?
das gahs ist al-le	*vas moos ikh toon*

Camping & Caravanning

● In Germany and Switzerland the speed of a car towing a caravan must not exceed 50 kph in built-up areas and 80 kph on other roads and motorways (Austria up to 100 kph on motorways).

● Places where you can fill water tanks and empty toilets, etc, are called **Entsorgungsstation** or **Wohnmobil Stellplatz**.

have you a list of campsites?
haben Sie eine Liste von Campingplätzen?
hah-ben zee *ine*-e *lis*-te fon *kam*ping-pletsen

have you any vacancies?
haben Sie noch Plätze frei?
hah-ben zee nokh *plet*-se fry

how much is it per night?
was kostet die Nacht?
vas *kos*tet dee nakht

we'd like to stay for ... nights
wir möchten ... Nächte bleiben
veer *mur'kh*-ten ... *nekh*-te *bly*-ben

where are the washrooms?
wo sind die Waschräume?
voh zint dee *vash*-roy-me

where can I empty the chemical toilet?
wo kann ich die chemische Toilette entsorgen?
voh kan ikh dee *khe*-mishe twa-*le*-te ent-*zor*-gen

is there a restaurant?
gibt es ein Restaurant?
gipt es ine restoh-*rong*

is there a shop?
gibt es einen Laden?
gipt es *ine*-en *lah*-den

can we park our caravan here overnight?
können wir unseren Wohnwagen hier über Nacht parken?
kur'-nen veer *oon*seren *vohn*-vahgen heer *oo*ber nakht *par*ken

can we camp here overnight? *(for tent)*
können wir über Nacht hier zelten?
kur'-nen veer *oo*ber nakht heer *tsel*-ten

Children

- In Germany children up to 4 must have their own special car seat and those up to 12 must have booster seats (and sit in the back). In Austria and Switzerland children must travel in the back with seatbelts.
- Restaurants often have children's dishes (**Kinderteller**).
- **Europa-Park** in the south of Germany is a theme park.

a child's ticket
eine Kinderkarte
ine-e **kin**der-kar-te

he/she is ... years old
er/sie ist...
er/zee ist...

is there a reduction for children?
gibt es Ermäßigung für Kinder?
*gipt es er-**may**-sigoong foor **kin**der*

where can I change the baby?
wo kann ich das Baby wickeln?
*voh kan ikh das **ba**by **vi**-keln*

can you warm this up?
können Sie das aufwärmen?
***kur'**-nen zee das **owf**-ver-men*

do you have a children's menu?
haben Sie eine Kinderkarte?
***hah**-ben zee **ine**-e **kin**der-kar-te*

do you have...?
haben Sie...?
***hah**-ben zee...*

a child's car seat
einen Kindersitz
ine-en **kin**-der-zits

a high chair
einen Kinderstuhl
ine-en **kin**der-shtool

a cot
ein Kinderbett
ine **kin**der-bet

is it ok to bring children here?
können wir die Kinder mitbringen?
***kur'**-nen veer dee **kin**der **mit**-bringen*

is there a playpark?
gibt es einen Spielplatz?
*gipt es **ine**-en **shpeel**-plats*

what's there for children to do?
was können die Kinder hier unternehmen?
*vas **kur'**-nen dee **kin**der heer oonter-**nay**men*

I have two children
ich habe zwei Kinder
*ikh **hah**-be tsvy **kin**der*

do you have children?
haben Sie Kinder?
***hah**-ben zee **kin**der*

Special Needs

- On all Intercity and on most Eurocity and fast trains, special wheelchair compartments are now available in second class. A wheelchair sign indicates facilities for the disabled.
- You can arrange help in advance for getting on and off trains. Ring the hotline 01805 512 512 to book it.
- The standard UK disabled badge is valid throughout the EU.

is it possible to visit ... with a wheelchair?
kann man ... auch im Rollstuhl besuchen?
*kan man ... aukh im **rol**-shtool be**zoo**khen*

do you have toilets for the disabled?
haben Sie Toiletten für Behinderte?
***hah**-ben zee twa-**le**-ten foor be-**hin**-der-te*

I need a bedroom on the ground floor
ich brauche ein Zimmer im Erdgeschoss
*ikh **brow**-khe ine **tsim**mer im **ert**-geshos*

is there a lift?
gibt es einen Aufzug?
*gipt es **ine**-en **owf**tsook*

where is the lift?
wo ist der Aufzug?
*voh ist der **owf**tsook*

I can't walk far
ich kann nicht weit laufen
*ikh kan nikht vite **low**-fen*

are there many steps?
sind es viele Stufen?
*zint es **fee**le **shtoo**fen*

is there an entrance for wheelchairs?
gibt es einen Eingang für Rollstuhlfahrer?
*gipt es **ine**-en **ine**-gang foor **rol**-shtool-fahrer*

can I travel on this train with a wheelchair?
kann ich als Rollstuhlfahrer in diesem Zug mitfahren?
*kan ikh als **rol**-shtool-fahrer in **dee**zem tsook **mit**-fahren*

is there a reduction for the disabled?
gibt es Ermäßigung für Behinderte?
*gipt es er-**may**-sigoong foor be-**hin**-der-te*

Exchange Visitors

● These phrases are intended for families hosting German-speaking visitors.
● Germans usually have lunch between noon and 1pm. Normally this is their main hot meal. Dinner, a lighter meal (usually bread and cold sliced meats and cheese), is at 7pm.

what would you like for breakfast?
was möchten Sie zum Frühstück?
*vas **mur'kh**-ten zee tsoom **froo**-shtook*

do you eat...?
essen Sie...?
es-sen zee...

what would you like to eat?
was möchten Sie essen?
*vas **mur'kh**-ten zee **es**-sen*

what would you like to drink?
was möchten Sie trinken?
*vas **mur'kh**-ten zee **trin**ken*

did you sleep well?
haben Sie gut geschlafen?
*hah-ben zee goot ges**hlah**fen*

what would you like to do today?
was möchten Sie heute unternehmen?
*vas **mur'kh**-ten zee **hoy**-te oonter-**nay**men*

I will pick you up at...
ich hole Sie um ... ab
*ikh **hoh**-le zee oom ... ap*

did you enjoy yourself?
hat es Ihnen gefallen?
*hat es **ee**nen ge**fal**len*

take care
passen Sie auf sich auf
*pa**ssen** zee owf zikh owf*

please be back no later than...
bitte seien Sie bis spätestens ... zurück
bi**-te **zy**-en zee bis **shpay**-testens ... tsoo**rook

we'll be in bed when you get back
wir werden schon schlafen, wenn Sie zurückkommen
*veer **vehr**-den shohn **shlah**fen ven zee tsoo**rook**-kommen*

Exchange Visitors

- These phrases are intended for those people staying with German-speaking families.
- You should use the polite (**Sie**) form with older people and those you do not know well.
- If invited to a German home, it is considered polite to take a little gift, such as a bunch of flowers.

I like...
ich mag...
ikh makh...

I don't like...
ich mag ... nicht
ikh makh ... nikht

that was delicious
das war sehr gut
das vahr zehr goot

thank you very much
vielen Dank
***fee**-len dank*

may I phone home?
darf ich nach Hause telefonieren?
*darf ikh nakh **how**-ze taylay-fo-**nee**ren*

can I have a key?
kann ich einen Schlüssel bekommen?
*kan ikh **ine**-en **shloo**-sel be-**kom**men*

can I borrow...?
kann ich ... borgen?
*kan ikh ... **bohr**-gen*

a hairdryer
einen Föhn
***ine**-en fur'n*

an iron
ein Bügeleisen
*ine boogel-**ize**-en*

can you take me by car?
können Sie mich mit dem Auto hinbringen?
***kur'**-nen zee mikh mit dem **ow**to **hin**-bringen*

what time do you get up?
wann stehen Sie auf?
*van **shtay**en zee owf*

I'm staying with...
ich wohne bei...
*ikh **voh**-ne by...*

I've had a great time
es hat mir sehr gut gefallen
*es haht meer zehr goot ge**fal**len*

Problems

- Germans may be slightly reserved, but they are helpful if approached.
- Many Germans speak good English (particularly the young).
- If you need to attract someone's attention, begin your request with **Entschuldigen Sie!**

excuse me!
entschuldigen Sie!
*ent-**shool**-di-gen zee*

can you help me?
können Sie mir helfen?
***kur'**-nen zee meer **helf**en*

do you speak English?
sprechen Sie Englisch?
***shpre**khen zee **eng**-lish*

I'm lost
ich habe mich verlaufen
*ikh **hah**-be mikh fer-**low**fen*

I'm late
ich habe mich verspätet
*ikh **hah**-be mikh ver**shpay**-tet*

I've missed...
ich habe ... verpasst
*ikh **hah**-be ... fer-**past***

I've lost...
ich habe ... verloren
*ikh **hah**-be ... fer-**lohr**en*

my suitcase...
mein Koffer...
*mine **ko**fer...*

leave me alone!
lassen Sie mich in Ruhe!
***las**sen zee mikh in **roo**-e*

I don't speak German
ich spreche kein Deutsch
*ikh **shpre**-khe kine doytch*

does anyone speak English?
spricht jemand Englisch?
*shprikht **yay**mant **eng**-lish*

how do I get to...?
wie komme ich zum/zur/nach...?
*vee **kom**me ikh tsoom/tsoor/nakh...*

I need to get to...
ich muss zum/zur/nach...
ikh moos tsoom/tsoor/nakh...

my connection
meinen Anschluss
***mine**-en **an**-shloos*

my passport
meinen Pass
***mine**-en pass*

is damaged
wurde beschädigt
***voor**-de be-**shay**-dikht*

my plane
mein Flugzeug
*mine **flook**-tsoyk*

my money
mein Geld
mine gelt

is missing
ging verloren
*geeng fer-**lohr**en*

go away!
hau ab!
how ap

Complaints

- Germans usually attach great importance to quality and good service. If they are not satisfied with something, they say so.
- If you complain, you can often get compensation (**Entschädigung**), e.g. for long delays on the trains.
- Germans automatically expect to receive good service and quality.

the light
das Licht
das likht

the lock
das Schloss
das shlos

... doesn't work
... funktioniert nicht
*... foonk-tsyoh-**neert** nikht*

the toilet
die Toilette
*dee twa-**le**-te*

the heating
die Heizung
*dee **hyt**-soong*

the room is ...
das Zimmer ist...
*das **tsim**mer ist...*

dirty
schmutzig
***shmoo**tsik*

too hot
zu warm
tsoo varm

too cold
zu kalt
tsoo kalt

too noisy
zu laut
tsoo lowt

too small
zu klein
tsoo kline

this isn't what I ordered
das habe ich nicht bestellt
*das **hah**-be ikh nikht be**shtelt***

I want to complain
ich möchte mich beschweren
*ikh **mur'kh**-te mikh be**shveh**ren*

the bill is not correct
die Rechnung stimmt nicht
*dee **rekh**-noong shtimt nikht*

I want my money back
ich möchte mein Geld zurück
*ikh **mur'kh**-te mine gelt tsoo**rook***

we've been waiting for a very long time
wir warten schon sehr lange
*veer **var**-ten shohn zehr **lang**-e*

this is broken
das ist kaputt
*das ist ka**poot***

can you repair it?
können Sie das reparieren?
***kur'**-nen zee das raypa-**ree**ren*

Emergencies

- In Germany, if you don't have time to check in the local telephone directory for the emergency ambulance service, the fire brigade also has an ambulance service. Ring 112.
- The Police emergency number is 110.
- If you need urgent medical help, go to the A&E (**Notaufnahme**) of the nearest hospital.

help!	**fire!**	**can you help me?**
Hilfe!	Feuer!	können Sie mir helfen?
hil-fe	*foy-er*	*kur'n-en zee meer hel-fen*

there's been an accident
ein Unfall ist passiert
ine oonfal ist paseert

these are my insurance details
hier sind meine Versicherungsangaben
here zint mine-e fer-zikh-e-roongs-an-gaben

someone is injured
es ist jemand verletzt worden
es ist yaymant ferletzt vorden

please call...	**the police**	**an ambulance**
bitte rufen Sie...	die Polizei	einen Krankenwagen
bi-te roofen zee...	*dee poli-tsye*	*ine-en kranken-vahgen*

the fire brigade
die Feuerwehr
dee foy-er-vehr

where's the police station?
wo ist die Polizeiwache?
voh ist dee poli-tsy-va-khe

I want to report a theft
ich möchte einen Diebstahl melden
ikh mur'kh-te ine-en deep-shtahl melden

my car has been stolen
mein Auto ist gestohlen worden
*mine **ow**to ist ge**shtoh**-len **vor**den*

my car has been broken into
mein Auto ist aufgebrochen worden
*mine **ow**to ist **owf**-gebro-khen **vor**den*

I've been robbed
ich bin beraubt worden
*ikh bin be-**rowpt vor**den*

I've been attacked
ich bin überfallen worden
*ikh bin oober-**fa**llen **vor**den*

I've been raped
ich bin vergewaltigt worden
*ikh bin fer-ge**val**-tikht **vor**den*

I need a report for my insurance
ich brauche einen Bericht für meine Versicherung
*ikh **brow**-khe **ine**-en be**rikht** foor **mine**-e fer**zikh**-eroong*

how much is the fine?
wie viel Strafe muss ich zahlen?
*** vee**feel **shtrah**-fe moos ikh **tsah**-len*

where do I pay it?
wo kann ich das bezahlen?
*voh kan ikh das be-**tsah**len*

I have no money
ich habe kein Geld
*ikh **hah**-be kine gelt*

I would like to phone my embassy
ich möchte mit meiner Botschaft telefonieren
*ikh **mur'kh**-te mit **mine**-er **boht**shaft taylay-fo-**nee**ren*

I'm very sorry
es tut mir sehr Leid
es toot meer zayr lite

Health

● Pharmacies will be able to provide advice on any health matters and deal with minor problems. Look out for the old fashioned 'A' sign.
● To get free emergency dental and medical care, you must take your stamped E111 form (available from local Post Offices).

have you something for...?
haben Sie etwas gegen...?
*hah-ben zee **et**vas **gay**-gen...*

car sickness
Reisekrankheit
ry-ze-krank-hite

diarrhoea
Durchfall
doorkh-fal

is it safe to give children?
kann man es bedenkenlos auch Kindern geben?
*kan man es be-**deng**-ken-lohs owkh **kin**dern **gay**ben*

I'm ill
ich bin krank
ikh bin krank

I need a doctor
ich brauche einen Arzt
*ikh **brow**-khe **ine**-en artst*

my son/my daughter has a high temperature
mein Sohn/meine Tochter hat hohes Fieber
*mine zohn/**mine**-e **tokh**ter hat **hoh**-es **fee**ber*

I'm on this medication
ich nehme dieses Medikament
*ikh **nay**-me **dee**zes medeeka**ment***

I have high blood pressure
ich habe hohen Blutdruck
*ikh **hah**-be **hoh**-en **bloot**-drook*

I have fallen
ich bin hingefallen
*ikh bin hin-ge-**fal**-en*

I'm diabetic
ich habe Zucker
*ikh **hah**-be **tsoo**ker*

I'm pregnant
ich bin schwanger
*ikh bin **shvan**ger*

I'm on the pill
ich nehme die Pille
*ikh **nay**-me dee **pi**-le*

I'm allergic to penicillin
ich bin allergisch gegen Penizillin
*ikh bin a-ler-gish **gay**-gen peni-tsi**leen***

my blood group is...
meine Blutgruppe ist...
***mine**-e blootgroo-pe ist...*

I'm breastfeeding
ich stille mein Baby
*ikh **shtil**le mine **ba**by*

is it safe to take?
kann man das bedenkenlos einnehmen?
*kan man das be-**deng**-ken-lohs **ine**-naymen*

will I/he/she have to go to hospital?
muss ich/er/sie ins Krankenhaus?
*moos ikh/er/zee ins **kran**ken-hows*

I need to go to casualty
ich muss zur Notaufnahme
*ikh moos tsoor **noht**-owf-nahme*

where is the hospital?
wo ist das Krankenhaus?
*voh ist das **kran**ken-hows*

when are visiting hours?
wann ist die Besuchszeit?
*van ist dee be**zookhs**-tsite*

which ward?
welche Station?
vel**-khe shtah-tsee-**ohn

I need a dentist
ich brauche einen Zahnarzt
*ikh **brow**-khe **ine**-en **tsahn**artst*

he/she has toothache
er/sie hat Zahnschmerzen
*er/zee hat **tsahn**-shmer-tsen*

can you do a temporary filling?
können Sie mir eine provisorische Plombe machen?
***kur'**-nen zee meer **ine**-e provi-**zo**rish-e **plom**-be **ma**khen*

I have an abscess
ich habe einen Abszess
*ikh **hah**-be **ine**-en apst**sess***

it hurts
das tut weh
das toot vay

can you repair my dentures?
können Sie mein Gebiss reparieren?
***kur'**-nen zee mine ge**biss** raypa-**ree**ren*

do I have to pay now?
muss ich das gleich bezahlen?
*moos ikh das **glykh** be**tsah**-len*

how much will it be?
wie teuer wird es?
*vee **toy**-er virt es*

I need a receipt for my insurance
ich brauche eine Quittung für meine Krankenkasse
*ikh **brow**-khe **ine**-e **kvi**-toong foor **mine**-e **kran**ken-ka-se*

Business

● Germany hosts many top international fairs such as the computer fair CEBIT in Hannover and the Frankfurt Book Fair. Book accommodation well in advance.

● There are a number of public holidays in Germany when all companies are closed. These include Whit Monday, Ascension Day and Reunification Day on 3 October.

my name is...
mein Name ist...
*mine **nah**-me ist...*

here's my card
hier ist meine Karte
*heer ist **mine**-e **kar**-te*

I work for...
ich arbeite für...
*ikh **arby**-te foor...*

I'd like to arrange a meeting
ich möchte eine Besprechung ausmachen
*ikh **mur'kh**-te **ine**-e be-**shpre**-khoong **ows**-makhen*

on April 4th at 11 o'clock
am vierten April um elf Uhr
*am **feer**-ten a**pril** oom elf oor*

can we meet for lunch?
können wir uns bei einem Mittagessen treffen?
***kur'**-nen veer oons by **ine**-em **mi**tahk-essen **tref**fen*

I'm staying at Hotel...
ich wohne im Hotel...
*ikh **voh**-ne im ho**tel**...*

how do I get to your office?
wie komme ich zu Ihrem Büro?
*vee **kom**me ikh tsoo **ee**-rem boo**roh***

here is some information about my company
hier sind einige Informationen über meine Firma
*heer zint **ine**-nee-ge infor-matsy**ohn**-en **oo**ber **mine**-e **feer**-ma*

I have an appointment with...
ich habe einen Termin mit...
*ikh **hah**-be **ine**-en ter-**meen** mit...*

at ... o'clock
um ... Uhr
oom ... oor

I'm delighted to meet you at last
schön, dass wir uns endlich persönlich kennen lernen
*shur'n das veer oons **ent**-likh per-**sur'n**-likh **ken**nen-layr-nen*

my German isn't very good
mein Deutsch ist nicht sehr gut
mine doytch ist nikht zehr goot

please speak slowly
bitte sprechen Sie langsam
bi-te shpre-khen zee lang-zahm

what is the name of the managing director?
wie ist der Name des Geschäftsführers?
vee ist der nah-me des geshefts-foorers

I'd like some information about the company
ich möchte einige Informationen über die Firma
ikh mur'kh-te ine-neege infor-matsyohn-en oober dee feer-ma

do you have a press office?
haben Sie eine Presseabteilung?
hah-ben zee ine-e pres-se-ap-tye-loong

I need an interpreter
ich brauche einen Dolmetscher
ikh brow-khe ine-en dol-met-sher

can you copy this for me?
können Sie das für mich kopieren?
kur'-nen zee das foor mikh kopee-ren

do you have an appointment?
haben Sie einen Termin?
hah-ben zee ine-en ter-meen

...isn't in the office at the moment
...ist im Augenblick nicht im Büro
...ist im owgen-blik nikht im booroh

he/she will be back in a few minutes
er/sie kommt in ein paar Minuten wieder
er/zee kommt in ein pahr minoo-ten veeder

I'll put you through.
ich verbinde
ikh fer-bin-de

can I take a message?
kann ich etwas ausrichten?
kan ikh et-vas ows-rikh-ten

Phoning

- Dialling codes from the UK: **Germany** 00 49, **Switzerland** 00 41, **Austria** 00 43.
  - Dialling code to the UK from Europe: 00 44.
  - Most phoneboxes take phonecards (**Telefonkarte**) which you can buy in newsagents' and phone shops.
  - The word for 'phone call' is **Anruf**.

a phonecard, please
eine Telefonkarte, bitte
*ine-e taylay-**fon**-kar-te **bi**-te*

I want to make a phone call
ich möchte telefonieren
*ikh **mur'kh**-te taylay-fo-**nee**ren*

Herr Braun, please
Herr Braun, bitte
*hayr brown **bi**-te*

extension ..., please
Apparat ..., bitte
*apa-**raht** ... **bi**-te*

can I speak to ...?
kann ich mit ... sprechen?
*kan ikh mit ... **shpre**-khen*

this is Jim Brown
hier ist Jim Brown
heer ist jim brown

I'll call back later
ich rufe später wieder an
*ikh **roo**-fe **shpay**ter **vee**der an*

I'll call back tomorrow
ich rufe morgen wieder an
*ikh **roo**-fe **mor**gen **vee**der an*

an outside line, please
eine Amtsleitung, bitte
*ine-e **amts**-lye-toong **bi**-te*

I can't get through
ich komme nicht durch
*ikh **kom**me nikht doorkh*

do you have a mobile?
haben Sie ein Handy?
*hah-ben zee ine **han**dy*

what is your mobile number?
wie lautet Ihre Handynummer?
*vee **lau**-tet **ee**-re **han**dy-noomer*

my mobile number is...
meine Handynummer ist...
*mine-e **han**dy-noomer ist...*

hello
hallo
*ha**lo***

who is calling?
wer spricht, bitte?
*ver shprikht **bi**-te*

it's engaged
es ist besetzt
*es ist be**zetst***

E-mail/Fax

- Internet cafés are found in most cities and often have special deals. The most common internet service providers are T-Online and AOL.
- German domain names end in .de for **Deutschland**.
- www dot is pronounced **veh veh veh poonkt**.
- The @ symbol is pronounced 'at', as in English.

I want to send an e-mail
ich möchte eine E-Mail schicken
*ikh **mur'kh**-te **ine**-e e-mail **shi**-ken*

my e-mail address is...
meine E-Mail Adresse ist...
***mine**-e **ee**-mail a-**dres**-se ist...*

what's your e-mail address?
wie ist Ihre E-Mail-Adresse?
*vee ist **ee**-re e-mail-a-**dre**-se*

did you get my e-mail?
haben Sie meine E-Mail bekommen?
***hah**-ben zee **mine**-e e-mail be-**kom**men*

the website is www.anyone.co.uk
die Website ist www.anyone.co.uk
dee website ist veh veh veh poonkt anyone poonkt tseh oh poonkt oo kah

I want to send a fax
ich möchte ein Fax schicken
*ikh **mur'kh**-te ine fax **shi**-ken*

did you get my fax?
haben Sie mein Fax bekommen?
***hah**-ben zee mine fax be-**kom**men*

can I send a fax from here?
kann ich von hier ein Fax schicken?
*kan ikh fon heer ine fax **shi**-ken*

what's your fax number?
wie ist Ihre Faxnummer?
*vee ist **ee**-re **fax**-noomer*

do you have a fax?
haben Sie ein Fax?
***hah**-ben zee ine fax*

Numbers

0	**null** *nool*		
1	**eins** *ines*	1st	**erste**
2	**zwei** *tsvy*		***er**-ste*
3	**drei** *dry*	2nd	**zweite**
4	**vier** *feer*		***tsvy**-te*
5	**fünf** *foonf*	3rd	**dritte**
6	**sechs** *zekhs*		***drit**-te*
7	**sieben** ***zee**ben*	4th	**vierte**
8	**acht** *akht*		***feer**-te*
9	**neun** *noyn*	5th	**fünfte**
10	**zehn** *tsayn*		***foonf**-te*
11	**elf** *elf*	6th	**sechste**
12	**zwölf** *tsvur'lf*		***zekhs**-te*
13	**dreizehn** ***dry**-tsayn*	7th	**siebte**
14	**vierzehn** ***feer**-tsayn*		***zeep**-te*
15	**fünfzehn** ***foonf**-tsayn*	8th	**achte**
16	**sechzehn** ***zekh**-tsayn*		***akh**-te*
17	**siebzehn** ***zeep**-tsayn*	9th	**neunte**
18	**achtzehn** ***akh**-tsayn*		***noyn**-te*
19	**neunzehn** ***noyn**-tsayn*	10th	**zehnte**
20	**zwanzig** ***tsvan**-tsikh*		***tsayn**-te*

21	**einundzwanzig** ***ine**-oont-tsvan-tsikh*
22	**zweiundzwanzig** ***tsvy**-oont-tsvan-tsikh*
30	**dreißig** ***dry**-sikh*
40	**vierzig** ***feer**-tsikh*
50	**fünfzig** ***foonf**-tsikh*
60	**sechzig** ***zekh**-tsikh*
70	**siebzig** ***zeep**-tsikh*
80	**achtzig** ***akh**-tsikh*
90	**neunzig** ***noyn**-tsikh*
100	**hundert** ***hoon**dert*
101	**hunderteins** ***hoon**dert-ines*
250	**zweihundertfünfzig** ***tsvy**-hoondert **foonf**-tsikh*
500	**fünfhundert** ***foonf**-hoondert*
1,000	**tausend** ***tow**zent*

Monday	montag **mohn**-tahk
Tuesday	dienstag **deens**-tahk
Wednesday	mittwoch **mit**-vokh
Thursday	donnerstag **don**ners-tahk
Friday	freitag **fry**-tahk
Saturday	samstag **zams**-tahk
Sunday	sonntag **zon**-tahk

January	januar **yan**-ooar
February	februar **feb**-rooar
March	märz mehrts
April	april ap-**reel**
May	mai mye
June	juni **yoo**-nee
July	juli **yoo**-lee
August	august ow-**goost**
September	september sep-**tem**ber
October	oktober ok-**to**ber
November	november no-**vem**ber
December	dezember dayt-**sem**ber

what's the date?
der Wievielte ist heute?
*der vee-**feel**-te ist **hoy**-te*

which day?
welcher Tag?
***vel**-kher tahk*

which month?
welcher Monat?
***vel**-kher **mohn**at*

it's the 5th of March 2005
heute ist der fünfte März zweitausendfünf
***hoy**-te ist der **foonf**-te merts **tsvy**towzent-foonf*

on Saturday
am Samstag
*am **zams**-tahk*

on Saturdays
samstags
***zams**-tahks*

every Saturday
jeden Samstag
***yay**-den **zams**-tahk*

this Saturday
diesen Samstag
***dee**zen **zams**-tahk*

next Saturday
nächsten Samstag
***naykh**-sten **zams**-tahk*

last Saturday
letzten Samstag
***lets**-ten **zams**-tahk*

please can you confirm the date?
können Sie bitte das Datum bestätigen?
***kur'**-nen zee **bi**-te das **dah**toom be**shtay**-teegen*

Time

- Central European Time is 1 hour ahead of the UK.
- In German the half hour is expressed by referring forwards to the next full hour as opposed to backwards to the last full hour as in English. You will also hear in Austria and eastern Germany **viertel** (quarter) **acht** meaning 'a quarter past 7' and **dreiviertel** (three quarters) **acht** meaning 'a quarter to 8'.

what time is it, please?
wie spät ist es, bitte?
*vee shpayt ist es **bi**-te*

am
morgens
***mor**gens*

pm
nachmittags/abends *(eve)*
***nakh**-mi-tahks/**ah**bents*

it's 1 o'clock
es ist ein Uhr
es ist ine oor

it's 3 o'clock
es ist drei Uhr
es ist dry oor

it's 6 o'clock
es ist sechs Uhr
es ist zekhs oor

it's half past 8
es ist halb neun
es ist halp noyn

it's half past 10
es ist halb elf
es ist halp elf

an hour
eine Stunde
*ine-e **shtoon**-de*

half an hour
eine halbe Stunde
*ine-e **hal**-be **shtoon**-de*

a quarter of an hour
eine Viertelstunde
*ine-e **feer**tel-**shtoon**-de*

three quarters of an hour
eine Dreiviertelstunde
*ine-e **dry**-feertel-**shtoon**-de*

until 8 o'clock
bis acht Uhr
bis akht oor

it is 10 past 9
es ist zehn nach neun
es ist tsehn nakh noyn

at 10 am
um 10 Uhr morgens
*oom tsayn oor **mor**gens*

at 4 pm
um 16 Uhr
*oom **zekh**-tsayn oor*

soon
bald
balt

later
später
shpay-ter

die deutsche Küche

As far as cuisine is concerned, Germany can be grouped into three main regions – northern, western and southern.

The northern region is the only one with a coastline so fish, especially herring, but also fish such as sole and plaice, appears frequently on the menu. Try *Krabbensalat*, shrimp salad, and don't miss *Matjeshering* (salted herring) especially in June when the new season starts and the herring is at its freshest. However, meat is still the most important item on the menu here, as it is in the rest of the country. There is also strong influence from Polish and Scandinavian cuisines.

The western region comprises the areas on both sides of the river Rhine and its famous valley, with strong French influence. The western region is more food conscious and it is said that the best German restaurants are to be found here. Some very local specialities involve the use of frogs' legs (*Froschschenkel*) and snails (*Schnecken*). The delicious *Schwarzwälder Schinken* (Black Forest ham) must not be missed.

The southern region of Germany is dominated by Bavaria. Here veal is popular, and the main speciality is *Kalbshaxe* (knuckles of veal). A pork speciality is *Eisbein* (knuckle of pork), and the favourite sausage is one made from pork, beef and seasonings (*Leberkäse*). Pasta is also popular, in various dishes, especially in Swabia where *Spätzle* (noodles) are poplular. *Sauerkraut* is also a favourite, served with pork. This region is rich in dairy products. Try also the *Kaiserschmarren* (pancakes with a rich filling) and *Strudel*, normally filled with apples.

In Germany the main meal of the day is usually *Mittagessen*, lunch. It starts with soup, followed by the main dish (meat with vegetables or salad and potato or rice, etc) and an optional dessert or fruit.

Dinner (*Abendessen*) consists of platters of cold meats and cheeses. On occasions Germans also have a hot meal, but not a heavy one.

Breakfast (*Frühstück*) generally consists of a variety of cold meats and cheeses, with different kinds of bread and jam and fresh coffee.

Ordering drinks

- There are many cafés and confectioners' shops (**Konditorei**) where coffee and cakes are served. Some bakeries also have a small café, usually standing. These usually open very early and are good places for breakfast.
- Tea is also available, especially in northern Germany, particularly Frisia where it is more popular.

a black coffee
einen schwarzen Kaffee
ine-en shvar-tsen kafay

a white coffee
einen Kaffee mit Sahne
ine-en kafay mit zah-ne

a tea
einen Tee
ine-en tay

with milk
mit Frischmilch
mit frish-milkh

with lemon
mit Zitrone
mit tsitroh-ne

a lager
ein helles Bier
ine he-les beer

a bitter
ein Altbier
ine alt-beer

a half pint
ein Kleines
ine kline-es

a pint
ein Großes
ine groh-ses

a bottle of mineral water
eine Flasche Mineralwasser
ine-e fla-she mi-nerahl-vasser

sparkling
mit Kohlensäure
mit kohlen-zoy-re

still
still
shtill

the wine list, please
die Weinkarte, bitte
dee vinekar-te bi-te

a bottle of house wine
eine Flasche Hauswein
ine-e fla-she howsvine

a glass of white wine/red wine
ein Glas Weißwein / Rotwein
ine glahs vicevine / rohtvine

a bottle of red wine
eine Flasche Rotwein
ine-e fla-she rohtvine

a bottle of white wine
eine Flasche Weißwein
ine-e fla-she vicevine

would you like a drink?
möchten Sie etwas trinken?
mur'kh-ten zee etvas trinken

what will you have?
was möchten Sie?
vas mur'kh-ten zee

- Many restaurants in Germany close one day a week (**Ruhetag**, or 'rest day'), often Mondays.
- If all you want is a quick snack, you can get things like hamburgers and sausages at an **Imbiss**.
- Eating places must display prices outside.
- Restaurants usually offer set-price meals.

I'd like to book a table
ich möchte einen Tisch reservieren
*ikh **mur'kh**-te **ine**-en tish ray-zer-**vee**ren*

for ... people
für ... Personen
*foor ... per-**zoh**nen*

for tonight
für heute Abend
*foor **hoy**-te **ah**bent*

at 8 pm
um acht Uhr
oom akht oor

the menu, please
die Speisekarte, bitte
*dee **shpy**-ze-kar-te **bi**-te*

is there a dish of the day?
gibt es ein Tagesgericht?
*gipt es ine **tah**ges-gerikht*

have you a set-price menu?
haben Sie eine Tageskarte?
***hah**-ben zee **ine**-e **tah**ges-kar-te?*

I'll have this
ich nehme das
*ikh **nay**-me das*

what do you recommend?
was können Sie empfehlen?
*vas **kur'**-nen zee emp-**fay**len*

I don't eat meat
ich esse kein Fleisch
*ikh **es**-se kine flysh*

do you have any vegetarian dishes?
haben Sie vegetarische Gerichte?
***hah**-ben zee vaygay-**ta**rish-e ge-**rikh**-te*

excuse me, please!
Entschuldigung, bitte!
*ent**shool**-digoong **bi**-te*

more bread
noch Brot
nokh broht

more water
noch Wasser
*nokh **vas**ser*

the bill, please
zahlen, bitte
***tsah**-len **bi**-te*

enjoy your meal!
guten appetit!
goo**-ten apay-**teet

cheers!
prost!
prohst

Special requirements

- Although meat is an important part of the traditional German diet, more and more restaurants are now offering vegetarian alternatives.
- Hygiene and quality control standards are very high and many restaurants try to use organic produce wherever possible.

are there any vegetarian restaurants here?
gibt es hier vegetarische Restaurants?
*gipt es heer vaygay-**ta**rish-e restoh-**rongs***

I'm vegetarian
ich bin Vegetarier
*ikh bin vaygay-**ta**ree-er*

I don't eat meat/pork
ich esse kein Fleisch/Schweinefleisch
*ikh **es**-se kine flysh/**shvy**-ne-flysh*

I don't eat fish/shellfish
ich esse keinen Fisch/keine Meeresfrüchte
*ikh **es**-se **kine**-en fish/**kine**-e **meh**res-frur'kh-te*

I'm allergic to shellfish
ich bin allergisch gegen Meeresfrüchte
*ikh bin a-**ler**-gish **gay**-gen **meh**res-frur'kh-te*

I am allergic to peanuts
ich bin allergisch gegen Erdnüsse
*ikh bin a-**ler**-gish **gay**-gen **ert**-noos-se*

I can't eat raw eggs
ich kann kein rohes Ei essen
*ikh kan kine **roh**-es eye **es**-sen*

I can't eat liver
ich kann keine Leber essen
*ikh kan **kine**-e **lay**-ber **es**-sen*

I am on a diet
ich bin auf Diät
*ikh bin owf dee-**ayt***

I don't drink alcohol
ich trinke keinen Alkohol
*ikh **trin**-ke **kine**-en **al**ko-hol*

what is in this?
was ist darin enthalten?
*vas ist da-**rin** ent-**hal**ten*

is it raw?
ist das roh?
ist das roh

IMBISS Germans are fond of snacks and there are numerous roadside stalls. There should be no worries over trying the food, as there are strict hygiene laws governing the operation of stalls.

Typical snacky food such as *Bratwurst* (fried sausage), *Bockwurst* (boiled sausage) and *Buletten* (thick hamburger, but without the roll).

Germany has a huge variety of sausages which are served at all times of the day. By law they are made with 100% meat.

A *Stehcafé* is a good place for coffee and cake, generally standing only. They are often attached to a baker's and the 7am opening means you can get breakfast.

A *Biergarten* is an open-air pub serving a selection of hearty meals. They are particularly popular in Bavaria where you can often bring your own picnic and spend the evening in a beergarden with the whole family.

shut on Mondays

In smaller towns restaurants tend to shut one day (generally Mondays). As a rule, eating places (including restaurants) have a menu with prices outside, so you will be prepared for the cost before going in. Restaurants usually offer set-price meals.

Some hotels have special offers. Here a Summer buffet. It includes (*inkl. Aperitif u. Parken*) aperitif and parking. The price is for 2 people.

You can find a great variety of cakes at a *Café Konditorei*, generally served with cream (*mit Sahne*) and very good coffee.

You find a wide variety of Chinese and Italian restaurants in Germany.

Turkish food (such as doner kebabs) tends to be sold in snackbars rather than restaurants.

Eating places

In butcher's shops there is often an area for a quick meal (generally eaten standing) such as this dish: *Wiener Würstchen mit Kartoffelsalat* (boiled frankfurter with potato salad).

Metzgerei is a southern German term for butcher's.

 BUTCHER'S

Winebars usually serve light (often cold) meals.

Weinstube

WINEBAR

durchgehend warme Küche

HOT MEALS SERVED ALL DAY

RATSKELLER
One of the unusual places where one can eat in Germany (and eat well) is the town hall (*Rathaus*), which often has a restaurant open to the public (usually in the basement), called the *Ratskeller* (council's cellar).

Bistro

A good place for breakfast, snacks, coffee and cakes.

Germany has a huge variety of bread and rolls. It is generally served at breakfast or with a light evening meal. Butter is usually served with bread. German butter is unsalted.

Reading the menu

Don't be overwhelmed by German words – they may be long, but they are made up of smaller bits of words. Try to work out what the item is by identifying what makes up the long word. So **Tomatencremesuppe** is cream of tomato soup. You will also come across English terms such as **Snacks**. There are also usually children's menus. Remember, German portions are quite large!

Speisekarte	_Menu_
Vorspeisen	**Starters**
Suppen	soups
Salate	salads
Knoblauchbrot	garlic bread
Fleisch	**Meat**
Wild und Geflügel	**Game & Poultry**
Fisch	**Fish**
Meeresfrüchte	seafood
Gemüse	**Vegetables**
Käse	**Cheese**
Dessert	**Dessert**
Getränke	**Drinks**

UNTIL 3PM

Mittags menue = lunch menu.
It's normally spelt
Mittagsmenü.

heiß

HOT

COLD

kalt

SNACK BOARD:

Our offer:

–sandwich

–roll with meat
or cheese
(**Bel.** is short for
'filled' **belegtes**)

–soup

–sweets

Look out for restaurant offers in local newspapers.

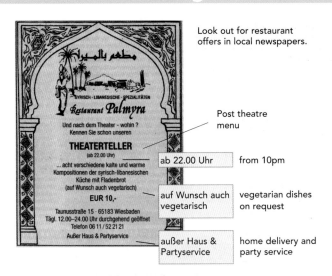

Post theatre menu

ab 22.00 Uhr — from 10pm

auf Wunsch auch vegetarisch — vegetarian dishes on request

außer Haus & Partyservice — home delivery and party service

DISH OF THE DAY

Tagesgericht für 7 € 50 Fisch oder Fleisch oder Geflügel	**dish of the day** 7 € 50 fish or meat or poultry

LUNCHTIME MENU

Mittagsmenü **Vorspeise + Hauptgericht** **+ Kaffee**	lunchtime menu starter + main course + coffee

kleine Speisekarte   SNACK MENU

BEER

There are over 1,000 breweries in Germany with more than half of them in Bavaria. Many cities have at least one brewpub. Wheat beers are a speciality of Bavaria along with smoked beer. It is best to sample the local beer in the place it has been brewed. In Cologne you should try the pale refreshing *Kölsch* and in Düsseldorf sample the darkish malty *Altbier*.

Pilsner
A typical lager available all over Germany.

Kölsch
A pale-coloured, light-textured, fruity-flavoured beer brewed in Cologne. Best drunk in a brewpub.

Weißbier
The Bavarians also brew dark versions of their wheat beers. These may contain some malted wheat that has been darkened by roasting. *Dunkel* means dark.

Hefe-Weißbier
A speciality beer from Bavaria with a fruity, slightly smoked aroma.

WINE

Wines are usually categorised according to three criteria: the overall growing area, the village or even the vineyard where they are produced, and the type of grape they are made from. Major grape varieties include *Riesling*, *Edelzwicker*, *Gewürztraminer* and *Müller-Thurgau*. The names of the villages and vineyards producing wines are innumerable. The name of the wine is often the name of the village (e.g. *Nierstein*) plus the name of the particular vineyard (e.g. *Gutes Domtal*) which combined become *Niersteiner Gutes Domtal*.

Meßmer

1996
SCHEUREBE
KABINETT
Burrweiler Altenforst
Gutsabfüllung

◆

Weingut
Herbert Meßmer D-76835 Burrweiler
Qualitätswein mit Prädikat A.P.Nr. 50160952597

750 ml   PFALZ   alc.11.0%vol

Qualitätsweine mit Prädikat
This is the mark of the highest quality wine. If you want a good German wine, choose this rather than *Tafelwein*, *Landwein* or *QbA* (wine from a specified region).

Weinkarte   **WINE LIST**

A service charge is generally included in the billl, so tipping is discretionary.

Getränke nicht inklusive

drink not included

Weißwein	**trocken**
vice-vine	*tro-ken*
white wine	dry
Roséwein	**halbtrocken**
rohzay-vine	*halp-tro-ken*
rosé wine	medium dry
Rotweine	**lieblich**
rohtvine	*leeb-likh*
red wine	sweet
Sekt	**Tafelwein**
zekt	*tahfel-vine*
sparkling wine	table wine

A

Aal *eel*
  Aalsuppe *eel soup*
Allgäuer Emmentaler *whole-milk hard cheese from the Allgäu*
Allgäuer Käsespätzle *cheese noodles from the Allgäu*
Alpzirler *cow's milk cheese from Austria*
Alsterwasser *lager shandy*
Altbier *top-fermented beer from the lower Rhine*
Ananas *pineapple*
Apfel *apple*
  Apfelkorn *apple brandy*
  Apfelkuchen *apple cake*
  Apfelmus *apple puree*
  Apfelsaft *apple juice*
  Apfelsalami *salami with apple*
  Apfelstrudel *flaky pastry filled with apples and spices*
  Apfelwein *cider (apple wine)*
Aprikose *apricot*
Arme Ritter *French toast*
Art *style or fashion of e.g. 'nach Art des Hauses'* ⇒ *à la maison*
Artischocken *artichokes*
Aubergine *aubergine*
Auflauf *baked dish, can be sweet or savoury*
Aufschnitt *sliced cold meats*
Austern *oysters*

B

Bäckerofen *'baker's oven', pork and lamb bake from Saarland*
Backpflaumen *prunes*
Banane *banana*
Bandnudeln *ribbon pasta*
Barack *apricot brandy*
Barsch *perch*
Bauernfrühstück *scrambled eggs, bacon, cooked diced potatoes, onions, tomatoes*

Baunzerl *little bread roll with distinctive cut on top (Austria)*
Bayrisch Kraut *shredded cabbage cooked with sliced apples, wine and sugar*
Beilage *side dish*
Bereich Bernkastel *area along the Moselle producing crisp white wines*
Bergkäse *cheese from the Alps*
Berliner *doughnut filled with jam*
Berliner Weiße *fizzy beer with fruit syrup added*
Berner Erbsensuppe *soup made of dried peas with pig's trotters*
Bienenstich *type of cake, baked on a tray with a coating of almonds and sugar and a cream filling*
Bierschinken *beer sausage with ham*
Bierteig *pastry made with beer*
Bierwurst *beer sausage*
Birchermüsli *muesli with yoghurt (Switzerland)*
Birne *pear*
  Birnen, Bohnen und Speck *(Northern Germany) pears, green beans and bacon*
  Birne Helene *dessert with vanilla ice cream, pear and chocolate sauce*
  Birnenmost *pear wine*
  Birnensekt *sparkling pear wine*
Blattsalat *green salad*
blau *rare (meat); poached (fish)*
Blauschimmelkäse *blue cheese*
Blumenkohl *cauliflower*
Blunz'n *black pudding (South Germany and Austria)*
Blutwurst *black pudding*
Bockbier *strong beer (light or dark), drunk especially in Bavaria*

84

Bockwurst *boiled sausage.*
A popular snack served with
a bread roll
Böhmische Knödel *sliced*
dumpling
Bohnen *beans*
Bohnensalat *bean salad*
Bohnensuppe *thick bean and*
bacon soup
Bosniakerl *wholemeal roll with*
caraway seeds
Brathähnchen *roast chicken*
Brathering *fried herring (eaten*
cold)
Bratkartoffeln *fried potatoes*
Bratwurst *fried sausage.*
A popular snack served with
a bread roll
Brauner *strong black coffee with*
a little milk
Bremer Kükenragout *Bremen*
chicken fricassée
Brezel *(or in Bavaria: Brezn)*
pretzel
Broiler *spit-roasted chicken*
(East German)
Brombeeren *blackberries*
Bröselknödel *soup with little*
dumplings prepared with bone
marrow and breadcrumbs
Brot *bread*
Brötchen *bread roll*
Brühwurst *thick frankfurter*
B'soffene *pudding soaked in*
mulled wine
Buletten *thick hamburgers (but*
without the bread)
Buletten mit Kartoffelsalat *thick*
hamburgers with potato salad
Bündnerfleisch *raw beef smoked*
and dried, served thinly sliced
Burgenländische Krautsuppe *thick*
cabbage and vegetable soup

Butter *butter*
Butterbrot *open sandwich*
Butterkäse *high-fat cheese*

C

Cervelat *fine beef and pork*
salami
Chindbettering *ring of bread*
Cremeschnitten *cream slices*
Champignons *button mushrooms*
Currywurst *sausage served with*
a spicy sauce. A popular snack
originally from Berlin

D

Damenkäse *mild buttery cheese*
Dampfnudeln *hot yeast*
dumplings with vanilla sauce
Danziger Goldwasser *schnapps*
containing tiny bits of gold leaf
Datteln *dates*
Deutsches Beefsteak *thick*
hamburger (but without the
bread)
dicke Bohnen *broad beans*
Doppelbockbier *like Bockbier,*
but still stronger
Dorsch *cod*
Dresdner Suppentopf *Dresden*
vegetable soup with dumplings
(East German)
Dunkles *dark beer*

E

Ei *egg*
Eier im Glas *soft boiled eggs*
served in a glass
Eierkuchen *pancakes*
Eierschwammerln *chanterelles*
Eierspeispfandl *special Viennese*
omelette
eingelegt *pickled*
Einmachsuppe *chicken or veal*
broth with cream and egg

Einspänner coffee with whipped cream served in a glass (Austria)

Eintopf stew

Eis ice cream

Eisbecher knickerbocker glory

Eisbein boiled pork knuckle often served with sauerkraut

Eiskaffee iced coffee served with vanilla ice cream

Eiswein a rich, naturally sweet, white wine made from grapes which are harvested only after a period of frost

Emmentaler Swiss Emmental, whole-milk hard cheese

Ennstaler blue cheese from mixed milk

Ente duck

Erbach area producing scented white wines mainly from Riesling grape

Erbsen peas

Erbsenpüree green pea purée

Erbsensuppe pea soup

Erdäpfel potatoes

Erdäpfelgulasch spicy sausage and potato stew

Erdäpfelknödel potato and semolina dumplings

Erdäpfelkren relish with potato and horseradish (Austria)

Erdäpfelnudeln fried, boiled potato balls tossed in fried breadcrumbs

Erdbeeren strawberries

erster Gang first course

Essig vinegar

Export Bier premium beer

F

Falscher Hase baked mince meatloaf

Fasan pheasant

Feigen figs

Fenchel fennel

fettarm low in fat

Fisch fish

Fischfilet fish fillet

Fischgerichte fish and seafood

Fischklöße fish dumplings

Fischsuppe fish soup

flambiert flambé

Fledermaus boiled beef in horseradish cream browned in the oven

Fleisch meat

Fleischgerichte meat dishes

Fleischklößchen meatballs

Fleischlaberln highly seasoned meat cake (Austria)

Fleischpflanzerl thick hamburgers (without the bread)

Fleischsalat sausage salad with onions

Fleischsuppe meat soup served with dumplings

Flunder flounder

Fondue melted cheese with wine and bread for dipping

Forelle trout

Forelle blau steamed trout with potatoes and vegetables

Forelle Müllerin trout fried in batter with almonds

Forelle Steiermark trout fillet with bacon in white sauce

Frikadelle thick hamburger (without the bread)

frisch fresh

Fritattensuppe beef broth with strips of pancake (Austria)

frittiert fried

Froschschenkel frogs' legs

Frucht fresh fruit

Früchtetee fruit tea

Fruchtsaft fruit juice

Fünfkernbrot wholemeal bread made with five different cereals

G

Gang course
Gans goose
  Gänseleber foie gras
  Gänseleberpastete goose
  liver pâté
Gebäck pastries
gebacken baked
gebackene Leber liver fried
  in breadcrumbs
gebraten roasted/fried
gedämpft steamed
Geflügel poultry
gefüllt stuffed/filled
  gefüllte Kalbsbrust stuffed
  breast of veal
  gefüllte Paprika peppers filled
  with mince
gegrillt grilled
  gegrillter Lachs grilled salmon
Gehacktes mince
gekocht boiled
  gekochtes Rindfleisch mit
  grüner Soße boiled beef with
  green sauce
gemischter Salat mixed salad
Gemüse vegetables
  Gemüse und Klöße vegetables
  and dumplings
  Gemüselasagne vegetable
  lasagne
  Gemüseplatte mixed vegetables
  Gemüsesuppe vegetable soup
geräuchert smoked
Gericht dish
geschmort braised
Geschnetzeltes thinly sliced meat
  in sauce served with potatoes
  or rice
Geselchtes smoked meats
  (Austria)
Gespritzter spritzer, white wine
  and soda water

Gewürzgurken gherkins
Gitziprägel baked rabbit in
  batter (a Swiss dish)
Glühwein mulled wine
Goldbarsch redfish
Graf Görz Austrian soft cheese
Grammeln croissant stuffed with
  bacon
Grießklößchensuppe soup with
  semolina dumplings
Grießtaler gnocchi
Grog hot rum
grüne Bohnen green beans
grüne Veltlinersuppe green wine
  soup
grüner Salat green salad
Grünkohl kale
Gruyère gruyère cheese
Güggeli roast chicken with
  onions and mushrooms in white
  wine sauce (Switzerland)
Gulasch stewed diced beef and
  pork with paprika served with
  dumplings and red cabbage
Gulaschsuppe spicy meat soup
  with paprika
Gulyas beef stew with paprika
Gumpoldskirchner spicy white
  wine from Austria
Gurke cucumber
  Gurkensalat cucumber salad
gutbürgerliche Küche traditional
  German cooking
Gyros kebab

H

Hackbraten mincemeat roast
Hackepeter auf Schrippen mit
  Zwiebeln spiced minced pork
  on rolls, with onions
Hackfleisch mince
Hähnchen chicken
  Hähnchenbrust chicken breast

halbtrocken *medium-dry*
Hamburger Rundstück *Hamburg meat roll*
Hammel *mutton*
Hartkäse *hard cheese*
Hase *hare*
Hasenbraten *roast hare*
Hasenpfeffer *peppered rabbit stew*
Hauptgericht *main course*
Hausbrauerei *house brewery*
hausgemacht *home-made*
Hausmannskost *good traditional home cooking*
Hawaitoast *toast with cooked ham, pineapple slice and melted cheese*
Hecht *pike*
Hefeweizen *wheat beer*
Heidschnuckenragout *lamb stew*
heiß *hot*
Helles *light beer*
Hering *herring*
  Heringsschmaus *herring in creamy sauce*
Herz *heart*
Heuriger *new wine*
Himbeeren *raspberries*
  Himbeergeist *raspberry brandy*
Hirn *brain*
Hirsch *venison*
Hockheim *strong white wines from the Rheingau*
Honig *honey*
Hühnchen *chicken*
Hühnerfrikasse *chicken fricassée*
Hühnerschenkel *chicken drumsticks*
Hühnerleber *chicken liver*
Hummer *lobster*

I

Ingwer *ginger*

J

Jägerschnitzel *cutlet served with mushrooms and wine sauce*
Jogurt *yoghurt*
Johannisbeeren *redcurrants*
Jura Omelette *bacon, potato and onion omelette*

K

Kabeljau *cod*
Kaffee *coffee*
  Kaffee komplett *coffee with milk and sugar*
  Kaffee mit Milch *coffee with milk*
Kaisermelange *black coffee with an egg yolk*
Kaiserschmarren *strips of pancake served with raisins, sugar and cinnamon*
Kakao *cocoa*
Kalb *veal*
  Kalbsbraten *roast veal*
  Kalbshaxe *knuckle of veal*
  Kalbskoteletts *veal cutlets*
  Kalbsleber *calf's liver*
  Kalbsschnitzel *veal escalope*
kalt *cold*
  kalte Platte *cold meat platter*
Kaninchen *rabbit*
Kapuziner *Austrian equivalent to a cappuccino which is black coffee with a drop of milk*
Karotten *carrots*
Karpfen *carp*
  Karpfen blau *poached carp*
  Karpfen in Bier *carp poached in beer with herbs*
Kartoffeln *potatoes*
  Kartoffelklöße *potato dumplings*
  Kartoffelpuffer *potato pancakes. A popular snack*

Kartoffelpüree *mashed potatoes*
Kartoffelsalat *potato salad*
Kartoffelsuppe *potato soup*
Käse *cheese*
  Käsebrötchen *roll with small bacon pieces in the dough and melted cheese on top*
  Käsefondue *dish made from melted cheese and flavoured with wine and kirsch into which you dip bread*
  Käsekuchen *cheesecake*
  Käsenudeln *noodles served with cheese*
  Käseplatte *cheese platter with various cheeses*
  Käsesuppe *cheese soup*
  Kässpätzle *cheese-covered dish of homemade noodles*
Kasseler *smoked pork*
  Kasseler Rippe mit Sauerkraut *smoked pork rib with sauerkraut*
Kastanienroulade *roulade with chestnut filling*
Katenspeck *streaky bacon*
Kaviar *caviar*
Kekse *biscuits*
Kirschen *cherries*
Kirschwasser *cherry schnapps*
Kirtagssuppe *soup with caraway seed thickened with potato*
Klops *rissole*
Klöße *dumplings*
Knackwurst *hot spicy sausage. A popular snack served with bread*
Knoblauch *garlic*
Knödel *dumpling*
  Knödelbeignets *fruit dumplings*
Knöderl *dumplings*
Kohl *cabbage*

Kohlrouladen *stuffed cabbage*
Kohlsprossen *Brussels sprouts*
Kölsch *top-fermented beer from Cologne*
Kompott *stewed fruit*
Königsberger Klopse *meatballs served in thick white sauce with capers*
Kopfsalat *lettuce salad*
Korn *rye spirit*
Kotelett *pork chop/cutlet dipped in breadcrumbs and deep fried*
Krabben *prawns*
  Krabbencocktail *prawn cocktail*
Kraftbrot *wheatgerm bread*
Kraftfleisch *corned beef*
Kraftsuppe *consommé*
Krapfen *doughnut*
Kräuter *herbs*
Kräutertee *herbal tea*
Krautwickerl *stuffed cabbage*
Kren *horseradish*
Kristallweizen *a kind of sparkling beer*
Kroketten *croquettes*
Kürbis *pumpkin*

L

Labskaus *cured pork, herring and potato stew*
Lachs *salmon*
  Lachsbrot *smoked salmon with bread*
Lamm *lamb*
Lammkeule *leg of lamb*
Languste *spiny lobster*
Lasagne *lasagne*
Lauch *leeks*
Leber *liver*
Leberkäse *pork liver meatloaf*
Leberknödelsuppe *light soup with chicken liver dumplings*
Leberpastete *liver paté*
Leberwurst *liver sausage*

Lebkuchen *gingerbread*
Leinsamenbrot *wholemeal bread with linseed*
Leipziger Allerlei *vegetable dish made from peas, carrots, cauliflower and cabbage (East German)*
Lendenbraten *roast loin*
Lieblich *sweet (wine)*
Likör *liqueur*
Limburger *strong cheese flavoured with herbs*
Limonade *lemonade*
Linsen *lentils*
Linsenspecksalat *lentil salad with bacon*
Linsensuppe *lentil and sausage soup*
Linzer Torte *latticed tart with jam topping*
Liptauer Quark *cream cheese with paprika and herbs*
Lunge *lungs*

M

Mais *sweetcorn*
Maiskolben *corn on the cob*
Makrele *mackerel*
Malzbier *dark malt beer*
Mandarine *tangerine*
Mandeln *almonds*
Marillenknödel *apricot dumplings (Austria)*
Marmelade *jam*
Maronitorte *chestnut tart*
Märzenbier *stronger beer brewed for special occasions*
Mastochsenhaxe *knuckle of beef (with sauce) from Sachsen-Anhalt (East German)*
Matjes *herring*
Maultaschen *ravioli-like pasta filled with pork, veal and spinach mixture*

Meeresfrüchte *seafood*
Meerrettich *horseradish*
Mehrkornbrötchen *rolls made with several kinds of wholemeal flour*
Melange *milky coffee*
Melone *melon*
Mettenden *sausage with a filling similar to mince*
Milch *milk*
Milchrahmstrudel *strudel filled with egg custard and soft cheese*
Milchreis *rice pudding*
Milchshake *milk shake*
Mineralwasser *mineral water*
Mirabellen *small yellow plums*
Mischbrot *grey bread made with rye and wheat flour*
Mittagstisch *lunch menu*
Mohn *poppy seed*
Mohnnudeln *noodles with poppy seeds, cinnamon, sugar and butter*
Mohntorte *gâteau with poppy seeds*
Möhren *carrots*
Möhrensalat *carrot salad*
Mohr im Hemd *chocolate pudding*
Most *fruit juice; (in the south) fruit wine*
Münchener *a kind of dark lager from Munich*
Muscheln *mussels*

N

Nachspeisen *desserts*
Nieren *kidneys*
Nierstein *village on the Rhine producing medium to sweet white Rheinwein*
Nockerln *small dumplings*

Nudeln *noodles*
  Nudelsuppe *noodle soup*
Nüsse *nuts*
  Nusskuchen *nut cake*
  Nusstorte *nut gâteau*

O

Obst *fruit*
  Obstkuchen *fruit cake*
  Obstsalat *fruit salad*
Ochsenschwanz *oxtail*
  Ochsenschwanzsuppe *oxtail soup*
Öl *oil*
Oppenheim *village on the Rhine producing fine white wines*
Orange *orange*
Orangensaft *orange juice*

P

Palatschinken *pancakes filled with curd mixture or jam or ice cream*
Pampelmuse *grapefruit*
paniert *coated with breadcrumbs*
Paprika *peppers*
Pellkartoffeln *small jacket potatoes served with their skins, often accompanied by Quark*
Pfannkuchen *pancakes*
Pfeffer *pepper*
  Pfefferkäse mit Schinken *ham and pepper cheese log*
Pfifferlinge *chanterelles*
Pfirsich *peach*
Pflaumen *plums*
  Pflaumenkuchen *plum tart*
Pils, Pilsner *a strong, slightly bitter lager*
Pilze *mushrooms*
Pilzsuppe *mushroom soup*
Pommes frites *chips*
Powidltascherl *ravioli-like pasta filled with plum jam (Austria)*

Preiselbeeren *cranberries*
Pumpernickel *very dark bread made with wholemeal coarse rye flour*
Punschpudding *pudding containing alcohol*
Pute *turkey*
  Putenschnitzel *turkey breast in breadcrumbs*

Q

Quark *curd cheese*

R

Raclette *melted cheese and potatoes*
Radler *beer with lemonade (Bavaria)*
Ragout *stew*
Rahm *sour cream*
Rahmschnitzel *cutlet with a creamy sauce*
Rahmsuppe *creamy soup*
Räucherkäse mit Schinken *smoked cheese with bacon pieces in it*
Räucherkäse mit Walnüssen *smoked cheese with pieces of walnut in it*
Räucherlachs *smoked salmon*
Räucherspeck *smoked bacon*
Reh *venison*
  Rehrücken *roast saddle of venison*
Reibekuchen *potato cakes*
Reis *rice*
Riesling *Riesling wine*
  Rieslingsuppe *wine soup made with Riesling*
Rind(fleisch) *beef*
  Rinderbraten *roast beef*
  Rinderrouladen *rolled beef (beef olives)*
Rippenbraten *roast spare ribs*

Risi lisi, Risibisi rice with peas
Rollmops marinated herring
  fillets rolled up with small
  pieces of onion, gherkins and
  white peppercorns
Rosenkohl Brussels sprouts
Roséwein rosé wine
Rosinen raisins
Rösti fried diced potatoes,
  onions and bacon
Rotbarsch rosefish
rote Bete beetroot
rote Grütze raspberry, red
  currant and wine jelly served
  with fresh cream
rote Rübe beetroot
Rotkohl red cabbage
Rotwein red wine
Roulade beef olive
Rübe turnip
Rührei scrambled eggs

S

Sachertorte rich chocolate
  gâteau
Saft juice
Sahne cream
Saison season e.g. je nach saison
  ⇒ depending on the season
Salat salad
Salz salt
Salzkartoffeln boiled potatoes
Sardellen anchovies
Sardinen sardines
Sauerbraten braised pickled
  beef served with dumplings
  and vegetables
Sauerkraut shredded pickled
  white cabbage
Scampi scampi
Schafskäse ewe's milk cheese
scharf spicy
Schaschlik shish kebab
Schellfisch haddock

Schnaps strong spirit
Schinken ham
  Schinkenkipferl ham-filled
  croissant
  Schinkenwurst ham sausage
Schlachtplatte mixture of cold
  sausages and meat
Schlagsahne whipped cream
Schmelzkäse cheese spread
Schmorgurken hotpot with
  cucumber and meat
Schnecke snail
Schnittlauch chives
  Schnittlauchbrot chives on bread
Schnitzel escalope served with
  potatoes and vegetables
Schokolade chocolate
Schokoladentorte chocolate
  gateaux
Scholle plaice
Schorle wine and sparkling water
Schwäbischer Apfelkuchen apple
  cake from Swabia
Schwammerlgulasch mushroom
  stew
Schwarzbrot rye bread
schwarze Johannisbeeren
  blackcurrants
schwarzer Tee black tea
Schwarzwälder Kirschtorte Black
  Forest gâteau
Schwarzwälder Schinken Black
  Forest ham
Schwarzwälder Torte fruit
  compote flan with cream
Schwein pork
  Schweinebraten roast pork
  Schweinefleisch pork
  Schweinehaxe knuckle of pork
  Schweinekotelett pork chop
  Schweinsrostbraten roast pork
Schwertfisch swordfish
Seezunge sole
Sekt sparkling wine like
  champagne

Selters(wasser) *sparkling mineral water*
Semmeln *bread rolls*
Semmelknödel *whole roll dumpling*
Senf *mustard*
Seniorenteller *small portion of a dish for senior citizens*
Sesam *sesame*
Scampi *scampi*
Slivovitz *plum schnapps*
Sonnenblumenbrot *wholemeal bread with sunflower seeds*
Soße *sauce*
Spanferkel *suckling pig*
Spargel *asparagus*
Spargelcremesuppe *cream of asparagus soup*
Spargelsalat *asparagus salad*
Spätzle *home-made noodles*
Speck *bacon (fat)*
Spezialität des Hauses *speciality of the house/chef's special*
Spiegelei *fried egg, sunny side up*
Spieß *kebab style*
Spinat *spinach*
Sprudel *sparkling mineral water*
Stachelbeeren *gooseberries*
Stachelbeertorte *gooseberry tart*
Stangl *croissant covered with cheese*
Starkbier *strong beer*
Steinbutt *turbot*
Steinpilze *wild mushroom found in the woods*
Steirischer Selchkäse *ewe's milk cheese (Austria)*
Steirisches Lammkarree mit Basilikum *lamb baked with basil (Austria)*
Sterz *Austrian polenta*
Stollen *spiced loaf with candied peel traditionally eaten at Christmas*
Strudel *strudel*
Sulz/Sülze *meat in aspic*
Suppen *soups*
süß *sweet*
süßsauer *sweet-and-sour*

T

Tafelspitz *boiled beef of various cuts*
Tafelspitzsulz *beef in aspic*
Tagesgericht *dish of the day*
Tagesppuppe *soup of the day*
Tee *tea*
Tee mit Milch *tea with milk*
Tee mit Zitrone *tea with lemon*
Thunfisch *tuna fish*
Thüringer Rostbratwurst *sausages from Thuringia, grilled or fried*
Tilsiter *savoury cheese with sharpish taste*
Tintenfisch *squid*
Tomaten *tomatoes*
Tomatensaft *tomato juice*
Tomatensoße *tomato sauce*
Topf *stew*
Topfen *curd cheese (Austria)*
Topfenknödel *curd cheese dumplings*
Topfennudeln *pasta with cheese*
Topfenstrudel *flaky pastry strudel with curd-cheese filling*
Torte *gateau*
Trauben *grapes*
Traubensaft *grape juice*
Trocken *dry (wine)*
Truthahn *turkey*
Türkischer *Turkish coffee*

U

überbacken *baked in the oven with cheese on top*

V

vegetarische Gerichte *vegetarian dishes*
Vollkorn- *wholemeal*
Vollkornbrot *wholemeal bread*
Vorspeisen *starters*

W

Wacholder *juniper*
Waldpilze *wild mushrooms*
Walnüsse *walnuts*
warm *warm*
  warmer Krautsalat *salad with warm cabbage and crunchy bacon*
Wasser *water*
Weichkäse *cream cheese*
Wein *wine*
Weinbrand *brandy*
Weinkarte *wine list*
Weißbrot *wheat bread*
Weiße *golden wheat beer*
Weißkohl *white cabbage*
Weißwein *white wine*
Weißwurst *white sausage (veal and pork with herbs)*
Weizenbier *wheat beer*
Wels *catfish*
Westfälischer Schinken *Westphalian ham*
Wiener *frankfurters*
Wiener Backhendl *roast chicken in breadcrumbs*
Wiener Fischfilets *fish fillets baked in sour cream sauce*
Wiener Hofburgtorte *chocolate gâteau*
Wiener Kartoffelsuppe *potato soup with mushrooms*
Wiener Sachertorte *Viennese chocolate cake*
Wiener Schnitzel *veal escalope fried in breadcrumbs*

Wiener Würstchen *frankfurter*
Wild *game*
  Wildbraten *roast venison*
  Wildgulasch *game stew*
Wildschwein *wild boar*
Wirsingkohl *Savoy cabbage*
Wurst *sausage*
Würstchen *frankfurter*
Würzfleisch *strips of meat roasted in a spicy sauce*

Z

Zander *pike-perch*
Ziegenkäse *goat's milk cheese*
Ziegett *mixed milk cheese*
Zigeunerschnitzel *cutlet in paprika sauce*
Zillertaler *cow's cheese from the Zillertal*
Zimt *cinnamon*
Zitrone *lemon*
  Zitronentee *lemon tea*
Zopf *braided bread loaf*
Zucchini *courgette*
Zucker *sugar*
Zuger Köteli *baked dace with herbs and wine*
Zunge *tongue*
Zürcher Geschnetzeltes *thinly sliced meat (veal or turkey), served with a wine sauce and mushrooms (and side dish such as Rösti) (Switzerland)*
Zwetschgen *plums*
  Zwetschgendatschi *damson tart*
  Zwetschgenknödel *plum dumplings*
Zwiebeln *onions*
  Zwiebelkuchen *onion flan*
  Zwiebelrostbraten *large steak with onions*
  Zwiebelsalami *salami with onion*
  Zwiebelsuppe *onion soup*

DICTIONARY
English-German
German-English

A

a *(with der words)* ein
  (with die words) eine
  (with das words) ein
abbey die Abtei
able: *to be able* können
abortion die Abtreibung
about *(concerning)* über
  about 4 o'clock ungefähr vier Uhr
above *(overhead)* oben
  (higher than) über
abroad im Ausland
abscess der Abszess
accelerator das Gaspedal
to accept akzeptieren
accident der Unfall
accident and emergency
  department die Notaufnahme
accommodation die Unterkunft
to accompany begleiten
account *(bill)* die Rechnung
  (in bank) das Konto
account number die Kontonummer
to ache: *it aches* es tut weh
acid die Säure
actor der Schauspieler
adaptor der Adapter
address die Adresse
  what is the address? wie lautet die
  Adresse?
address book das Adressbuch
adhesive tape das Klebeband
admission fee der Eintrittspreis
adult der/die Erwachsene
  for adults für Erwachsene
advance: *in advance* im Voraus
advertisement *(in paper)* die Anzeige
to advise raten
A&E die Notaufnahme
aeroplane das Flugzeug
aerosol die Spraydose
afraid: *to be afraid of* Angst haben
  vor
after *(afterwards)* danach
  after lunch nach dem Mittagessen
afternoon der Nachmittag
  this afternoon heute Nachmittag

tomorrow afternoon morgen
  Nachmittag
  in the afternoon am Nachmittag
aftershave das Rasierwasser
again wieder
against gegen
age das Alter
agency die Agentur
ago: *a week ago* vor einer Woche
to agree vereinbaren
agreement die Vereinbarung
AIDS das Aids
air das Luft
airbag der Airbag
airbed die Luftmatratze
air conditioning die Klimaanlage
air freshener der Lufterfrischer
airline die Fluggesellschaft
air mail: *by air mail* per Luftpost
airplane das Flugzeug
airport der Flughafen
airport bus der Flughafenbus
air ticket das Flugticket
aisle der Gang
alarm die Alarmanlage
alarm call der Weckruf
alarm clock der Wecker
alcohol der Alkohol
alcohol-free alkoholfrei
alcoholic alkoholisch
all alle
allergic: *to be allergic to* allergisch
  sein gegen
  I'm allergic to... ich bin allergisch
  gegen...
allergy die Allergie
to allow erlauben
  to be allowed dürfen
all right *(agreed)* in Ordnung
  are you all right? geht es Ihnen
  gut?
almost fast
alone allein
Alps die Alpen
already schon
also auch
altar der Altar

aluminium foil die Alufolie
always immer
a.m. vormittags
am: *I am* ich bin
amber *(traffic lights)* das Gelb
ambulance der Krankenwagen
America Amerika
American *adj* amerikanisch
m/f der/die Amerikaner(in)
amount: *total amount* die
Gesamtsumme
anaesthetic die Narkose
local anaesthetic die örtliche
Betäubung
general anaesthetic die Vollnarkose
anchor der Anker
and und
angina die Angina
angry zornig
animal das Tier
ankle der Knöchel
anniversary der Jahrestag
to announce bekannt geben
announcement die
Bekanntmachung
annual jährlich
another *(additional)* noch ein/noch
eine/noch ein
(different) ein anderer/eine
andere/ein anderes
another beer please noch ein Bier
bitte
answer die Antwort
to answer antworten
answerphone der Anrufbeantworter
antacid das säurebindende Mittel
antibiotic das Antibiotikum
antifreeze das Frostschutzmittel
antihistamine das Antihistamin
anti-inflammatory das entzündungs-
hemmende Mittel
antiques die Antiquitäten
antique shop der Antiquitätenladen
antiseptic das Antiseptikum
any jegliche(r/s)
have you any apples? haben Sie
Äpfel?

anybody jeder
anything irgendetwas
anywhere irgendwo
apartment das Appartement
appendicitis die
Blinddarmentzündung
apple der Apfel
appointment der Termin
I have an appointment ich habe
einen Termin
approximately ungefähr
apricot die Aprikose
April der April
apron die Schürze
architect der/die Architekt(in)
are sind ; seid ; bin
arm der Arm
armbands *(to swim)* die
Schwimmflügel
armchair der Sessel
to arrange vereinbaren
to arrest verhaften
arrival die Ankunft
to arrive ankommen
art die Kunst
art gallery die Kunsthalle
arthritis die Arthritis
artichokes die Artischocken
artificial künstlich
artist der/die Künstler(in)
ashtray der Aschenbecher
to ask *(question)* fragen
(for something) bitten um
asleep: *to be asleep* schlafen
to fall asleep einschlafen
asparagus der Spargel
aspirin das Aspirin
asthma das Asthma
I have asthma ich habe Asthma
at: *at the hotel* im Hotel
at home zu Hause
at 8 o'clock um acht Uhr
at once sofort
at night am Abend
ATM der Geldautomat
to attack angreifen

attractive attraktiv
aubergine die Aubergine
auction die Auktion
audience das Publikum
August der August
aunt die Tante
au pair das Au-pair-Mädchen
Australia Australien
Australian *adj* australisch
  m/f der/die Australier(in)
Austria Österreich
Austrian *adj* österreichisch
  m/f der/die Österreicher(in)
author der/die Autor(in)
automatic automatisch
automatic car das Automatikauto
auto-teller der Geldautomat
autumn der Herbst
available erhältlich
avalanche die Lawine
avenue die Allee
average der Durchschnitt
to avoid *(obstacle)* ausweichen
  (person) meiden
awake wach
away weg
awful schrecklich
axe die Axt
axle *(car)* die Achse

B

baby das Baby
baby food die Babynahrung
baby milk die Babymilch
baby's bottle die Babyflasche
baby seat *(in car)* der Kindersitz
babysitter der/die Babysitter(in)
baby wipes die Babytücher
back *(of body, hand)* der Rücken
backpack der Rucksack
bacon der Speck
bad *(weather, news)* schlecht
  (fruit, vegetables) verdorben
bag die Tasche
baggage das Gepäck

baggage allowance das Freigepäck
baggage reclaim die
  Gepäckausgabe
bait *(for fishing)* der Köder
baked gebacken
baker's die Bäckerei
balcony der Balkon
ball der Ball
ballet das Ballett
balloon der Ballon
Baltic Sea die Ostsee
banana die Banane
band *(musical)* die Band
bandage der Verband
bank die Bank
  (river) das Ufer
bank account das Bankkonto
banknote der Geldschein
bar die Bar
barbecue der Grill
  to have a barbecue eine Grillparty
  geben
barber der Herrenfriseur
to bark bellen
barn die Scheune
basement das Untergeschoss
basket der Korb
basketball der Basketball
Basle Basel
bat *(racquet)* der Schläger
bath das Bad
  tub die Badewanne
  to have a bath ein Bad nehmen
bathing cap die Badekappe
bathroom das Badezimmer
  with bathroom mit Bad
battery die Batterie
bay *(along coast)* die Bucht
B&B Übernachtung mit Frühstück
to be sein
beach der Strand
  private beach der Privatstrand
  sandy beach der Sandstrand
  nudist beach der FKK-Strand
beach hut der Strandkorb
beans die Bohnen

beard der Bart
beautiful schön
because weil
to become werden
bed das Bett
  double bed das Doppelbett
  single bed das Einzelbett
  twin beds zwei Einzelbetten
bed and breakfast Übernachtung
  mit Frühstück
bedclothes die Bettwäsche
bedroom das Schlafzimmer
bee die Biene
beef das Rindfleisch
beer das Bier
before vor
  before breakfast vor dem Frühstück
to begin beginnen
behind hinter
beige beige
to believe glauben
bell *(church)* die Glocke
  (door) die Klingel
to belong to gehören zu
below unterhalb
belt der Gürtel
bend *(in road)* die Kurve
berth *(train, ship)* die Kabine
beside *(next to)* neben
best: *the best* der/die/das beste
bet die Wette
to bet on wetten auf
better besser
  better than besser als
between zwischen
bib *(baby's)* das Lätzchen
bicycle das Fahrrad
  by bicycle mit dem Fahrrad
bicycle repair kit das
  Fahrradflickzeug
big groß
  bigger than größer als
bike *(push bike)* das Fahrrad
  (motorbike) das Motorrad
bike lock das Fahrradschloss
bikini der Bikini

bill *(account)* die Rechnung
bin *(dustbin)* der Mülleimer
bin liner der Müllbeutel
binoculars das Fernglas
bird der Vogel
biro der Kugelschreiber
birth die Geburt
birth certificate die Geburtsurkunde
birthday der Geburtstag
  happy birthday! alles Gute zum
  Geburtstag!
  my birthday is on... ich habe am ...
  Geburtstag
birthday card die Geburtstagskarte
birthday present das
  Geburtstagsgeschenk
biscuits die Kekse
bit *(piece)* das Stück
  a bit (a little) ein bisschen
bite *(by insect)* der Biss
  (of food) der Bissen
to bite beißen
  (insect) stechen
bitten *(by insect)* gestochen
  I've been bitten ich bin gestochen
  worden
bitter *(taste)* bitter
black schwarz
black ice das Glatteis
blanket die Decke
bleach das Bleichmittel
to bleed bluten
blender der Mixer
blind *(person)* blind
blind *(for window)* das Rollo
blister die Blase
blocked *(pipe, road)* verstopft
blond *(person)* blond
blood das Blut
blood group die Blutgruppe
blood pressure der Blutdruck
blood test der Bluttest
blouse die Bluse
to blow-dry föhnen
blue blau
  dark blue dunkelblau
  light blue hellblau

blunt *(knife, blade)* stumpf

boar das Wildschwein

to board *(plane, train, etc)* einsteigen

boarding card/pass die Bordkarte

boarding house die Pension

boat *(large)* das Schiff
  (small) das Boot

boat trip die Bootsfahrt

body der Körper
  (dead) die Leiche

to boil kochen

boiled gekocht

boiler der Boiler

bomb die Bombe

bone der Knochen
  fish bone die Gräte

bonnet *(car)* die Motorhaube

book das Buch
  book of tickets die Mehrfahrtenkarte

to book buchen

booking *(in hotel, train, etc)* die Reservierung

booking office *(train)* der Fahrkartenschalter

bookshop die Buchhandlung

boot *(car)* der Kofferraum

boots *(long)* die Stiefel
  (ankle) die Schnürschuhe

border *(country)* die Grenze

boring langweilig

born: I was born in 1960 ich bin neunzehn-hundertsechzig geboren

to borrow borgen

boss der/die Chef(in)

both beide

bottle die Flasche
  a bottle of wine eine Flasche Wein
  a half-bottle eine kleine Flasche

bottle opener der Flaschenöffner

bowl *(soup, etc)* die Schüssel

bow tie die Fliege

box *(of wood)* die Kiste
  (of cardboard) der Karton

box office die Kasse

boy der Junge

boyfriend der Freund

bra der BH

bracelet das Armband

to brake bremsen

brake fluid die Bremsflüssigkeit

brake light das Bremslicht

brake pads die Bremsbeläge

brakes die Bremsen

branch *(of tree)* der Ast
  (of bank, etc) die Filiale

brand *(make)* die Marke

brass das Messing

brave mutig

bread das Brot
  brown bread das Schwarzbrot
  French bread das Baguette
  sliced bread geschnittenes Brot
  white bread das Weißbrot

bread roll das Brötchen

to break *(object)* zerbrechen

breakable zerbrechlich

breakdown *(car)* die Panne

breakdown van die Pannenhilfe

breakfast das Frühstück
  when is breakfast? wann gibt es Frühstück?

breast die Brust

to breast-feed stillen

to breathe atmen

brick der Ziegel

bride die Braut

bridegroom der Bräutigam

bridge die Brücke

briefcase die Aktentasche

to bring bringen

Britain Großbritannien

British britisch

brochure die Broschüre

broken gebrochen

broken down *(car, etc)* kaputt

bronchitis die Bronchitis

bronze die Bronze

brooch die Brosche

broom der Besen

brother der Bruder

brother-in-law der Schwager

brown braun
bruise der Bluterguss
brush die Bürste
   (for floor) der Besen
bubble bath das Schaumbad
bucket der Eimer
buffet das Buffet
buffet car der Speisewagen
to build bauen
building das Gebäude
bulb (electric) die Glühbirne
bumbag die Gürteltasche
bumper die Stoßstange
bunch (flowers) der Blumenstrauß
   (grapes) die Weintraube
bureau de change die Wechselstube
burger der Hamburger
burglar der/die Einbrecher(in)
burn die Brandwunde
to burn verbrennen
bus der Bus
bus station der Busbahnhof
bus stop die Bushaltestelle
bus ticket der Busfahrschein
bus tour die Busfahrt
business das Geschäft
   on business geschäftlich
business address die
   Geschäftsadresse
business card die Visitenkarte
businessman/woman der
   Geschäftsmann/die Geschäftsfrau
business trip die Dienstreise ; die
   Geschäftsreise
busy beschäftigt
but aber
butcher's die Fleischerei
butter die Butter
button der Knopf
to buy kaufen
by (beside) bei
   (via) über
   by bus mit dem Bus
   by car mit dem Auto
   by ship mit dem Schiff
   by train mit dem Zug
bypass die Umgehungsstraße

C

cab (taxi) das Taxi
cabaret das Varieté
cabin (on ship) die Kabine
   inside cabin Innenkabine
   outside cabin Außenkabine
cabin crew die Besatzung
cable car die Seilbahn
café das Café
   internet café das Internet-Café
cake der Kuchen
cake shop die Konditorei
calculator der Taschenrechner
calendar der Kalender
call (on phone) der Anruf
to call (on phone) anrufen
calm (person) ruhig
   (weather) windstill
camcorder der Camcorder
camera die Kamera
camera shop das Fotogeschäft
to camp campen
camping gas das Campinggas
camping mat die Isomatte
camping stove der Campingkocher
campsite der Campingplatz
can die Dose
can opener der Dosenöffner
can (to be able) können
   I can/we can ich kann/wir können
Canada Kanada
Canadian adj kanadisch
   m/f der/die Kanadier(in)
canal der Kanal
to cancel stornieren
cancellation die Stornierung
cancer der Krebs
candle die Kerze
canoe das Kanu
cap (hat) die Mütze
   (diaphragm) das Diaphragma
capital (city) die Hauptstadt
car das Auto
car alarm die Autoalarmanlage
car ferry die Autofähre

car hire die Autovermietung
car insurance die Kfz-Versicherung
car keys die Autoschlüssel
car park der Parkplatz
car parts die Ersatzteile
car radio das Autoradio
car seat *(children's)* der Kindersitz
car wash die Waschanlage
caravan der Wohnwagen
carburettor der Vergaser
card *(greetings)* die (Glückwunsch)karte
 (playing) die Spielkarte
cardboard die Pappe
cardigan die Strickjacke
careful vorsichtig
 be careful! passen Sie auf!
carpet der Teppich
carriage *(railway)* der Wagen
carrot die Karotte
to carry tragen
carton der Karton
case *(suitcase)* der Koffer
cash das Bargeld
to cash *(cheque)* einlösen
cash desk die Kasse
cash dispenser der Geldautomat
cashier der/die Kassierer(in)
cashpoint der Geldautomat
casino das Kasino
casserole dish die Kasserolle
cassette die Kassette
cassette player der Kassettenrekorder
castle das Schloss
 (medieval fortress) die Burg
casualty department die Unfallstation
cat die Katze
cat food das Katzenfutter
catalogue der Katalog
catalytic converter *(car)* der Katalysator
to catch *(bus, train)* nehmen
cathedral der Dom
Catholic katholisch

cauliflower der Blumenkohe
cave die Höhle
cavity *(in tooth)* das Loch
CD die CD
CD player der CD-Spieler
ceiling die Decke
celery der Sellerie
cellar der Keller
cellphone das Handy
cemetery der Friedhof
cent *(euro)* der Cent
centimetre der Zentimeter
central zentral
central heating die Zentralheizung
central locking *(car)* die Zentralverriegelung
centre das Zentrum
century das Jahrhundert
ceramic die Keramik
cereal *(breakfast)* die Cornflakes
certain *(sure)* sicher
certificate die Bescheinigung
chain die Kette
chair der Stuhl
chairlift der Sessellift
chambermaid das Zimmermädchen
champagne der Champagner
change *(money)* das Wechselgeld
to change *(to alter)* ändern
 (bus, train, etc) umsteigen
 to change money Geld wechseln
 to change clothes sich umziehen
changing room die Umkleidekabine
Channel *(English)* der Kanal
chapel die Kapelle
charcoal die Holzkohle
charge *(fee)* die Gebühr
to charge berechnen
 please charge it to my account bitte setzen Sie es auf meine Rechnung
charger *(for battery, etc)* das Ladegerät
charter flight der Charterflug
cheap billig
cheap rate der Billigtarif

to check überprüfen
(passports) kontrollieren
to check in einchecken
(at hotel) sich an der Rezeption anmelden
check-in der Check-in
cheers! *(toast)* Prost!
cheese der Käse
chef der Koch/die Köchin
chemical toilet die chemische Toilette
chemist's die Drogerie
(for medicines) die Apotheke
cheque der Scheck
cheque book das Scheckheft
cheque card die Scheckkarte
cherry die Kirsche
chest *(body)* die Brust
chewing gum der Kaugummi
chicken das Hühnchen
chickenpox die Windpocken
child das Kind
children die Kinder
for children für Kinder
chimney der Schornstein
chin das Kinn
china das Porzellan
chips *(french fries)* die Pommes frites
chocolate die Schokolade
chocolates die Pralinen
choir der Chor
to choose auswählen
chopping board das Küchenbrett
Christian name der Vorname
Christmas Weihnachten
merry Christmas! frohe Weihnachten!
Christmas card die Weihnachtskarte
Christmas Eve Heiligabend
church die Kirche
cigar die Zigarre
cigarette die Zigarette
cigarette lighter das Feuerzeug
cigarette papers das Zigarettenpapier

cinema das Kino
circle *(theatre)* der Rang
circuit breaker der Unterbrecher
(for protection) der Schutzschalter
cistern *(of toilet)* der Spülkasten
city die Stadt
city centre das Stadtzentrum
class: *first class* erste Klasse
second class zweite Klasse
clean sauber
to clean säubern
cleaning lady die Putzfrau
clear klar
client der Kunde/die Kundin
cliff *(along coast)* die Klippe
(in mountains) der Felsen
to climb *(mountains)* klettern
climbing boots die Bergschuhe
clingfilm® die Frischhaltefolie
clinic die Klinik
cloakroom die Garderobe
clock die Uhr
to close schließen
closed geschlossen
cloth *(rag)* der Lappen
(fabric) der Stoff
clothes die Kleider
clothes line die Wäscheleine
clothes peg die Wäscheklammer
clothes shop das Bekleidungsgeschäft
cloudy bewölkt
club der Club
clutch *(car)* die Kupplung
coach *(bus)* der Bus
coach station der Busbahnhof
coach trip die Busreise
coal die Kohle
coast die Küste
coastguard die Küstenwache
coat der Mantel
coat hanger der Kleiderbügel
cockroach die Kakerlake
cocoa der Kakao
code der Kode

coffee der Kaffee
  black coffee schwarzer Kaffee
  white coffee Kaffee mit Milch
  decaffeinated coffee koffeinfreier
  Kaffee
coil *(IUD)* die Spirale
coin die Münze
Coke® die Cola
colander das Sieb
cold kalt
  I'm cold mir ist kalt
  it's cold es ist kalt
cold *(illness)* die Erkältung
  I have a cold ich habe mich erkältet
cold sore der Ausschlag
collar der Kragen
collar bone das Schlüsselbein
colleague der Kollege/die Kollegin
to collect *(person)* abholen
  (something) (etwas) sammeln
collection die Sammlung
Cologne Köln
colour die Farbe
colour-blind farbenblind
colour film der Farbfilm
comb der Kamm
to come kommen
  (to arrive) ankommen
to come back zurückkommen
to come in hereinkommen
  come in! herein!
comedy die Komödie
comfortable bequem
company *(firm)* die Firma
compartment *(in train)* das Abteil
compass der Kompass
to complain sich beschweren
complaint die Klage
complete vollständig
to complete vervollständigen
compulsory obligatorisch
computer der Computer
computer disk *(floppy)* die Diskette
computer game das Computerspiel
computer program das
  Computerprogramm

concert das Konzert
concert hall die Konzerthalle
concession die Ermäßigung
concussion die Gehirnerschütterung
conditioner *(hair)* der Conditioner
condom das Kondom
conductor der Schaffner/die
  Schaffnerin
conference die Konferenz
to confirm bestätigen
  please confirm bitte bestätigen Sie
confirmation *(flight, etc)* die
  Bestätigung
confused verwirrt
congratulations! herzlichen
  Glückwünsch!
connection *(train, etc)* die
  Verbindung
constipated verstopft
consulate das Konsulat
contact *(person)* der/die
  Ansprechpartner(in)
to contact kontaktieren
contact lens cleaner der
  Kontaktlinsenreiniger
contact lenses die Kontaktlinsen
to continue weitermachen
contraceptive das Verhütungsmittel
contract der Vertrag
convenient: *is it convenient?* passt
  es so?
convulsions die Krämpfe
to cook kochen
cooked gekocht
cooker der Herd
cookies die Kekse
cool kühl
cool-box *(for picnic)* die Kühlbox
copy *(duplicate)* die Kopie
to copy kopieren
cork der Korken
corkscrew der Korkenzieher
corner die Ecke
cornflakes die Cornflakes
corridor der Flur
cosmetics die Kosmetikartikel

cost *(price)* die Kosten
to cost kosten
  how much does it cost? wie viel
  kostet es?
costume *(swimming)* der Badeanzug
cot das Kinderbett
cottage das Ferienhäuschen
cotton die Baumwolle
cotton bud das Wattestäbchen
cotton wool die Watte
couchette der Liegewagen
cough der Husten
to cough husten
cough sweets die Hustenbonbons
counter *(shop, bar)* die Theke
country das Land
countryside die Landschaft
couple *(two people)* das Paar
  a couple of... ein paar...
courgettes die Zucchini
courier service der Kurierdienst
course *(of study)* der Kurs
  (of meal) der Gang
cousin der Cousin/die Cousine
cover charge *(in restaurant)* die
  Gedeckkosten
cow die Kuh
crafts das Kunsthandwerk
craftsperson der Handwerker/die
  Handwerkerin
cramps die Krämpfe
crash *(collision)* der Zusammenstoß
to crash einen Unfall haben
crash helmet der Sturzhelm
cream *(lotion)* die Creme
  (on milk) die Sahne
  soured cream saure Sahne
  whipped cream Schlagsahne
cream cheese der Frischkäse
credit card die Kreditkarte
crime das Verbrechen
crisps die Chips
to cross *(road)* überqueren
cross-channel ferry die Kanalfähre
cross-country skiing der Skilanglauf
crossing *(sea)* die Überfahrt

crossroads die Kreuzung
crossword puzzle das
  Kreuzworträtsel
crowd die Menge
crowded überfüllt
crown die Krone
cruise die Kreuzfahrt
crutches die Krücken
to cry *(weep)* weinen
crystal das Kristall
cucumber die Gurke
cufflinks die Manschettenknöpfe
cul-de-sac die Sackgasse
cup die Tasse
cupboard der Schrank
curlers die Lockenwickler
currency die Währung
current *(electric)* der Strom
  (water) die Strömung
curtains die Vorhänge
cushion das Kissen
custom *(tradition)* der Brauch
customer der Kunde/die Kundin
customs *(duty)* der Zoll
cut die Schnittwunde
to cut schneiden
cutlery das Besteck
cutlet das Schnitzel
to cycle Rad fahren
cycle track der Radweg
cycling das Radfahren
cyst die Zyste
cystitis die Blasenentzündung

D

daily *(each day)* täglich
dairy products die Milchprodukte
dam der Damm
damage der Schaden
damp feucht
dance der Tanz
to dance tanzen
danger die Gefahr
dangerous gefährlich

dark dunkel
after dark nach Einbruch der Dunkelheit
date das Datum
date of birth das Geburtsdatum
daughter die Tochter
daughter-in-law die Schwiegertochter
dawn die Morgendämmerung
day der Tag
every day jeden Tag
per day pro Tag
dead tot
deaf taub
dear *(in letter)* liebe(r/s)
(expensive) teuer
debts die Schulden
decaffeinated coffee der koffeinfreie Kaffee
December der Dezember
deckchair der Liegestuhl
to declare erklären
nothing to declare nichts zu verzollen
deep tief
deep freeze die Tiefkühltruhe
deer das Reh
to defrost entfrosten
to de-ice enteisen
delay die Verspätung
delayed verspätet
delicatessen das Feinkostgeschäft
delicious köstlich
demonstration die Demonstration
dental floss die Zahnseide
dentist der Zahnarzt/die Zahnärztin
dentures das Gebiss
deodorant das Deo
to depart abfahren
department die Abteilung
department store das Kaufhaus
departure die Abfahrt
(plane) der Abflug
departure lounge die Abflughalle
deposit die Anzahlung
to describe beschreiben

description die Beschreibung
desk der Schreibtisch
dessert der Nachtisch
details die Details
detergent das Waschmittel
detour der Umweg
to develop *(photos)* entwickeln
diabetes der Diabetes
diabetic person der Diabetiker/die Diabetikerin
to dial wählen
dialling code die Vorwahl
dialling tone der Wählton
diamond der Diamant
diarrhoea der Durchfall
diapers die Windeln
diaphragm *(contraception)* das Diaphragma
diary der Terminkalender
dice der Würfel
dictionary das Wörterbuch
to die sterben
diesel der Diesel
diet die Diät
I'm on a diet ich muss eine Diät einhalten
special diet spezielle Diät
different verschieden
difficult schwierig
digital camera die Digitalkamera
digital radio das Digitalradio
to dilute verdünnen
dinghy *(rubber)* das Schlauchboot
dining room das Esszimmer
dinner *(evening meal)* das Abendessen
to have dinner zu Abend essen
diplomat der Diplomat/die Diplomatin
direct *(route)* direkt
(train, etc) durchgehend
directions: *to ask for directions* nach dem Weg fragen
directory *(phone)* das Telefonbuch
directory enquiries die Auskunft
dirty schmutzig

disability die Behinderung
disabled *(person)* behindert
to disagree nicht zustimmen
to disappear verschwinden
disco die Disko
discount der Rabatt
to discover entdecken
disease die Krankheit
dish die Schale
  (food) das Gericht
dishtowel das Geschirrtuch
dishwasher die
  Geschirrspülmaschine
disinfectant das Desinfektionsmittel
disk die Diskette
to dislocate auskugeln
disposable wegwerfbar
distance die Entfernung
distilled water das destillierte
  Wasser
district der Bezirk
to disturb stören
to dive tauchen
diversion die Umleitung
diving das Tauchen
divorced geschieden
DIY shop der Baumarkt
dizzy schwindelig
to do machen
doctor der Arzt/die Ärztin
documents die Dokumente
dog der Hund
dog food das Hundefutter
dog lead die Hundeleine
doll die Puppe
dollar der Dollar
domestic *(flight)* Inlands-
donor card der
  Organspenderausweis
door die Tür
doorbell die Klingel
dormitory der Schlafsaal *(in hostel)*;
  das Studentenwohnheim *(student
  residence)*
double Doppel-
double bed das Doppelbett

double room das Doppelzimmer
doughnut der Berliner
down: to go down nach unten gehen
downstairs unten
drain der Abfluss
draught *(of air)* der Durchzug
  there's a draught hier zieht es
draught lager das Fassbier
drawer die Schublade
drawing die Zeichnung
dress das Kleid
to dress *(get dressed)* sich anziehen
dressing *(for food)* die Soße
  (for wound) das Verbandsmaterial
dressing gown der Morgenmantel
drill *(tool)* der Bohrer
drink das Getränk
to drink trinken
drinking water das Trinkwasser
to drive fahren
driver *(of car)* der Fahrer/die Fahrerin
driving licence der Führerschein
to drown ertrinken
drug das Medikament
  (narcotic) die Droge
drunk betrunken
dry trocken
to dry trocknen
dry cleaner's die Reinigung
dryer der Wäschetrockner
due: when's he due? wann soll er
  ankommen?
dummy *(for baby)* der Schnuller
during während
dust der Staub
duster das Staubtuch
dustpan and brush Schaufel und
  Handfeger
duty-free zollfrei
duvet die Bettdecke
duvet cover der Bettbezug
to dye färben
dynamo *(car)* die Lichtmaschine
  (bike) der Dynamo*

E

each jede(r/s)
ear das Ohr
earache die Ohrenschmerzen
  I have earache ich habe
  Ohrenschmerzen
earlier früher
early früh
to earn verdienen
earphones die Kopfhörer
earrings die Ohrringe
earth die Erde
earthquake das Erdbeben
east der Osten
Easter Ostern
easy leicht
to eat essen
economy class die Touristenklasse
egg das Ei
  fried egg das Spiegelei
  hard-boiled egg hart gekochte Ei
  scrambled egg Rührei
  soft-boiled egg weich gekochte Ei
either ... or entweder ... oder
elastic band das Gummiband
Elastoplast® das Pflaster
elbow der Ellbogen
electric elektrisch
electric blanket die Heizdecke
electric razor der Elektrorasierer
electric shock der elektrische Schlag
electrician der Elektriker
electricity meter der Stromzähler
elevator der Fahrstuhl
e-mail die E-Mail
to e-mail e-mailen
e-mail address die E-Mail-Adresse
embassy die Botschaft
emergency der Notfall
emergency exit der Notausgang
emery board die Nagelfeile
empty leer
end das Ende
engaged *(to marry)* verlobt
  (toilet, telephone) besetzt

engine der Motor
engineer der Ingenieur/die
  Ingenieurin
England England
English *adj* englisch
Englishman/woman der
  Engländer/die Engländerin
to enjoy *(to like)* mögen
  enjoy your meal! guten Appetit!
enough genug
  that's enough das reicht
enquiry desk die Auskunft
to enter eintreten
entertainment das Entertainment
entrance der Eingang
entrance fee der Eintrittspreis
envelope der Umschlag
epileptic der Epileptiker/die
  Epileptikerin
epileptic fit der epileptische Anfall
equal gleich
equipment die Ausrüstung
eraser der Radiergummi
error der Fehler
escalator die Rolltreppe
to escape entkommen
essential wesentlich
estate agent's der
  Grundstücksmakler
euro der Euro
euro cent der Eurocent
Europe Europa
European europäisch
European Union die Europäische
  Union
evening der Abend
  this evening heute Abend
  tomorrow evening morgen Abend
  in the evening am Abend
evening dress das Abendkleid
evening meal das Abendessen
every *(each)* jede(r/s)
everyone jeder
everything alles
everywhere überall

examination (medical) die Untersuchung
(school) die Prüfung
example: for example zum Beispiel
excellent ausgezeichnet
except außer
excess baggage das Übergepäck
exchange der Austausch
to exchange tauschen
(money) wechseln
exchange rate der Wechselkurs
exciting aufregend
excursion der Ausflug
excuse me! (sorry) Entschuldigung!
exhaust der Auspuff
exhibition die Ausstellung
exit der Ausgang
expense Account das Spesenkonto
expenses die Spesen
expensive teuer
expert der Experte/die Expertin
to expire (ticket, etc) ungültig werden
to explain erklären
explanation die Erklärung
explosion die Explosion
export der Export
to export exportieren
express (train) der Schnellzug
express (parcel, etc) per Express
extension lead das Verlängerungskabel
extra (spare) übrig
(more) noch ein(e)
an extra towel ein zusätzliches Handtuch
eye das Auge
eyebrows die Augenbrauen
eye drops die Augentropfen
eye liner der Eyeliner
eye shadow der Lidschatten

F

fabric der Stoff
face das Gesicht
face cloth der Waschlappen
facial die Gesichtspflege

facilities die Einrichtungen
factory die Fabrik
to faint ohnmächtig werden
fainted ohnmächtig
fair (hair) blond
(just) gerecht
fair (trade fair) die Messe
(funfair) der Jahrmarkt
fake unecht
fall (autumn) der Herbst
to fall fallen
I have fallen ich bin hingefallen
false teeth das Gebiss
family die Familie
famous berühmt
fan (electric) der Ventilator
(football, music) der Fan
fan belt der Keilriemen
fancy dress die Verkleidung
far weit
how far is it? wie weit ist es?
fare (train, bus, etc) der Fahrpreis
farm der Bauernhof
farmer der Bauer/die Bäuerin
farmhouse das Bauernhaus
fashionable modern
fast schnell
too fast zu schnell
to fasten: to fasten the seatbelt sich anschnallen
fat (big) dick
fat das Fett
saturated fat gesättigte Fettsäuren
unsaturated fat ungesättigte Fettsäuren
father der Vater
father-in-law der Schwiegervater
fault (defect) der Fehler
it wasn't my fault das war nicht meine Schuld
favour der Gefallen
favourite Lieblings-
fax das Fax
by fax per Fax
to fax faxen
fax number die Faxnummer

February der Februar
to feed füttern
feeding bottle die Babyflasche
to feel fühlen
   I don't feel well ich fühle mich nicht wohl
   I feel sick mir ist schlecht
feet die Füße
female weiblich
ferry die Fähre
festival das Festival
to fetch *(bring)* holen
fever das Fieber
few: *a few* ein paar
fiancé(e) der/die Verlobte
field das Feld
fig die Feige
to fight kämpfen
file *(nail)* die Feile
   (computer) die Datei
   (for papers) der Ordner
to fill füllen
to fill in *(form)* ausfüllen
to fill up *(tank)* voll tanken
fillet das Filet
filling *(in tooth)* die Plombe
film der Film
Filofax® der Terminkalender
filter der Filter
to find finden
fine *(to be paid)* die Geldstrafe
finger der Finger
to finish beenden
fire das Feuer
fire alarm der Feuermelder
fire brigade die Feuerwehr
fire engine das Feuerwehrauto
fire escape die Feuertreppe
fire exit der Notausgang
fire extinguisher der Feuerlöscher
fireplace der Kamin
fireworks das Feuerwerk
firm *(company)* die Firma
first erste(r/s)
first aid die erste Hilfe

first class *(travel)* erste Klasse
first name der Vorname
fish der Fisch
to fish angeln
fishing permit der Angelschein
fishing rod die Angel
fishmonger's die Fischhandlung
fit *(seizure)* der Anfall
to fit passen
   it doesn't fit es passt nicht
to fix reparieren
   can you fix it? können Sie es reparieren?
fizzy sprudelnd
flag die Fahne
flames die Flammen
flash das Blitzlicht
flashlight *(torch)* die Taschenlampe
flask *(thermos)* die Thermosflasche
flat *(level)* flach
flat die Wohnung
flat battery die leere Batterie
flat tyre die Reifenpanne
flavour der Geschmack
   what flavour? welchen Geschmack?
flaw der Defekt
fleas die Flöhe
flesh das Fleisch
flex die Verlängerungsschnur
flight der Flug
flip-flops die Badelatschen
flippers die Schwimmflossen
flood die Flut
   flash flood die Überschwemmung
floor *(of building)* die Etage
   (of room) der Boden
   which floor? auf welcher Etage?
   on the ground floor im Erdgeschoss
   on the first floor in der ersten Etage
floorcloth der Scheuerlappen
flour das Mehl
flowers die Blumen
flu die Grippe
fly die Fliege
to fly fliegen

fly sheet das Überzelt
fog der Nebel
foggy neblig
foil die Folie
to fold falten
to follow folgen
food das Essen
food poisoning die Lebensmittelvergiftung
foot der Fuß
  on foot zu Fuß
football der Fußball
football match das Fußballspiel
football player der Fußballer
footpath der Fußweg
for für
  for me für mich
  for him/her für ihn/sie
forbidden verboten
forehead die Stirn
foreign ausländisch
foreigner der Ausländer/die Ausländerin
forest der Wald
forever für immer
to forget vergessen
fork *(for eating)* die Gabel
  (in road) die Gabelung
form *(document)* das Formular
fortnight zwei Wochen
forward vorwärts
fountain der Brunnen
fox der Fuchs
fracture der Bruch
fragile zerbrechlich
fragrance das Parfüm
frame *(picture)* der Rahmen
France Frankreich
free *(not occupied)* frei
  (costing nothing) umsonst
freezer die Tiefkühltruhe
French *adj* französisch
French beans die grünen Bohnen
French fries die Pommes frites
Frenchman/woman der Franzose/die Französin

frequent häufig
fresh frisch
fresh water das frische Wasser
Friday der Freitag
fridge der Kühlschrank
fried gebraten
friend der Freund/die Freundin
friendly freundlich
frog der Frosch
from von
  from Scotland aus Schottland
  from England aus England
front die Vorderseite
  in front of vor
front door die Eingangstür
frost der Frost
frozen gefroren
fruit das Obst
  dried fruit das Trockenobst
fruit juice der Fruchtsaft
to fry braten
frying pan die Bratpfanne
fuel *(petrol)* das Benzin
fuel gauge die Tankanzeige
fuel pump *(in car)* die Benzinpumpe
  (at petrol station) die Zapfsäule
fuel tank der Tank
full voll
  (occupied) besetzt
  I'm full ich bin satt!
full board die Vollpension
fumes die Abgase
fun der Spaß
funeral die Beerdigung
funfair der Jahrmarkt
funny *(amusing)* komisch
fur der Pelz
furnished möbliert
furniture die Möbel
fuse die Sicherung
fuse box der Sicherungskasten
future die Zukunft

G

gallery die Galerie
game das Spiel
  (meat) das Wild

garage *(private)* die Garage
  (for repairs) die Werkstatt
  (petrol station) die Tankstelle
garden der Garten
garlic der Knoblauch
gas das Gas
gas cooker der Gasherd
gastritis die Gastritis
gate *(airport)* das Gate
gay *(person)* der/die Homosexuelle
gearbox das Getriebe
gears das Getriebe
  first gear der erste Gang
  second gear der zweite Gang
  third gear der dritte Gang
  fourth gear der vierte Gang
  neutral der Leerlauf
  reverse der Rückwärtsgang
generous großzügig
gents' *(toilet)* die Herrentoilette
genuine echt
German *adj* deutsch
  m/f der/die Deutsche
German measles die Röteln
Germany Deutschland
to get *(to obtain)* bekommen
  (to fetch) holen
to get in(to) *(bus, etc)* einsteigen
to get off *(bus, etc)* aussteigen
gift das Geschenk
gift shop der Geschenkeladen
girl das Mädchen
girlfriend die Freundin
to give geben
to give back zurückgeben
glacier der Gletscher
glass das Glas
  a glass of water ein Glas Wasser
glasses *(spectacles)* die Brille
glasses case das Brillenetui
gloves die Handschuhe
glue der Klebstoff
to go *(on foot)* gehen
  (in car) fahren
  I'm going to... ich fahre nach...
  we're going to... wir fahren nach...
  to go home nach Hause fahren
  to go on foot zu Fuß gehen

to go back zurückgehen
to go in hineingehen
to go out ausgehen
God Gott
goggles *(swimming)* die Taucherbrille
  (skiing) die Schneebrille
gold das Gold
golf das Golf
golf ball der Golfball
golf clubs die Golfschläger
golf course der Golfplatz
good gut
  (pleasant) schön
good afternoon guten Tag
goodbye auf Wiedersehen
good day guten Tag
good evening guten Abend
good morning guten Morgen
good night gute Nacht
goose die Gans
grandchild das Enkelkind
granddaughter die Enkelin
grandfather der Großvater
grandmother die Großmutter
grandparents die Großeltern
grandson der Enkel
Grapefruit die Grapefruit
grapes die Trauben
grass das Gras
grated *(cheese)* gerieben
gram das Gramm
grater die Reibe
great *(big)* groß
  (wonderful) großartig
Great Britain Großbritannien
green grün
greengrocer's der Gemüseladen
greetings card die Grußkarte
grey grau
grill der Grill
to grill grillen
grilled gegrillt
grocer's der Lebensmittelladen
ground der Boden

ground floor das Erdgeschoss
  on the ground floor im Erdgeschoss
groundsheet der Zeltboden
group die Gruppe
guarantee die Garantie
guard *m/f (on train)* der Schaffner/
  die Schaffnerin
guest der Gast
guesthouse die Pension
guide *m/f (tour guide)* der
  Fremdenführer/die
  Fremdenführerin
guidebook der Reiseführer
guided tour die Führung
guitar die Gitarre
gun die Waffe
gym das Fitnesscenter
gym shoes die Turnschuhe

H

haemorrhoids die Hämorrhoiden
hail der Hagel
hair die Haare
hairbrush die Haarbürste
haircut der Haarschnitt
hairdresser der Friseur
hairdryer der Föhn
hair dye die Tönung
hair gel das Haargel
hairgrip die Haarklemme
hair spray das Haarspray
half halb
  a half bottle eine kleine Flasche
  half an hour eine halbe Stunde
half board die Halbpension
half fare der halbe Fahrpreis
half price der halbe Preis
ham der Schinken
  (cooked) Kochschinken
  (cured) geräucherter Schinken
hamburger der Hamburger
hammer der Hammer
hand die Hand
handbag die Handtasche
handbrake *(car)* die Handbremse
hand-made handgearbeitet

handicapped behindert
handkerchief das Taschentuch
handle der Griff
handlebars der Lenker
hand luggage das Handgepäck
hands-free phone das Telefon mit
  Freisprechanlage
handsome gut aussehend
hang gliding das Drachenfliegen
hangover der Kater
to hang up auflegen
to happen passieren
  what happened? was ist passiert?
happy glücklich
  happy birthday! alles Gute zum
  Geburtstag!
harbour der Hafen
hard *(difficult)* schwierig
  (not soft) hart
hardware shop die
  Eisenwarenhandlung
to harm schädigen
harvest die Ernte
hat der Hut
to have haben
  I have... ich habe...
  we have... wir haben...
  do you have...? haben Sie...?
to have to müssen
hay fever der Heuschnupfen
he er
head der Kopf
headache die Kopfschmerzen
  I have a headache ich habe
  Kopfschmerzen
headlights die Scheinwerfer
headphones die Kopfhörer
health die Gesundheit
health food shop das Reformhaus
healthy gesund
to hear hören
hearing aid das Hörgerät
heart das Herz
heart attack der Herzinfarkt
heartburn das Sodbrennen
to heat up *(food, milk)* aufwärmen

heater das Heizgerät
  (*radiator*) der Heizkörper
heating die Heizung
heavy schwer
heel der Absatz
heel bar der Schuhreparatur-Service
  (*shoemaker*) der Schuster
height die Höhe
helicopter der Hubschrauber
hello hallo
helmet (*for bike*) der Schutzhelm
help! Hilfe!
to help helfen
hem der Saum
hepatitis die Hepatitis
her (*with der words*) ihr
  (*with das words*) ihr
  (*with die words*) ihre
  to her zu ihr
herbal tea der Kräutertee
herbs die Kräuter
here hier
  here is... hier ist...
hernia der Eingeweidebruch
hi! hallo!
to hide verstecken
high hoch
  (*number, speed*) groß
high blood pressure der hohe
  Blutdruck
high chair der Kinderstuhl
high tide die Flut
hill der Hügel
hill-walking das Bergwandern
him ihm
hip die Hüfte
hip replacement die künstliche
  Hüfte
hire die Vermietung
  car hire die Autovermietung
  bike hire die Fahrradvermietung
  boat hire der Bootsverleih
  ski hire der Skiverleih
to hire mieten
hire car das Mietauto

his (*with der words*) sein
  (*with das words*) sein
  (*with die words*) seine
historic historisch
history die Geschichte
to hit schlagen
to hitchhike trampen
hobby das Hobby
to hold halten
  to contain enthalten
hold-up (*traffic jam*) der Stau
hole das Loch
holiday der Feiertag
  holidays der Urlaub
  on holiday in den Ferien
home das Zuhause
  at home zu Hause
homepage die Homepage
homesick (*to be*) Heimweh haben
  I'm homesick ich habe Heimweh
homosexual homosexuell
honest ehrlich
honey der Honig
honeymoon die Flitterwochen
hood (*of jacket*) die Kapuze
hook der Haken
to hope hoffen
  I hope so hoffentlich
  I hope not hoffentlich nicht
horn (*car*) die Hupe
hors d'œuvre die Vorspeise
horse das Pferd
horse racing das Pferderennen
to horse ride reiten
hosepipe der Schlauch
hospital das Krankenhaus
hostel das Wohnheim
  (*youth hostel*) die Jugendherberge
hot heiß
  I'm hot mir ist heiß
  it's hot (*weather*) es ist heiß
hot-water bottle die Wärmflasche
hotel das Hotel
hour die Stunde
  1 hour eine Stunde
  2 hours zwei Stunden
  half an hour eine halbe Stunde

house das Haus
housewife/husband die Hausfrau/der Hausmann
house wine der Hauswein
housework die Hausarbeit
how wie
how much? wie viel?
how many? wie viele?
how are you? wie geht es Ihnen?
hungry *(to be)* hungrig
to hunt jagen
hunting permit die Jagderlaubnis
hurry: *I'm in a hurry* ich habe es eilig
to hurt *(be painful)* weh tun
my back hurts mir tut der Rücken weh
that hurts das tut weh
husband der Mann
hut *(beach)* der Strandkorb
(mountain) die Hütte
hypodermic needle die Spritze

I

I ich
ice das Eis
with/without ice mit/ohne Eis
ice box die Kühlbox
ice cream das Eis
ice cube der Eiswürfel
ice rink die Eisbahn
to ice-skate Schlittschuh laufen
ice skates die Schlittschuhe
iced: *iced coffee* der Eiskaffee
iced tea der Eistee
idea die Idee
identity card der Personalausweis
if wenn
ignition die Zündung
ignition key der Zündschlüssel
ill krank
I'm ill ich bin krank
illness die Krankheit
immediately sofort
immersion heater der Boiler
immunisation die Immunisierung

to import importieren
important wichtig
impossible unmöglich
to improve verbessern
in in
in 2 hours in zwei Stunden
in Vienna in Wien
in front of vor
included inbegriffen
inconvenient unpassend
to increase vergrößern
indicator *(in car)* der Blinker
indigestion die Magenverstimmung
indigestion tablets die Magentabletten
indoors drinnen
infection die Infektion
infectious ansteckend
information die Auskunft
information desk der Informationsschalter
information office das Informationsbüro
ingredients die Zutaten
inhaler *(for medication)* der Inhalationsapparat
injection die Spritze
to injure verletzen
injured *(person)* verletzt
injury die Verletzung
ink die Tinte
inn das Gasthaus
inner tube der Schlauch
inquiries die Auskunft
inquiry desk der Auskunftsschalter
insect das Insekt
insect bite der Insektenstich
insect repellent das Insektenschutzmittel
inside in
instant coffee der Pulverkaffee
instead of anstelle von
insulin das Insulin
insurance die Versicherung
to insure versichern
insured versichert

to intend to vorhaben
interesting interessant
international international
   (arrivals, departures) Ausland
internet das Internet
internet café das Internet-Café
interpreter der Dolmetscher/
   die Dolmetscherin
interval die Pause
into in
   into town in die Stadt
   into the centre ins Zentrum
to introduce vorstellen
invitation die Einladung
to invite einladen
invoice die Rechnung
Ireland Irland
Irish *adj* irisch
Irishman/woman der Ire/die Irin
iron *(for clothes)* das Bügeleisen
   (metal) das Eisen
to iron bügeln
ironing board das Bügelbrett
ironmonger's die
   Eisenwarenhandlung
is ist
island die Insel
it er/sie/es
Italian *adj* italienisch
   m/f der Italiener/die Italienerin
Italy Italien
to itch jucken
item das Ding

J

jack *(for car)* der Wagenheber
jacket die Jacke
jacuzzi der Whirlpool
jam *(food)* die Marmelade
jammed blockiert
January der Januar
jar *(honey, jam, etc)* das Glas
jaundice die Gelbsucht
jaw der Kiefer
jealous eifersüchtig
jeans die Jeans

jellyfish die Qualle
jet ski das Wassermotorrad
jetty die Mole
Jew der Jude/die Jüdin
jeweller's der Juwelier
jewellery der Schmuck
Jewish jüdisch
job *(employment)* die Stelle
to jog joggen
to join *(club)* beitreten
to join in mitmachen
joint *(of body)* das Gelenk
to joke scherzen
joke der Witz
journalist der Journalist/die
   Journalistin
journey die Reise
judge der Richter/die Richterin
jug der Krug
juice der Saft
   carton of juice der Saftkarton
July der Juli
to jump springen
jumper der Pullover
jump leads *(for car)* das
   Starthilfekabel
junction *(road)* die Kreuzung
June der Juni
just: *just two* nur zwei
   I've just arrived ich bin gerade
   angekommen

K

to keep *(retain)* behalten
kettle der Wasserkocher
key der Schlüssel
keyring der Schlüsselring
to kick *(ball)* schießen
   (person) treten
kidneys die Nieren
to kill töten
kilo das Kilo
kilometre der Kilometer
kind *(person)* nett
kind *(sort)* die Art
kiosk der Kiosk

kiss der Kuss
to kiss küssen
kitchen die Küche
kitchen paper das Küchenpapier
kite der Drachen
knee das Knie
kneehighs die Kniestrümpfe
knickers der Slip
knIfe das Messer
to knit stricken
to knock stoßen
to knock down (in car) überfahren
to knock over (object) umstoßen
knot der Knoten
to know (facts) wissen
  (be acquainted with) kennen
  I don't know ich weiß nicht
to know how to können
kosher koscher

L

label das Schild
lace (shoe) der Schnürsenkel
ladder die Leiter
ladies' (toilet) die Damentoilette
lady die Dame
lager das helle Bier
  bottled lager das Flaschenbier
  draught lager das Fassbier
lake der See
lamb das Lammfleisch
lamp (for table) die Lampe
to land landen
landlady die Vermieterin
landlord der Vermieter
landslide der Erdrutsch
lane die Gasse
  (of motorway/road) die Spur
language die Sprache
language school die Sprachenschule
laptop der Laptop
large groß
last (final) letzte(r/s)
  the last bus der letzte Bus
  last night gestern Abend
  last time letztes Mal

late spät
  the train is late der Zug hat
  Verspätung
later später
to laugh lachen
launderette der Waschsalon
laundry service der
  Wäschereiservice
lavatory die Toilette
law das Gesetz
lawn der Rasen
lawyer der Rechtsanwalt/die
  Rechtsanwältin
laxative das Abführmittel
layby die Haltebucht
lazy faul
lead (metal) das Blei
to lead führen
lead-free bleifrei
leaf das Blatt
leak (of gas, liquid) das Leck
to leak: it's leaking es hat ein Leck
to learn lernen
lease (rental) der Mietvertrag
leather das Leder
to leave (a place)
  weggehen/wegfahren
  when does the train leave? wann
  fährt der Zug ab?
leek der Lauch
left: on the left links
  to the left nach links
left-luggage locker das Schließfach
left-luggage office die
  Gepäckaufbewahrung
leg das Bein
lemon die Zitrone
lemon tea der Zitronentee
lemonade die Limonade
to lend leihen
length (size) die Länge
  (duration) die Dauer
lens die Linse
lenses (contact) die Kontaktlinsen
lesbian lesbisch

less weniger
  less than weniger als
lesson die Unterrichtsstunde
to let *(to allow)* erlauben
  (room, house) vermieten
letter *(written)* der Brief
  (of alphabet) der Buchstabe
letterbox der Briefkasten
lettuce der Kopfsalat
library die Bibliothek
lid der Deckel
lie *(untruth)* die Lüge
to lie down sich hinlegen
lifebelt der Rettungsring
lifeboat das Rettungsboot
lifeguard der
  Rettungsschwimmer/die
  Rettungsschwimmerin
life insurance die
  Lebensversicherung
life jacket die Schwimmweste
life raft die Rettungsinsel
lift *(elevator)* der Aufzug
  can I have a lift? können Sie mich
  mitnehmen?
lift pass der Liftpass
light *(not heavy)* leicht
light das Licht
  have you a light? haben Sie Feuer?
light bulb die Glühbirne
lighter das Feuerzeug
lighthouse der Leuchtturm
lightning der Blitz
like *(preposition)* wie
to like mögen
  I like coffee ich trinke gern Kaffee
  I don't like... ich mag ... nicht
  we'd like... wir möchten...
lilo® die Luftmatratze
lime *(fruit)* die Limone
line *(row, of railway)* die Linie
  (telephone) die Leitung
linen das Leinen
lingerie die Unterwäsche
lips die Lippen
lip-reading das Lippenlesen

lipstick der Lippenstift
liqueur der Likör
list die Liste
to listen to zuhören
litre der Liter
  litre of milk ein Liter Milch
litter *(rubbish)* der Abfall
little *(small)* klein
  a little... ein bisschen...
to live *(exist)* leben
  (reside) wohnen
  I live in London ich wohne
  in London
liver die Leber
living room das Wohnzimmer
loaf of bread das Brot
local *(wine, speciality)* hiesig
lock das Schloss
to lock zuschließen
locker *(luggage)* das Schließfach
locksmith der Schlosser
log *(for fire)* der Holzscheit
log book *(car)* die Zulassung
long lang
  for a long time lange Zeit
long-sighted weitsichtig
to look after sich kümmern um
to look at anschauen
to look for suchen
loose *(screw, tooth)* locker
  it's come loose es hat sich gelockert
lorry der Lastwagen
to lose verlieren
lost *(object)* verloren
  I've lost my wallet ich habe meine
  Brieftasche verloren
  I'm lost (on foot) ich habe mich
  verlaufen
  I'm lost (in car) ich habe mich
  verfahren
lost property office das Fundbüro
lot: *a lot* viel
lotion die Lotion
lottery das Lotto
loud laut

lounge *(hotel/airport)* die Lounge
  (in house) das Wohnzimmer
love die Liebe
to love lieben
  I love you ich liebe dich
  I love swimming ich schwimme gern
lovely schön
low niedrig
low-alcohol alkoholarm
low-fat fettarm
low tide die Ebbe
luck das Glück
lucky glücklich
luggage das Gepäck
luggage rack die Gepäckablage
luggage tag der Kofferanhänger
luggage trolley der Gepäckwagen
lump *(swelling)* die Beule
lunch das Mittagessen
lunch break die Mittagspause
lung die Lunge
luxury der Luxus

M

machine die Maschine
mad verrückt
magazine die Zeitschrift
magnet der Magnet
magnifying glass die Lupe
maid *(in hotel)* das Zimmermädchen
maiden name der Mädchenname
mail die Post
  by mail per Post
main *(principal)* Haupt-
main course *(of meal)* das Hauptgericht
main road die Hauptstraße
to make machen
  (meal) zubereiten
make-up das Make-up
male männlich
man der Mann
  men die Männer
manager der Geschäftsführer/die Geschäftsführerin

manual *(gear change)* das Schaltgetriebe
many viele
map die Karte
  (of region, country) die Landkarte
  (of town) der Stadtplan
March der März
margarine die Margarine
marina der Jachthafen
mark *(stain)* der Fleck
market der Markt
market place der Marktplatz
marmalade die Orangenmarmelade
married verheiratet
  I'm married ich bin verheiratet
  are you married? sind Sie verheiratet?
to marry heiraten
mascara die Wimperntusche
mass *(in church)* die Messe
mast der Mast
matches die Streichhölzer
material das Material
matter: it doesn't matter das macht nichts
  what's the matter? was ist los?
mattress die Matratze
May der Mai
mayonnaise die Mayonnaise
maximum das Maximum
me *(direct object)* mich
  (indirect object) mir
meal das Essen
to mean bedeuten
  what does this mean? was bedeutet das?
measles die Masern
to measure messen
meat das Fleisch
  I don't eat meat ich esse kein Fleisch
mechanic der Mechaniker/die Mechanikerin
medical insurance die Krankenversicherung
medical treatment die medizinische Behandlung

medicine die Medizin
medieval mittelalterlich
medium rare (meat) halb durch
to meet (by chance) treffen
 (arranged) sich treffen mit
 pleased to meet you! sehr erfreut!
meeting das Treffen
 (business) die Besprechung
melon die Melone
to melt schmelzen
member (of club, etc) das Mitglied
memory das Gedächtnis
memory card die Speicherkarte
men die Männer
to mend reparieren
meningitis die Hirnhautentzündung
menu die Speisekarte
 set menu die Tageskarte
message die Nachricht
metal das Metall
meter der Zähler
metre der Meter
metro die U-Bahn
metro station die U-Bahn-Station
microwave oven die Mikrowelle
midday der Mittag
 at midday am Mittag
middle die Mitte
middle-aged in den mittleren
 Jahren
midge die Mücke
midnight die Mitternacht
 at midnight um Mitternacht
migraine die Migräne
 I have a migraine ich habe Migräne
mile die Meile
milk die Milch
 fresh milk frische Milch
 full cream milk Vollfettmilch
 hot milk heiße Milch
 long-life milk H-Milch
 powdered milk das Milchpulver
 semi-skimmed milk Halbfettmilch
 skimmed milk Magermilch
 soya milk die Sojamilch
 with/without milk mit/ohne Milch
millimetre der Millimeter

mince (meat) das Hackfleisch
mind: *do you mind if...?* haben Sie
 etwas dagegen, wenn...?
 I don't mind es ist mir egal
mineral water das Mineralwasser
minibar die Minibar
minimum das Minimum
minister (church) der Pfarrer/die
 Pfarrerin
 (political) der Minister/die
 Ministerin
mint (herb) die Minze
 (sweet) das Pfefferminzbonbon
minute die Minute
mirror der Spiegel
miscarriage die Fehlgeburt
to miss (train, etc) verpassen
Miss Fräulein
missing (object) verschwunden
 my son's missing mein Sohn ist weg
mistake der Fehler
misty dunstig
misunderstanding das
 Missverständnis
to mix mischen
mixer der Mixer
mobile phone das Handy
modem das Modem
modern modern
moisturizer die Feuchtigkeitscreme
mole (on skin) das Muttermal
moment: *just a moment* einen
 Moment, bitte
monastery das Kloster
Monday der Montag
money das Geld
 I have no money ich habe kein Geld
moneybelt die Gürteltasche
money order die Postanweisung
month der Monat
 this month diesen Monat
 last month letzten Monat
 next month nächsten Monat
monthly monatlich
monument das Denkmal
moon der Mond

mooring der Anlegeplatz
mop *(floor)* der Mopp
moped das Moped
more mehr
  more than mehr als
  more wine noch etwas Wein
morning der Morgen
  in the morning am Morgen
  this morning heute Morgen
morning-after pill die Pille danach
mosque die Moschee
mosquito die Stechmücke
mosquito net das Moskitonetz
mosquito repellent das
  Insektenschutzmittel
most: *most of* das meiste von
moth *(clothes)* die Motte
mother die Mutter
mother-in-law die Schwiegermutter
motor der Motor
motorbike das Motorrad
motorboat das Motorboot
motorway die Autobahn
mould der Schimmel
mountain der Berg
mountain bike das Mountainbike
mountain rescue die Bergwacht
mountaineering das Bergsteigen
mouse die Maus
moustache der Schnurrbart
mouth der Mund
to move bewegen
  it isn't moving es bewegt sich nicht
movie der Kinofilm
to mow mähen
Mr Herr
Mrs Frau
Ms Frau
much viel
  too much zu viel
muddy schlammig
mugging der Überfall
mumps der Mumps
Munich München
muscle der Muskel
museum das Museum

mushrooms die Pilze
music die Musik
musical das Musical
mussel die Muschel
must müssen
  I must ich muss
  we must wir müssen
  you musn't du darfst nicht
mustard der Senf
my *(with der words)* mein
  (with das words) mein
  (with die words) meine

N

nail *(fingernail)* der Fingernagel
  (metal) der Nagel
nailbrush die Nagelbürste
nail file die Nagelfeile
nail polish/varnish der Nagellack
nail polish remover der
  Nagellackentferner
nail scissors die Nagelschere
name der Name
  what is your name? wie ist Ihr
  Name?
nanny das Kindermädchen
napkin die Serviette
nappy die Windel
narrow eng
national national
nationality die Nationalität
natural natürlich
nature die Natur
nature reserve das
  Naturschutzgebiet
navy blue marineblau
near *(place, time)* nahe
  near the bank in der Nähe der
  Bank
  is it near? ist es in der Nähe?
necessary notwendig
neck der Hals
necklace die Halskette
nectarine die Nektarine
to need brauchen
  I need... ich brauche...
  we need... wir brauchen...
  I need to go ich muss gehen

needle die Nadel
  needle and thread Nadel und Faden
neighbour der Nachbar/die Nachbarin
nephew der Neffe
net das Netz
  the Net das Internet
never nie
  I never drink wine Wein trinke ich nie
new neu
news die Nachrichten
newsagent's der Zeitungsladen
newspaper die Zeitung
newsstand der Zeitungskiosk
New Year (1 Jan) Neujahr
  happy New Year! ein gutes neues Jahr!
New Year's Eve Silvester
New Zealand Neuseeland
next nächste(r/s)
  next to neben
  next week nächste Woche
  the next bus der nächste Bus
nice (person) nett
  (place, holiday) schön
niece die Nichte
night die Nacht
  at night am Abend
  last night gestern Abend
  per night pro Nacht
  tonight heute Abend
night club der Nachtklub
nightdress das Nachthemd
no nein
  no thanks nein danke
  no problem kein Problem
  (without) ohne
  no sugar ohne Zucker
  no ice ohne Eis
nobody niemand
noise der Lärm
noisy laut
  it's very noisy es ist sehr laut
non-alcoholic alkoholfrei
none keine(r/s)
non-smoker der Nichtraucher

non-smoking Nichtraucher-
north der Norden
Northern Ireland Nordirland
North Sea die Nordsee
nose die Nase
not nicht
  I do not know ich weiß nicht
note (banknote) der Geldschein
  (written) die Notiz
note pad der Notizblock
nothing nichts
  nothing else nichts weiter
notice (sign) das Schild
novel der Roman
November der November
now jetzt
nowhere nirgends
nuclear nuklear
nudist beach der FKK-Strand
number die Zahl
number plate das Nummernschild
nurse die Krankenschwester/der Krankenpfleger
nursery die Kinderbetreuung
nursery school die Vorschule
nut (to eat) die Nuss
  (for bolt) die Schraubenmutter

O

oar das Ruder
oats der Hafer
to obtain erhalten
occupation (work) der Beruf
ocean der Ozean
October der Oktober
odd (strange) seltsam
of von
  a glass of water ein Glas Wasser
  made of... aus...
off (light, radio, etc) aus
  (rotten) schlecht
office das Büro
off-season die Nebensaison
often oft
  how often? wie oft?
oil das Öl

oil filter der Ölfilter
ointment die Salbe
OK okay
old alt
  how old are you? wie alt sind Sie?
  I'm... years old ich bin... Jahre alt
old age pensioner der Rentner/die Rentnerin
on *(light, radio, etc)* an
on auf
  on the table auf dem Tisch
  on time pünktlich
once einmal
  at once sofort
onion die Zwiebel
only nur
open geöffnet
to open öffnen
opera die Oper
operation *(surgical)* die Operation
operator *(phone)* die Vermittlung
opposite gegenüber
  opposite the bank gegenüber der Bank
  quite the opposite ganz im Gegenteil
optician's der Optiker
or oder
orange *(colour)* orange
orange *(fruit)* die Orange
orange juice der Orangensaft
orchestra das Orchester
order *(in restaurant)* die Bestellung
to order *(food)* bestellen
organic organisch
to organize organisieren
other: *the other one* der/die/das andere
  have you got any others? haben Sie noch andere?
our *(with der words)* unser
  (with das words) unser
  (with die words) unsere
out *(light, etc)* aus
  she's out sie ist nicht da
out of order kaputt
outdoor *(pool, etc)* im Freien

outside draußen
oven der Herd
ovenproof dish die feuerfeste Form
over *(on top of, above)* über
to overbook überbuchen
to overcharge zu viel berechnen
overdone *(food)* verkocht
overdose die Überdosis
to overheat überhitzen
to overload überladen
to oversleep verschlafen
to overtake überholen
to owe schulden
  I owe you... ich schulde Ihnen...
  you owe me... Sie schulden mir...
owner der Besitzer/die Besitzerin
oxygen der Sauerstoff

P

pace das Tempo
pacemaker der Herzschrittmacher
to pack *(luggage)* packen
package das Paket
package tour die Pauschalreise
packet das Paket
padded envelope der gefütterte Umschlag
paddling pool das Planschbecken
padlock das Vorhängeschloss
page die Seite
paid bezahlt
  I've paid ich habe bezahlt
pain der Schmerz
painful schmerzhaft
painkiller das Schmerzmittel
to paint malen
painting *(picture)* das Bild
pair das Paar
palace der Palast
pale blass
pan *(saucepan)* der Kochtopf
  (frying pan) die Bratpfanne
pancake der Pfannkuchen
panniers *(for bike)* die Satteltaschen
panties die Unterhose

pants (underwear) der Slip
panty liner die Slipeinlage
paper das Papier
paper hankies die Papiertaschentücher
paper napkins die Papierservietten
paralysed gelähmt
parcel das Paket
pardon? wie bitte?
I beg your pardon! Entschuldigung!
parents die Eltern
park der Park
to park parken
parking disk die Parkscheibe
parking fine der Strafzettel
parking meter die Parkuhr
parking ticket (fine) der Strafzettel
(to display) der Parkschein
partner (business) der Geschäftspartner/die Geschäftspartnerin
(boy/girlfriend) der Partner/die Partnerin
party (celebration) die Party
(political) die Partei
pass der Pass
passenger der Passagier
passport der Reisepass
passport control die Passkontrolle
password das Passwort
pasta die Nudeln
pastry der Teig
(cake) das Gebäck
path der Weg
patient (in hospital) der Patient/die Patientin
pavement der Bürgersteig
to pay zahlen
I'd like to pay ich möchte zahlen
where do I pay? wo kann ich bezahlen?
payment die Bezahlung
payphone das Münztelefon
peace der Frieden
peach der Pfirsich
peak rate der Höchsttarif

peanut allergy die Erdnussallergie
pear die Birne
pearls die Perlen
peas die Erbsen
pedal das Pedal
pedalo (pedal boat) das Tretboot
pedestrian der Fußgänger/die Fußgängerin
pedestrian crossing der Fußgängerübergang
to pee austreten
to peel (fruit) schälen
peg (clothes) die Wäscheklammer
(tent) der Hering
pen der Füller
pencil der Bleistift
penfriend der Brieffreund/die Brieffreundin
penicillin das Penizillin
penis der Penis
penknife das Taschenmesser
pension die Rente
pensioner der Rentner/die Rentnerin
people die Leute
pepper (spice) der Pfeffer/die Paprikaschote
per pro
per day pro Tag
per hour pro Stunde
per person pro Person
perfect perfekt
performance die Vorstellung
perfume das Parfüm
perhaps vielleicht
period (menstruation) die Periode
perm die Dauerwelle
permit die Genehmigung
person die Person
personal organizer der Terminplaner
personal stereo der Walkman®
pet das Haustier
pet food das Tierfutter
pet shop die Zoohandlung

petrol das Benzin
  4-star petrol Superbenzin
  unleaded petrol bleifreies Benzin
petrol cap der Tankdeckel
petrol pump *(at petrol station)* die Tanksäule
  (in car) die Benzinpumpe
petrol station die Tankstelle
petrol tank der Tank
pharmacy die Apotheke
to phone telefonieren
phone das Telefon
  by phone per Telefon
phonebook das Telefonbuch
phonebox die Telefonzelle
phone call der Anruf
phonecard die Telefonkarte
photocopy die Fotokopie
  I need a photocopy ich brauche eine Fotokopie
to photocopy fotokopieren
photograph das Foto
  to take a photograph fotografieren
phrase book der Sprachführer
piano das Klavier
to pick *(choose)* auswählen
  (pluck) pflücken
pickpocket der Taschendieb
picnic das Picknick
  to have a picnic ein Picknick machen
picture *(painting)* das Bild
  (photo) das Foto
pie *(sweet)* der Obstkuchen
  (savoury) die Pastete
piece das Stück
pier die Pier
pig das Schwein
pill die Pille
  to be on the Pill die Pille nehmen
pillow das Kopfkissen
pillowcase der Kopfkissenbezug
pilot der Pilot/die Pilotin
pin die Stecknadel
PIN number die Geheimzahl
pineapple die Ananas

pink rosa
pipe *(smoker's)* die Pfeife
  (drain, etc) das Rohr
pity: *what a pity* wie schade
pizza die Pizza
place der Platz
place of birth der Geburtsort
plain *(unflavoured)* einfach
plait der Zopf
plane *(airplane)* das Flugzeug
plant die Pflanze
plaster *(sticking)* das Pflaster
  (for broken limb) der Gips
plastic *(made of)* Plastik-
plastic bag der Plastikbeutel
plate der Teller
platform *(at station)* der Bahnsteig
  which platform? welcher Bahnsteig?
play *(theatre)* das Stück
to play spielen
play area die Spielecke
playground der Spielplatz
play park der Spielplatz
playroom das Spielzimmer
please bitte
pleased erfreut
  pleased to meet you sehr erfreut
pliers die Zange
plug *(electrical)* der Stecker
  (in sink) der Stöpsel
to plug in einstecken
plum die Pflaume
plumber der Klempner
plumbing die Installationen
  (water pipes) die Wasserleitungen
p.m. nachmittags
poached *(egg, fish)* pochiert
pocket die Tasche
points *(in car)* die Unterbrecherkontakte
poison das Gift
poisonous giftig
police *(force)* die Polizei
policeman/woman der Polizist/die Polizistin

police station das Polizeirevier
polish *(shoe)* die Schuhcreme
(furniture) die Möbelpolitur
pollen der Pollen
polluted verschmutzt
pony das Pony
pony trekking das Ponyreiten
pool der Swimmingpool
pool attendant der Bademeister
poor arm
pop socks die Kniestrümpfe
popular beliebt
pork das Schweinefleisch
port *(seaport)* der Hafen
porter *(for door)* der Portier
(station) der Gepäckträger
portion die Portion
portrait das Portrait
possible möglich
post: *by post* per Post
to post aufgeben
postbox der Briefkasten
postcard die Ansichtskarte
postcode die Postleitzahl
postman der Briefträger/die
Briefträgerin
post office das Postamt
poster das Poster
to postpone verschieben
pot *(cooking)* der Topf
potato die Kartoffel
baked potato die Folienkartoffel
boiled potatoes die Salzkartoffeln
fried potatoes die Bratkartoffeln
mashed potatoes das
Kartoffelpüree
roast potatoes die Bratkartoffeln
sautéed potatoes die Röstkartoffeln
potato peeler der Kartoffelschäler
potato salad der Kartoffelsalat
pothole das Schlagloch
pottery die Töpferwaren
pound das Pfund
to pour eingießen
powder: *in powder form*
pulverförmig

powdered milk die Trockenmilch
power *(electricity)* der Strom
power cut der Stromausfall
pram der Kinderwagen
to pray beten
to prefer vorziehen
pregnant schwanger
I'm pregnant ich bin schwanger
to prepare vorbereiten
to prescribe verschreiben
prescription das Rezept
present *(gift)* das Geschenk
president der Präsident
pressure: *tyre pressure* der
Reifendruck
blood pressure der Blutdruck
pretty hübsch
price der Preis
price list die Preisliste
priest der Priester
print *(photo)* der Abzug
printer der Drucker
prison das Gefängnis
private privat
prize der Preis
probably wahrscheinlich
problem das Problem
professor der Professor/die
Professorin
programme das Programm
prohibited verboten
to promise versprechen
to pronounce aussprechen
how's it pronounced? wie spricht
man das aus?
protein das Eiweiß
Protestant protestantisch
to provide zur Verfügung stellen
public öffentlich
public holiday der gesetzliche
Feiertag
pudding die Nachspeise
to pull ziehen
to pull a muscle sich einen Muskel
zerren
to pull over *(car)* anhalten

pullover der Pullover
pump (bike, etc) die Luftpumpe
  (in petrol station) die Tanksäule
puncture die Reifenpanne
puncture repair kit das
  Reifenflickzeug
puppet die Puppe
puppet show das Puppenspiel
purple violett
purpose der Zweck
  on purpose absichtlich
purse der Geldbeutel
to push stoßen
pushchair die Kinderkarre
to put (place) stellen
to put back verschieben
pyjamas der Pyjama

Q

quality die Qualität
quantity die Quantität
quarantine die Quarantäne
to quarrel streiten
quarter das Viertel
quay der Kai
queen die Königin
query die Frage
question die Frage
queue die Schlange
to queue anstehen
quick(ly) schnell
quiet ruhig
quilt die Bettdecke
quite (rather) ziemlich
  it's quite good es ist ganz gut
  it's quite expensive es ist ziemlich
  teuer
quiz show das Quiz

R

rabbit das Kaninchen
rabies die Tollwut
race das Rennen
race course die Rennbahn
racquet der Schläger

radiator (car) der Kühler
  (heater) der Heizkörper
radio das Radio
radishes die Radieschen
railcard die Bahncard
railway die Eisenbahn
railway station der Bahnhof
rain der Regen
to rain regnen
  it's raining es regnet
raincoat der Regenmantel
raisins die Rosinen
rake die Harke
rape die Vergewaltigung
to rape vergewaltigen
rare (unique) selten
  (steak) blutig
raspberry die Himbeere
rash (skin) der Ausschlag
rate (price) der Preis
rate of exchange der Wechselkurs
raw roh
razor der Rasierapparat
razor blades die Rasierklingen
to read lesen
ready fertig
  to get ready sich fertig machen
real echt
to realize erkennen
rearview mirror der Rückspiegel
receipt die Quittung
receiver der Hörer
reception (desk) der Empfang ; die
  Rezeption
receptionist der Empfangschef/die
  Empfangsdame
to recharge (battery) wieder aufladen
recipe das Rezept
to recognize erkennen
to recommend empfehlen
to record aufnehmen
to recover genesen
to recycle recyceln
red rot
to reduce reduzieren
reduction die Ermäßigung

refund die Rückerstattung
to refund rückerstatten
to refuse ablehnen
region das Gebiet
to register *(at hotel)* sich anmelden
registered letter das Einschreiben
registration form das Anmeldeformular
to reimburse entschädigen
relation *(family)* der/die Verwandte
to remain *(to stay)* bleiben
to remember sich erinnern
  I don't remember ich kann mich nicht erinnern
remote control die Fernbedienung
to remove entfernen
rent die Miete
to rent mieten
repair die Reparatur
to repair reparieren
to repeat wiederholen
to reply antworten
report der Bericht
to report berichten
request die Bitte
to request erbitten
to require benötigen
to rescue retten
reservation die Reservierung ; die Buchung
to reserve reservieren ; buchen
reserved reserviert
residence permit die Aufenthaltsgenehmigung
rest *(repose)* die Ruhe
  (remainder) der Rest
to rest ruhen
restaurant das Restaurant
restaurant car der Speisewagen
retired pensioniert
to return *(in car)* zurückfahren
  (on foot) zurückgehen
  (return something) zurückgeben
return ticket *(train)* die Rückfahrkarte
  (plane) das Rückflugticket
to reverse *(car)* rückwärts fahren

to reverse the charges ein R-Gespräch führen
reverse charge call das R-Gespräch
reverse gear der Rückwärtsgang
rheumatism der Rheumatismus
rib die Rippe
ribbon das Band
rice der Reis
rich *(person)* reich
  (food) reichhaltig
to ride *(horse)* reiten
right *(correct)* richtig
right: *on the right* rechts
  to the right nach rechts
right of way die Vorfahrt
ring der Ring
to ring klingeln
  it's ringing es klingelt
  to ring s.o. jemanden anrufen
ripe reif
river der Fluss
road die Straße
road map die Straßenkarte
road sign das Straßenschild
roast Rost-
roll *(bread)* das Brötchen
roller blades die Rollerblades
romantic romantisch
roof das Dach
roof-rack der Dachgepäckträger
room *(in house, hotel)* das Zimmer
  (space) der Platz
  double room das Doppelzimmer
  family room das Familienzimmer
  single room das Einzelzimmer
room number die Zimmernummer
room service der Zimmerservice
root die Wurzel
rope das Seil
rose *(flower)* die Rose
rotten *(fruit, etc)* verfault
round rund
roundabout *(traffic)* der Kreisverkehr
row *(in theatre, etc)* die Reihe
to row *(boat)* rudern
rowing *(sport)* das Rudern

rubber *(eraser)* der Radiergummi
  (material) das Gummi
rubber gloves die
  Gummihandschuhe
rubbish der Abfall
rubella die Röteln
rucksack der Rucksack
ruin *(eg castle)* die Ruine
ruler *(measuring)* das Lineal
to run rennen
rush hour die Rushhour
rusty rostig
rye bread das Roggenbrot

S

sad traurig
saddle der Sattel
safe *(for valuables)* der Safe
safe ungefährlich
  is it safe? ist das ungefährlich?
safety die Sicherheit
safety belt der Sicherheitsgurt
safety pin die Sicherheitsnadel
sail das Segel
to sail segeln
sailboard das Segelbrett
sailing *(sport)* das Segeln
sailing boat das Segelboot
salad der Salat
  green salad grüner Salat
  mixed salad gemischter Salat
  potato salad Kartoffelsalat
  tomato salad Tomatensalat
salad dressing die Salatsoße
salary das Gehalt
sale *(in general)* der Verkauf
  (seasonal bargains) der
  Schlussverkauf
salesperson der Verkäufer/die
  Verkäuferin
salt das Salz
salt water das Salzwasser
salty salzig
same gleich
sand der Sand
sandals die Sandalen

sandwich das Sandwich
sanitary pads die Damenbinden
satellite dish die Satellitenschüssel
satellite TV das Satellitenfernsehen
Saturday der Samstag
sauce die Soße
  tomato sauce die Tomatensoße
saucepan der Kochtopf
sauna die Sauna
sausage die Wurst
to save *(person)* retten
  (money) sparen
savoury pikant
to say sagen
scales die Waage
to scan einscannen
scarf *(headscarf)* das Kopftuch
  (round neck) das Halstuch
scenery die Landschaft
schedule der Plan
school die Schule
  primary school die Grundschule
  secondary school die Oberschule
scissors die Schere
score der Endstand
Scot der Schotte/die Schottin
Scotland Schottland
Scottish schottisch
screen der Bildschirm
screen wash das Scheibenputzmittel
screw die Schraube
screwdriver der Schraubenzieher
search engine die Suchmaschine
sedative das Beruhigungsmittel
to see sehen
to select auswählen
selection die Auswahl
self-catering für Selbstversorger
self-employed freiberuflich
self-service die Selbstbedienung
to sell verkaufen
  do you sell...? verkaufen Sie...?
sell-by date das Haltbarkeitsdatum
Sellotape® der Tesafilm®
to send schicken

senior citizen der Rentner/die Rentnerin

separated (couple) getrennt

September der September

septic tank die Klärgrube

serious schlimm

to serve (dish) servieren

service (in shop, etc) die Bedienung
is service included? ist die Bedienung inbegriffen?

service station die Raststätte

set menu die Tageskarte

settee das Sofa

several verschiedene

to sew nähen

sex das Geschlecht
(intercourse) der Sex

shade der Schatten
in the shade im Schatten

to shake schütteln

shallow (water) seicht

shampoo das Shampoo

shampoo and set Waschen und Föhnen

to share teilen

sharp scharf

to shave rasieren

she sie

sheep das Schaf

sheet (on bed) das Betttuch

shell (seashell) die Muschel
(egg, nut) die Schale

sheltered geschützt

to shine scheinen

shingles die Gürtelrose

ship das Schiff

shirt das Hemd

shock der Schock

shock absorber der Stoßdämpfer

shoe der Schuh

shoelaces die Schnürsenkel

shoe polish die Schuhcreme

shoe shop der Schuhladen

shop der Laden

to shop einkaufen

shop assistant der Verkäufer/die Verkäuferin

shopping das Einkaufen
to go shopping einkaufen gehen

shopping centre das Einkaufszentrum

shore das Ufer

short kurz

shortage der Mangel

short circuit der Kurzschluss

short cut die Abkürzung

shorts die Shorts

short-sighted kurzsichtig

shoulder die Schulter

to shout rufen

show (theatrical) die Aufführung

to show zeigen

shower (bath) die Dusche
(of rain) der Schauer

shower cap die Duschhaube

shower gel das Duschgel

to shrink einlaufen

shut (closed) geschlossen

to shut schließen

shutter (on window) der Fensterladen

sick (ill) krank
(nauseous) übel
I feel sick mir ist schlecht

sick bag die Spucktüte

side die Seite

side dish die Beilage

sidelight das Standlicht

sidewalk der Bürgersteig

sight die Sehenswürdigkeit

sightseeing tour die Besichtigungstour

sign (notice) das Schild

to sign unterschreiben

signature die Unterschrift

signpost der Wegweiser

silk die Seide

silver das Silber

to sing singen

single (unmarried) ledig
(not double) Einzel-
(ticket) einfach

single bed das Einzelbett
single room das Einzelzimmer
sink (kitchen) das Spülbecken
sister die Schwester
sister-in-law die Schwägerin
to sit sitzen
  sit down please! bitte setzen
  Sie sich!
size (clothes, shoes) die Größe
to skate (on ice) Schlittschuh laufen
skates (ice) die Schlittschuhe
  (roller) die Rollschuhe
skateboard das Skateboard
skating rink die Eisbahn
ski der Ski
to ski Ski fahren
ski boots die Skistiefel
skiing das Skilaufen
ski instructor der Skilehrer/die
  Skilehrehrin
ski jump die Sprungschanze
ski lift der Skilift
ski pants die Skihose
ski pass der Skipass
ski run/piste die Abfahrt
ski stick/pole der Skistock
ski suit der Skianzug
skin die Haut
skirt der Rock
sky der Himmel
sledge der Schlitten
to sleep schlafen
  to sleep in verschlafen
  to sleep late ausschlafen
sleeper (on train) der Schlafwagen
sleeping bag der Schlafsack
sleeping car der Schlafwagen
sleeping pills die Schlaftabletten
slice die Scheibe
slide (photograph) das Dia
to slip rutschen
slippers die Hausschuhe
slow(ly) langsam
to slow down langsamer werden
small klein
smaller than kleiner als

smell der Geruch
  (unpleasant) der Gestank
to smell riechen
smile das Lächeln
to smile lächeln
smoke der Rauch
to smoke rauchen
  I don't smoke ich bin
  Nichtraucher(in)
smoke alarm der Feuermelder
smoked (food) geräuchert
smokers (sign) Raucher
smooth weich
snack der Snack
  to have a snack einen Imbiss essen
snack bar die Snackbar
snake die Schlange
snake bite der Schlangenbiss
to sneeze niesen
snorkel der Schnorchel
snow der Schnee
to snow: it's snowing es schneit
to snowboard Snowboard fahren
snow chains die Schneeketten
snow tyres die Winterreifen
snowed up eingeschneit
soap die Seife
soap powder das Waschmittel
socket die Steckdose
socks die Socken
soda water das Soda
sofa das Sofa
sofa bed das Sofabett
soft weich
soft drink das alkoholfreie Getränk
soldier der Soldat
sole (of shoe) die Sohle
soluble löslich
some einige
someone irgendjemand
something etwas
son der Sohn
son-in-law der Schwiegersohn
song das Lied

soon bald
  as soon as possible so bald wie
  möglich
sore throat die Halsschmerzen
sorry: *I'm sorry!* tut mir leid!
sort die Sorte
  what sort? welche Sorte?
soup die Suppe
sour sauer
soured cream die saure Sahne
south der Süden
souvenir das Souvenir
spa das Bad
space der Platz
spade der Spaten
Spain Spanien
Spanish *adj* spanisch
spanner der Schraubenschlüssel
spare parts die Ersatzteile
spare room das Gästezimmer
spare tyre der Ersatzreifen
spare wheel das Ersatzrad
sparkling perlend
  sparkling water das Sprudelwasser
  sparkling wine der Schaumwein
spark plugs die Zündkerzen
to speak sprechen
  do you speak English? sprechen Sie
  Englisch?
special speziell
special offer das Sonderangebot
specialist der Spezialist/die
  Spezialistin
speciality die Spezialität
speed die Geschwindigkeit
speed limit die Geschwindigkeitsbegrenzung
  to exceed the speed limit die
  Geschwindigkeitsbegrenzung
  überschreiten
speedometer der Tachometer
to spell: *how's it spelt?* wie
  buchstabiert man das?
to spend ausgeben
spice das Gewürz
spicy würzig

to spill verschütten
spinach der Spinat
spin dryer die Wäscheschleuder
spine das Rückgrat
splinter der Splitter
spoilt verdorben
sponge der Schwamm
spoon der Löffel
sport der Sport
sports centre das Fitnesscenter
sports shop das Sportgeschäft
spot der Fleck
sprain die Verstauchung
spring *(season)* der Frühling
  (metal) die Feder
spring onions die Frühlingszwiebeln
square *(in town)* der Platz
stadium das Stadion
staff das Personal
stain der Fleck
stairs die Treppe
stale *(bread)* trocken
stalls *(in theatre)* das Parkett
stamp die Briefmarke
to stand stehen
star der Stern
  (film) der Star
to start *(begin)* anfangen
starter *(in meal)* die Vorspeise
  (in car) der Anlasser
station der Bahnhof
stationer's die
  Schreibwarenhandlung
statue die Statue
stay der Aufenthalt
  enjoy your stay! angenehmen
  Aufenthalt!
to stay *(to remain)* bleiben
steak das Steak
to steal stehlen
steamed gedünstet
steel der Stahl
steep steil
steeple der Kirchturm
step der Schritt
stepdaughter die Stieftochter

stepfather der Stiefvater
stepmother die Stiefmutter
stepson der Stiefsohn
stereo die Stereoanlage
sterling das Pfund Sterling
steward/stewardess der Steward/die Stewardess
to stick *(with glue)* kleben
sticking plaster das Heftpflaster
still *(yet)* noch
(motionless) still
  still water stilles Wasser
sting der Stachel
to sting stechen
stitches: *the wound needs stitches* die Wunde muss genäht werden
stock cube der Brühwürfel
stockings die Strümpfe
stolen gestohlen
stomach der Magen
stomach ache die Magenschmerzen
stone der Stein
stop *(sign)* das Stoppschild
to stop halten
stopover die Zwischenlandung
store *(shop)* das Geschäft
storey das Geschoss
storm der Sturm
story die Geschichte
straight away sofort
straight on geradeaus
strange *(odd)* seltsam
straw *(for drinking)* der Strohhalm
strawberries die Erdbeeren
stream der Bach
street die Straße
street map der Stadtplan
strength die Stärke
stress der Stress
strike *(of workers)* der Streik
string die Schnur
striped gestreift
stroke der Schlaganfall
  to have a stroke einen Schlaganfall haben

strong stark
  strong coffee starker Kaffee
  strong tea starker Tee
stuck: *it's stuck* es klemmt
student der Student/die Studentin
student discount die Studentenermäßigung
stuffed gefüllt
stung gestochen
stupid dumm
subscription *(fee)* der Beitrag
subsidiary die Tochtergesellschaft
subtitles die Untertitel
subway die Unterführung
suddenly plötzlich
suede das Wildleder
sugar der Zucker
sugar-free zuckerfrei
to suggest vorschlagen
suit *(man's)* der Anzug
  (woman's) das Kostüm
suitcase der Koffer
sum die Summe
summer der Sommer
summer holidays die Sommerferien
summit der Gipfel
sun die Sonne
to sunbathe sonnenbaden
sunblock die Sonnencreme
sunburn der Sonnenbrand
Sunday der Sonntag
sunglasses die Sonnenbrille
sunny sonnig
sunrise der Sonnenaufgang
sunroof das Sonnendach
sunscreen das Sonnenschutzmittel
sunset der Sonnenuntergang
sunshade der Sonnenschirm
sunstroke der Sonnenstich
suntan die Sonnenbräune
suntan lotion das Sonnenöl
supermarket der Supermarkt
supper das Abendessen
supplement *(to pay)* der Zuschlag
to supply zur Verfügung stellen

sure: *I'm sure* ich bin mir sicher
to surf surfen
   to surf the Net im Internet surfen
surfboard das Surfbrett
surgery die Operation
surname der Nachname
surprise die Überraschung
to survive überleben
suspension *(in car)* die Aufhängung
to swallow verschlucken
to sweat schwitzen
sweater der Pullover
sweatshirt das Sweatshirt
sweet *(not savoury)* süß
sweetener der Süßstoff
sweets die Süßigkeiten
to swell anschwellen
to swim schwimmen
swimming costume der Badeanzug
swimming pool das Schwimmbad
swimsuit der Badeanzug
swing *(for children)* die Schaukel
Swiss *adj* schweizerisch
   m/f der Schweizer/die Schweizerin
switch der Schalter
to switch off *(light)* ausschalten
   (machine) abschalten
   (gas, water) abstellen
to switch on *(light, machine)* einschalten
   (gas, water) anstellen
Switzerland die Schweiz
swollen geschwollen
synagogue die Synagoge
syringe die Spritze

T

table der Tisch
tablecloth die Tischdecke
tablet *(pill)* die Tablette
table tennis das Tischtennis
table wine der Tafelwein
to take nehmen
   (medicine) einnehmen
   how long does it take? wie lange dauert es?

take-away food das Essen zum Mitnehmen
to take off abfliegen
talc der Körperpuder
to talk to sprechen mit
tall groß
tampons die Tampons
tangerine die Mandarine
tank *(petrol)* der Tank
   (fish) das Aquarium
tap der Wasserhahn
tap water das Leitungswasser
tape die Kassette
tape measure das Maßband
tape recorder der Kassettenrekorder
target das Ziel
taste der Geschmack
to taste probieren
   can I taste it? darf ich es probieren?
tax die Steuer
taxi das Taxi
taxi driver der Taxifahrer/die Taxifahrerin
taxi rank der Taxistand
tea der Tee
   herbal tea Kräutertee
   tea with milk Tee mit Milch
tea bag der Teebeutel
teapot die Teekanne
teaspoon der Teelöffel
tea towel das Geschirrtuch
to teach unterrichten
teacher der Lehrer/die Lehrerin
team das Team
tear *(in material)* der Riss
teat *(on bottle)* der Sauger
teenager der Teenager
teeth die Zähne
telegram das Telegramm
telephone das Telefon
to telephone telefonieren
telephone box die Telefonzelle
telephone call der Anruf
telephone card die Telefonkarte

telephone directory das Telefonbuch

telephone number die Telefonnummer

television das Fernsehen

to tell erzählen

temperature die Temperatur
  to have a temperature Fieber haben

temporary provisorisch

tenant der Mieter

tendon die Sehne

tennis das Tennis

tennis ball der Tennisball

tennis court der Tennisplatz

tennis racket der Tennisschläger

tent das Zelt

tent peg der Hering

terminal das Terminal

terrace die Terrasse

to test testen

testicles die Hoden

tetanus injection die Tetanusimpfung

to text jemandem eine SMS schicken

text message die SMS

than als

to thank danken
  thank you danke
  thanks very much vielen Dank

that das
  that one das dort

the der, die, das

theatre das Theater

theft der Diebstahl

their *(with der words)* ihr
  (with das words) ihr
  (with die words) ihre

them ihnen

there *(over there)* dort

there is/there are es gibt

these diese
  these ones diese hier

they sie

thick *(not thin)* dick

thief der Dieb

thigh der Oberschenkel

thin dünn

thing das Ding
  my things meine Sachen

to think denken

thirsty durstig
  to be thirsty Durst haben

this dies
  this one das hier

thorn der Dorn

those jene
  those ones jene dort

thread der Faden

throat die Kehle

throat lozenges die Halspastillen

through durch

to throw away wegwerfen

thumb der Daumen

thunder der Donner

thunderstorm das Gewitter

Thursday der Donnerstag

ticket die Karte
  (train, bus, etc) die Fahrkarte
  (entrance fee) die Eintrittskarte
  a single ticket eine einfache Fahrkarte
  a return ticket eine Rückfahrkarte

ticket inspector der Schaffner/die Schaffnerin

ticket office der Fahrkartenschalter

tide die Gezeiten
  high tide die Flut
  low tide die Ebbe

tidy ordentlich

to tidy up aufräumen

tie die Krawatte

tight eng

tights die Strumpfhose

tile die Fliese

till *(cash desk)* die Kasse

till *(until)* bis
  till 2 o'clock bis zwei Uhr

time *(of day)* die Zeit
  what time is it? wie spät ist es?

timer die Schaltuhr

timetable der Fahrplan

tin *(can)* die Dose
tinfoil die Alufolie
tin-opener der Dosenöffner
to tip Trinkgeld geben
tip *(to waiter, etc)* das Trinkgeld
tipped *(cigarettes)* Filter-
tired müde
tissues die Papiertaschentücher
to zu (zum/zur)
  (with names of places) nach
  to London nach London
  to the airport zum Flughafen
toadstool der Giftpilz
toast der Toast
tobacco der Tabak
tobacconist's die
  Tabakwarenhandlung
today heute
toddler das Kleinkind
toe die Zehe
together zusammen
toilet die Toilette
  disabled toilet die
  Behindertentoilette
toilet brush die Toilettenbürste
toilet paper das Toilettenpapier
toiletries die Toilettenartikel
toll *(motorway)* die Maut
tomato die Tomate
  tinned tomatoes die Dosentomaten
tomato juice der Tomatensaft
tomorrow morgen
  tomorrow morning morgen früh
  tomorrow afternoon morgen
  Nachmittag
  tomorrow evening morgen Abend
tongue die Zunge
tonic water das Tonic
tonight heute Abend
tonsillitis die Mandelentzündung
too *(also)* auch
  too big zu groß
  too small zu klein
  too noisy zu laut
tools das Werkzeug
toolkit der Werkzeugkasten
tooth der Zahn

toothache die Zahnschmerzen
  I have toothache ich habe
  Zahnschmerzen
toothbrush die Zahnbürste
toothpaste die Zahnpasta
toothpick der Zahnstocher
top: *the top floor* das oberste
  Stockwerk
top *(of mountain)* der Gipfel
  (lid) der Deckel
  (clothing) das Oberteil
  on top of... oben auf...
topless oben ohne
torch *(flashlight)* die Taschenlampe
torn zerrissen
total *(amount)* die Endsumme
to touch anfassen
tough *(meat)* zäh
tour die Fahrt
  guided tour die Führung
tour guide der Reiseführer/die
  Reiseführerin
tour operator der Reiseveranstalter
tourist der Tourist/die Touristin
tourist information die
  Touristeninformation
tourist office das
  Fremdenverkehrsbüro
tourist route die Touristenroute
tourist ticket die Touristenkarte
to tow *(car)* abschleppen
towbar *(car)* die Abschleppstange
tow rope das Abschleppseil
towel das Handtuch
tower der Turm
town die Stadt
town centre das Stadtzentrum
town hall das Rathaus
town plan der Stadtplan
toxic giftig
toy das Spielzeug
toy shop der Spielzeugladen
tracksuit der Jogginganzug
traditional traditionell
traffic der Verkehr
traffic jam der Stau

traffic lights die Ampel
traffic policeman der Verkehrspolizist
trailer der Anhänger
train der Zug
 by train mit dem Zug
trainers die Turnschuhe
tram die Straßenbahn
tranquilliser das Beruhigungsmittel
to translate übersetzen
to travel reisen
travel agent's das Reisebüro
travel documents die Reisepapiere
travel guide der Reiseführer
travel insurance die Reiseversicherung
travel sickness die Reisekrankheit
traveller's cheques die Reisechecks
tray das Tablett
tree der Baum
trip der Ausflug
trolley *(luggage)* der Gepäckwagen
 (shopping) der Einkaufswagen
trousers die Hose
truck der Laster
true wahr
trunk der Koffer
trunks die Badehose
to try versuchen
to try on anprobieren
T-shirt das T-Shirt
Tuesday der Dienstag
tumble dryer der Wäschetrockner
tuna der Tunfisch
tunnel der Tunnel
to turn *(right/left)* abbiegen
to turn around umdrehen
to turn off *(light)* ausmachen
 (TV, radio, etc) ausschalten
 (tap) zudrehen
to turn on *(light)* anmachen
 (TV, radio, etc) anschalten
 (tap) aufdrehen
turnip die Steckrübe
turquoise *(colour)* türkis
tweezers die Pinzette

twice zweimal
twin-bedded room das Zweibettzimmer
twins die Zwillinge
to type Maschine schreiben
typical typisch
tyre der Reifen
tyre pressure der Reifendruck
Tyrol das Tirol

U

ugly hässlich
ulcer das Geschwür
umbrella der Regenschirm
 (sun) der Sonnenschirm
uncle der Onkel
uncomfortable unbequem
unconscious bewusstlos
under unter
undercooked nicht gar
underground die U-Bahn
underpants die Unterhose
underpass die Unterführung
understand verstehen
 I don't understand ich verstehe nicht
underwear die Unterwäsche
unemployed arbeitslos
to unfasten aufmachen
United Kingdom das Vereinigte Königreich
United States die Vereinigten Staaten
university die Universität
unleaded petrol das bleifreie Benzin
unlikely unwahrscheinlich
to unlock aufschließen
to unpack auspacken
unpleasant unangenehm
to unplug herausziehen
to unscrew aufschrauben
until bis
unusual ungewöhnlich
up: *to get up* aufstehen
upside down verkehrt herum
upstairs oben

urgent dringend
urine der Urin
us uns
to use benutzen
useful nützlich
usual(ly) gewöhnlich
U-turn die Wende

V

vacancy (in hotel) Zimmer frei
vacant frei
vacation der Urlaub
vaccination die Impfung
vacuum cleaner der Staubsauger
vagina die Vagina
valid gültig
valuable wertvoll
valuables die Wertsachen
value der Wert
valve das Ventil
van der Lieferwagen
vase die Vase
VAT die Mehrwertsteuer (MWST)
vegan: *I'm vegan* ich bin Veganer
vegetables das Gemüse
vegetarian vegetarisch
  I'm vegetarian ich bin Vegetarier
vehicle das Fahrzeug
vein die Ader
Velcro® das Klettband
vending machine der Automat
venereal disease die
  Geschlechtskrankheit
ventilator der Ventilator
very sehr
vest das Unterhemd
vet der Tierarzt
via über
to video (from TV) auf Video
  aufnehmen
  (to film) filmen
video das Video
video camera die Videokamera
video cassette/tape die
  Videokassette
video game das Videospiel
video recorder der Videorekorder

Vienna Wien
view die Aussicht
villa die Villa
village das Dorf
vinegar der Essig
vineyard der Weinberg
virus der Virus
visa das Visum
  to apply for a visa ein Visum
  beantragen
visit der Besuch
to visit (person) besuchen
  (place) besichtigen
visiting hours (hospital) die
  Besuchszeit
visitor der Besucher
vitamin das Vitamin
voice die Stimme
volcano der Vulkan
volleyball der Volleyball
voltage die Spannung
to vomit erbrechen
voucher der Gutschein

W

wage der Lohn
waist die Taille
waistcoat die Weste
to wait for warten auf
waiter/waitress der Kellner/die
  Kellnerin
waiting room der Warteraum
to wake up aufwachen
Wales Wales
walk der Spaziergang
  to go for a walk einen Spaziergang
  machen
to walk spazieren gehen
  (go on foot) zu Fuß gehen
walking boots die Wanderschuhe
walking stick der Wanderstock
Walkman® der Walkman®
wall die Mauer
wallet die Brieftasche
to want wollen
  I want... ich möchte...
  we want... wir möchten...

war der Krieg
ward (hospital) die Station
wardrobe der Kleiderschrank
warehouse die Lagerhalle
warm warm
  it's warm es ist warm
to warm up (milk, etc) aufwärmen
warning triangle das Warndreieck
to wash waschen
  (to wash oneself) sich waschen
wash and blow dry Waschen und
  Föhnen
washing machine die
  Waschmaschine
washing powder das Waschpulver
washing-up bowl die
  Abwaschschüssel
washing-up liquid das Spülmittel
wasp die Wespe
wasp sting der Wespenstich
waste bin der Abfalleimer
to watch zuschauen
watch die Armbanduhr
water das Wasser
  hot water warmes Wasser
  cold water kaltes Wasser
  drinking water Trinkwasser
  mineral water Mineralwasser
  sparkling water Sprudelwasser
  still water stilles Wasser
water heater das Heißwassergerät
watermelon die Wassermelone
waterproof wasserdicht
water sports der Wassersport
to water ski Wasserski fahren
water wings die Schwimmflügel
waves (on sea) die Wellen
way der Weg
way in (entrance) der Eingang
way out (exit) der Ausgang
we wir
weak schwach
  (tea, coffee) dünn
to wear tragen
weather das Wetter
weather forecast die
  Wettervorhersage

website die Webseite
website address die Internetadresse
wedding die Hochzeit
wedding anniversary der
  Hochzeitstag
wedding present das
  Hochzeitsgeschenk
Wednesday der Mittwoch
week die Woche
  last week letzte Woche
  next week nächste Woche
  this week diese Woche
weekday der Werktag
weekend das Wochenende
weekly wöchentlich
weekly ticket das Wochenticket
to weigh wiegen
weight das Gewicht
welcome willkommen
well gut
  he's not well ihm geht es nicht gut
well (for water) der Brunnen
well-done (steak) durch
wellington boots die Gummistiefel
Welsh adj walisisch
  m/f der Waliser/die Waliserin
west der Westen
wet nass
wetsuit der Taucheranzug
what was
wheat der Weizen
wheel das Rad
wheelchair der Rollstuhl
wheel clamp die Parkralle
when wann
where wo
which: *which man?* welcher Mann?
  which woman? welche Frau?
  which book? welches Buch?
while während
  in a while bald
white weiß
who wer
whole vollständig
wholemeal bread das Vollkornbrot
whose wessen

why warum
wide breit
widow die Witwe
widower der Witwer
wife die Frau
wig die Perücke
to win gewinnen
wind der Wind
windmill die Windmühle
window das Fenster
  (of shop) das Schaufenster
windscreen die Windschutzscheibe
windscreen wipers die
  Scheibenwischer
to windsurf surfen
windy: *it's windy* es ist windig
wine der Wein
  dry wine trockener Wein
  house wine Hauswein
  red wine Rotwein
  rosé wine Roséwein
  sparkling wine Schaumwein
  sweet wine süßer Wein
  white wine Weißwein
wine list die Weinkarte
wing der Flügel
wing mirror der Seitenspiegel
winter der Winter
wire der Draht
with mit
without ohne
to withdraw cash Geld abheben
witness der Zeuge
woman die Frau
wonderful wunderbar
wood *(material)* das Holz
wooden hölzern
woods *(forest)* der Wald
wool die Wolle
word das Wort
work die Arbeit
work permit die
  Arbeitsgenehmigung
to work *(person)* arbeiten
  (machine) funktionieren
world die Welt
worried besorgt
worse schlechter

worth: *it's worth £50* es ist fünfzig
  Pfund wert
to wrap up einwickeln
wrapping paper das
  Geschenkpapier
wrist das Handgelenk
to write schreiben
  please write it down bitte schreiben
  Sie das auf
writing paper das Briefpapier
wrong falsch
  what's wrong? was stimmt nicht?

X

X-ray die Röntgenaufnahme
to x-ray röntgen

Y

yacht die Jacht
year das Jahr
  this year dieses Jahr
  next year nächstes Jahr
  last year letztes Jahr
yearly jährlich
yellow gelb
Yellow Pages die Gelben Seiten
yes ja
yesterday gestern
yet: *not yet* noch nicht
yoghurt der Jogurt
  plain yoghurt Naturjogurt
yolk das Eigelb
you *(polite sing. and pl.)* Sie
  (familiar sing.) du ; ihr *(pl.)*
young jung
your dein/Ihr
  (with der words) dein/Ihr
  (with das words) dein/Ihr
  (with die words) deine/Ihre
youth hostel die Jugendherberge

Z

zebra crossing der Zebrastreifen
zero null
zip der Reißverschluss
zone die Zone
zoo der Zoo
zoom lens der Zoom

A

Aal *m* eel
ab off ; from
 ab 8 Uhr from 8 o'clock
 ab Mai from May onward
abbestellen to cancel
abbiegen to turn *(right/left)*
Abbildung *f* illustration
abblenden to dip *(lights)*
Abblendlicht *nt* dipped headlights
Abend *m* evening
Abendessen *nt* evening meal
abends in the evening(s)
aber but
abfahren to depart ; to leave
Abfahrt *f* departures
Abfahrtszeit *f* departure time
Abfall *m* rubbish
Abfertigungsschalter *m* check-in
 desk
abfliegen to take off
Abflug *m* flight departures
 Abflug Inland domestic departures
 Abflug Ausland international
 departures
Abflughalle *f* departure lounge
Abflugzeit *f* departure time
Abfluss *m* drain
Abführmittel *nt* laxative
abholen to fetch ; to claim *(baggage, etc)*
 abholen lassen to send for
Abkürzung *f* short cut
abladen to dump ; to offload
ablaufen to expire
ablehnen to refuse
Abonnement *nt* subscription
Abreise *f* departure
absagen to cancel
Absatz *m* heel
abschalten to switch off *(machine)*
abschicken to dispatch
Abschleppdienst *m* breakdown
 service
abschleppen to tow *(car)*
Abschleppseil *nt* towrope

Abschleppstange *f* towbar
Abschleppwagen *m* breakdown van
Absender *m* sender
abstellen to turn off ; to park car
Abszess *m* abscess
Abtei *f* abbey
Abteil *nt* compartment
Abteilung *f* department
Abtreibung *f* abortion
Abtreibungspille *f* abortion pill
Abzug *m* print *(photo)*
Achse *f* axle
achten auf to pay attention to
Achtung *f* caution ; danger
Ader *f* vein
Adler *m* eagle
Adressbuch *nt* address book
Adresse *f* address
adressieren to address
Affe *m* monkey
ähnlich similar
Aktentasche *f* briefcase
Akzent *m* accent *(pronunciation)*
akzeptieren to accept
Alarmanlage *f* alarm
Alge *f* seaweed
Alkohol *m* alcohol
alkoholfrei non-alcoholic
alkoholisch alcoholic *(drink)*
alle all ; everybody ; everyone
 alle zwei Tage every other day
Allee *f* avenue
allein alone
Allergie *f* allergy
allergisch gegen allergic to
Allerheiligen *nt* All Saints' Day
alles everything ; all
allgemein general ; universal
Alpen *pl* Alps
alt old
Altar *m* altar
Altbier *nt* top-fermented dark beer
Alter *nt* age *(of person)*
ältere(r/s) older ; elder
Altglascontainer *m* bottle bank
Alufolie *f* aluminium foil

am **at** ; **in** ; **on**
  am Bahnhof **at the station**
  am Abend **in the evening**
  am Freitag **on Friday**
Ameise f **ant**
Amerika nt **America**
Amerikaner(in) m/f **American**
amerikanisch adj **American**
Ampel f **traffic light**
Amtszeichen nt **dialling tone**
Amüsierviertel nt **nightclub district**
an **at** ; **on** (light, radio, etc) ; **near**
  Frankfurt an 1300 **arriving**
  Frankfurt at 1300
  an/aus **on/off**
Ananas f **pineapple**
anbauen **to grow** (cultivate)
anbieten **to offer**
andere(r/s) **other**
ändern **to change** (to alter)
Änderung f **change**
Anfall m **fit** (seizure)
Anfang m **start** (beginning)
anfangen **to begin** ; **to start**
Anfänger(in) m/f **beginner**
Anfängerhügel m **nursery slope**
Anfrage f **enquiry**
Angaben pl **details** ; **directions** (to a
  place)
angeben **to give**
Angebot nt **offer**
  im Angebot **on offer**
Angehörige(r) m/f **relative**
angeln **to fish**
Angeln nt **fishing** ; **angling**
  Angeln verboten **no fishing**
Angelrute f **fishing rod**
Angelschein m **fishing permit**
angenehm **pleasant**
Angestellte(r) m/f **employee**
Angina f **angina**
angreifen **to attack**
Angst haben vor **to be afraid of**
Anhänger m **trailer** ; **fan** (supporter)
Anker m **anchor**
ankommen **to arrive**
ankündigen **to announce**

Ankunft f **arrivals**
Anlage f **park** ; **grounds** ; **facilities**
  öffentliche Anlage **public park**
Anlasser m **starter** (in car)
Anlegeplatz m **mooring**
Anlegestelle f **landing stage** ; **jetty**
anmachen **to turn on**
Anmeldeformular nt **registration
  form**
Anmeldung f **registration** ;
  reception (place)
Annahme f **acceptance** ; **reception**
annehmen **to assume** ; **to accept**
anprobieren **to try on**
Anruf m **phone call**
Anrufbeantworter m **answerphone**
anrufen **to phone**
anschalten **to turn on**
anschauen **to look at**
Anschlagbrett nt **notice board**
Anschluss m **connection** (train, etc)
Anschlussflug m **connecting flight**
anschnallen **to fasten**
Anschrift f **address**
anschwellen **to swell**
Ansicht f **view**
Ansichtskarte f **picture postcard**
Ansprechpartner(in) m/f **contact
  person**
anstatt **instead of**
ansteckend **infectious**
anstehen **to queue**
anstellen **to switch on** (gas, water)
Anteil m **share** (part)
Antenne f **aerial**
Antibiotikum nt **antibiotic**
antik **ancient**
Antiquitäten pl **antiques**
Antiquitätenladen m **antique shop**
Antiseptikum nt **antiseptic**
Antwort f **answer** ; **reply**
antworten **to answer** ; **to reply**
Anweisungen pl **instructions**
Anzahl f **number**
Anzahlung f **deposit**

Anzeige f **advertisement** ; **report**
  (to police)
Anzug(-züge) m **suit(s)** *(man's)*
anzünden **to light** ; **to set fire to**
Apfel (Äpfel) m **apple(s)**
Apfelsaft m **apple juice**
Apfelsine(n) f **orange(s)**
Apfelwein m **cider**
Apotheke f **pharmacy**
Apparat m **appliance** ; **camera** ;
  extension
Aprikose(n) f **apricot(s)**
April m **April**
Aquarium nt **fish tank**
Arbeit f **employment** ; **work**
arbeiten **to work** *(person)*
arbeitslos **unemployed**
Architekt(in) m/f **architect**
Architektur f **architecture**
arm **poor**
Arm m **arm**
Armband nt **bracelet**
Armbanduhr f **watch**
Ärmelkanal m **English Channel**
Art f **type** ; **sort** ; **manner**
Arthritis f **arthritis**
Artikel m **article** ; **item**
Artischocke f **artichoke**
Arznei f **medicine**
Arzt (Ärztin) m/f **doctor**
Aschenbecher m **ashtray**
Aspirin nt **aspirin**
Ast m **branch** *(of tree)*
Asthma nt **asthma**
Atlantik m **Atlantic Ocean**
atmen **to breathe**
attraktiv **attractive**
Aubergine f **aubergine**
auch **also** ; **too** ; **as well**
auf **onto** ; **on** ; **upon** ; **on top of**
  auf Deutsch in German
  auf Wiedersehen goodbye
aufdrehen **to turn on** *(tap)*
Aufenthalt m **stay** ; **visit**
Aufenthaltsgenehmigung f
  residence permit

Aufenthaltsraum m **lounge**
Auffahrt f **slip-road**
Aufführung f **performance** ; **show**
aufgeben **to quit** ; **to post** ; **to check
  in** *(baggage)*
aufhalten **to delay** ; **to hold up**
  sich aufhalten to stay
auflegen **to hang up**
aufmachen **to open** *(shop, bank etc)* ;
  to unfasten
  sich aufmachen to set off
aufregend **exciting**
aufschließen **to unlock**
aufschrauben **to unscrew**
aufschreiben **to write down**
aufstehen **to get up**
Aufstieg m **ascent**
aufwachen **to wake up**
aufwärmen **to heat up** *(food, milk)*
Aufzug m **lift/elevator**
Auge(n) nt **eye(s)**
Augenblick m **moment** ; **instant**
Augentropfen pl **eye drops**
August m **August**
Auktion f **auction**
Au-pair-Mädchen nt **au pair**
aus **off** *(light, radio, etc)* ; **made of...** ;
  from ; **out of**
Ausdruck m **expression** ; **print-out** ;
  term *(word)*
Ausfahrt f **exit** *(motorway)*
Ausfall m **failure** *(mechanical)*
Ausflug(-flüge) m **trip(s)** ;
  excursion(s)
Ausfuhr f **export(s)**
ausführen **to export** ; **to carry out**
  (job)
ausfüllen **to fill in** *(form)*
  bitte nicht ausfüllen please leave
  blank *(on form)*
Ausgabe f **issue** *(of magazine)* ; **issuing
  counter**
Ausgaben pl **expenses**
Ausgang m **exit** ; **gate** *(at airport)*
ausgeben **to spend** *(money)*
ausgehen **to go out** *(for amusement)*
ausgeschaltet **off** *(radio)*

ausgestellt **issued at** *(passport)*
ausgezeichnet **excellent**
auskugeln **to dislocate** *(joint)*
Auskunft **information**
Ausland *nt* **foreign countries ;
abroad ; international**
 aus dem Ausland **from overseas**
Ausländer(in) *m/f* **foreigner**
ausländisch **foreign**
Auslandsgespräch *nt* **international
call**
auslassen **to leave out ; to omit**
auslaufen **to sail** *(ship)*
ausmachen **to turn off** *(light)* **; to put
out** *(fire, etc)*
Ausnahme *f* **exception**
auspacken **to unpack**
Auspuffrohr *nt* **exhaust pipe**
Ausrüstung *f* **kit ; equipment**
ausschalten **to switch off** *(light, TV,
radio)*
Ausschank *m* **bar ; drinks**
Ausschlag *m* **cold sore ; skin rash**
ausschließlich **excluding ;
exclusive(ly)**
Außenkabine *f (on ferry)* **outside
cabin**
Außenseite *f* **outside**
Außenspiegel *m* **outside mirror**
außer Betrieb **out of order**
äußerlich **exterior**
Aussicht *f* **view ; prospect**
aussprechen **to pronounce**
Ausstattung *f* **equipment** *(of car)*
aussteigen **to get out of** *(vehicle)*
Ausstellung *f* **show ; exhibition**
Ausstellungsdatum *nt* **date of issue**
Austausch *m* **exchange**
Australien *nt* **Australia**
Australier(in) *m/f* **Australian**
australisch *adj* **Australian**
Ausverkauf *m* **sale**
ausverkauft **sold out**
Auswahl *f* **choice**
auswählen **to choose**
auswärts essen **to eat out**

ausweichen **to avoid**
Ausweis *m* **identity card ; pass**
 (permit)
auszahlen **to pay**
Auto(s) *nt* **car(s)**
Autobahn *f* **motorway**
Autobahngebühr *f* **toll**
Autofähre *f* **car-ferry**
Autokarte *f* **road map**
Automat *m* **vending machine**
 Automat wechselt **change given**
Automatikauto *nt* **automatic car**
automatisch **automatic**
Automobilklub *m* **automobile
association**
Autor(in) *m/f* **author**
Autoreisezug *m* **motorail service**
Autoschlüssel *pl* **car keys**
Autovermietung *f* **car hire**

B

Baby *nt* **baby**
Babyflasche *f* **baby's bottle**
Babymilch *f* **baby milk**
Babynahrung *f* **baby food**
Babyraum *m* **mother and baby
room**
Babysitter(in) *m/f* **babysitter**
Babytücher *pl* **baby wipes**
Bach *m* **stream**
Bäckerei *f* **baker's**
Backofen *m* **oven**
Bad *nt* **bath ; spa**
Badeanzug *m* **swimsuit**
Badehose *f* **swimming trunks**
Badekappe *f* **bathing cap**
Badelatschen *pl* **flip flops**
baden **to bathe ; to swim**
 Baden verboten **no swimming**
Badewanne *f* **bath(tub)**
Badezimmer *nt* **bathroom**
Baguette *nt* **French bread**
Bahn *f* **railway ; rink**
 per Bahn **by rail**
Bahnhof *m* **station ; depot**
Bahnlinie *f* **line** *(railway)*

Bahnsteig *m* platform
Bahnübergang *m* level crossing
bald soon
Balkon *m* balcony
Ball *m* ball
Ballett *nt* ballet
Ballon *m* balloon
Banane(n) *f* banana(s)
Band (Bänder) *nt* ribbon(s) ; tape(s)
Band *f* band *(musical)*
Bank *f* bank ; bench
Bankkonto *nt* bank account
Bar *f* nightclub ; bar
Bär *m* bear *(animal)*
Bargeld *nt* cash
Bart *m* beard
Basel Basle
Batterie *f* battery
Bauarbeiten *pl* roadworks ;
  construction work
bauen to build
Bauer (Bäuerin) *m/f* farmer
Bauernhaus *nt* farmhouse
Bauernhof *m* farm(yard)
Baum *m* tree
Baumarkt *m* DIY shop
Baumwolle *f* cotton *(fabric)*
Baustelle *f* roadworks ; construction
  site
Bayern *nt* Bavaria
beachten to observe ; to obey
beantworten to answer
Bedarfshaltestelle *f* request stop
bedeckt cloudy *(weather)*
Bedeutung *f* meaning
bedienen to serve ; to operate
  sich bedienen to help oneself
Bedienung *f* service charge
Bedingung *f* condition
Beefsteak *nt* steak
  deutsches Beefsteak hamburger;
  beefburger
beenden to end ; to finish
Beerdigung *f* funeral
Beere *f* berry
beginnen to begin

begrüßen to greet ; to welcome
behalten to keep *(retain)*
Behandlung *f* treatment
beheizt heated
behindert disabled *(person)*
Behindertentoilette *f* toilet for
  disabled
Behinderung *f* obstruction ; handicap
bei near ; by *(beside)* ; at ; on ;
  during
beide both
Beilage *f* side-dish ; vegetables ;
  side-salad
Bein *nt* leg
Beisel *nt* pub *(Austria)*
Beispiel(e) *nt* example(s)
  zum Beispiel for example
beißen to bite
Beitrag *m* contribution ;
  subscription *(to club)*
beitreten to join *(club)*
Bekleidungsgeschäft *nt* clothes shop
bekommen to get *(receive, obtain)*
beladen to load *(truck, ship)*
Belastung *f* load
belegt no vacancies
Beleuchtung *f* lighting
Belgien *nt* Belgium
beliebt popular
Belohnung *f* reward
benachrichtigen to inform
Benachrichtigung *f* advice note
benötigen to require
benutzen to use
Benzin *nt* petrol
bequem comfortable
Beratungsstelle *f* advice centre
berechtigt zu entitled to
Berechtigte(r) *m/f* authorized person
bereit ready
Bereitschaftsdienst *m* emergency
  service
Berg(e) *m* mountain(s)
bergab downhill
bergauf uphill
Bergführer(in) *m/f* mountain guide

Bergschuhe *pl* **climbing boots**
Bergtour *f* **hillwalk ; climb**
Bergwacht *f* **mountain rescue**
Bergwanderung *f* **hill-walking**
Bericht(e) *m* **report(s) ; bulletin(s)**
berichten **to report**
Berliner *m* **doughnut**
Beruf *m* **profession ; occupation**
beruflich **professional**
Beruhigungsmittel *nt* **tranquilliser**
berühmt **famous**
berühren **to handle ; to touch**
beschädigen **to damage**
beschäftigt **busy**
Beschäftigung *f* **employment ;
   occupation**
Bescheinigung *f* **certificate**
beschreiben **to describe**
Beschreibung *f* **description**
Besen *m* **brush** *(for sweeping floor)*
besetzt **engaged ; occupied**
besichtigen **to visit** *(place)*
Besichtigungen *pl* **sightseeing**
Besichtigungstour *f* **guided tour**
Besitzer(in) *m/f* **owner**
besondere(r/s) **particular ; special**
besorgt **worried**
Besprechung *f* *(business)* **meeting**
besser **better**
Besserung(en) *f* **improvement(s)**
   gute Besserung **get well soon**
bestätigen **to confirm**
Bestätigung *f* **confirmation** *(flight,
   etc)*
beste(r/s) **best**
Besteck *nt* **cutlery**
bestellen **to book ; to order**
Bestellung *f* **order**
Bestimmungen *pl* **regulations**
Bestimmungsort *m* **destination**
besuchen **to visit** *(person)*
Besucher(in) *m/f* **visitor**
Besuchszeit *f* **visiting hours**
beten **to pray**
Betrag *m* **amount**
   Betrag erhalten **payment received**

betreten **to enter**
Betrieb *m* **business**
betrunken **drunk**
Bett(en) *nt* **bed(s)**
Bettbezug *m* **duvet cover**
Bettdecke *f* **duvet ; quilt**
Betttuch *nt* **sheet** *(on bed)*
Bettzeug *nt* **bedclothes**
Beule *f* **lump** *(swelling)*
bewacht **guarded**
bewegen **to move**
Bewohner(in) *m/f* **resident**
bewölkt **cloudy**
bewusstlos **unconscious**
bezahlen **to pay ; to settle bill**
bezahlt **paid**
Bezahlung *f* **payment**
Bezirk *m* **district**
bezüglich **concerning**
BH *m* **bra**
Bibliothek *f* **library**
Biene *f* **bee**
Bienenstich *m* **bee sting ; type of
   cream cake**
Bier *nt* **beer**
   Bier vom Fass **draught beer**
Biergarten *m* **beer garden**
Bierkeller *m* **beer cellar**
Bierstube *f* **pub that specializes
   in beer**
bieten **to offer**
Bikini *m* **bikini**
Bild(er) *nt* **picture(s)**
Bilderrahmen *m* **picture frame**
Bildschirm *m* **screen** *(TV, computer)*
billig **cheap ; inexpensive**
billiger **cheaper**
Billigtarif *m* **cheap rate**
Birne(n) *f* **pear(s) ; lightbulb(s)**
bis **until ; till**
   bis jetzt **up till now**
   bis zu 6 **up to 6**
   bis bald **see you soon**
bisschen: *ein bisschen* **a little ;
   a bit of**
bitte **please**

bitte? **pardon?**

bitten um **to ask for**

bitter *(taste)*

blass **pale**

Blase f **blister**

Blasenentzündung f **cystitis**

Blatt (Blätter) nt **sheet(s)** *(of paper)* ;
leaf (leaves)

blau **blue**

Blaue Zone f **limited parking zone**
(parking disk required)

Blei nt **lead** *(metal)*

bleiben **to stay** *(to remain)*

Bleichmittel nt **bleach**

Bleiersatz-Zusatz nt **lead additive**

bleifreies Benzin nt **unleaded petrol**

Bleistift m **pencil**

blind **blind** *(person)*

Blinddarmentzündung f **appendicitis**

Blinker m **indicator** *(in car)*

Blitz m **lightning**

Blitzlicht nt **flash** *(for camera)*

blockiert **jammed** *(camera, lock)*

Blockschrift f **block letters**

blond **fair** *(hair)* ; **blond**

Blumen pl **flowers**

Blumenladen m **florist's shop**

Bluse f **blouse**

Blut nt **blood**

Blutdruck m **blood pressure**

bluten **to bleed**

Bluterguss m **bruise**

Blutgruppe f **blood group**

blutig **rare** *(steak)*

Bluttest m **blood test**

Blutvergiftung f **blood poisoning**

Bockbier nt **strong beer**

Boden m **floor** *(of room)* ; **ground**

Bodensee m **Lake Constance**

Bohnen pl **beans**
grüne Bohnen **french beans**

Bohrer m **drill** *(tool)*

Boiler m **immersion heater**

Bombe f **bomb**

Bonbon nt **sweet**

Boot nt **boat** *(small)*

Bootsfahrt f **cruise**

Bootsrundfahrt f **round boat trip**

Bootsverleih m **boat hire**

Bordkarte f **boarding pass**

borgen **to borrow**

Böschung f **embankment**

botanischer Garten m **botanical
gardens**

Botschaft f **embassy**

Bowle f **punch** *(drink)*

Brandwunde f **burn** *(on skin)*

Brat- **fried** ; **roast**

braten **to fry** ; **to roast**

Bratkartoffeln pl **fried potatoes**

Bratpfanne f **frying pan**

Bratwurst f **sausage**

Brauch m **custom** *(tradition)*

brauchen **to need**

Brauerei f **brewery**

braun **brown**

Bräune f **suntan**

Braut f **bride**

Bräutigam m **bridegroom**

Brechreiz m **nausea**

breit **wide**

Bremse(n) f **brake(s)**

bremsen **to brake**

Bremsflüssigkeit f **brake fluid**

Bremslicht nt **brake light**

brennen **to burn**

Brief m **letter** *(message)*

Briefkasten m **letterbox** ; **postbox**

Briefmarke(n) f **stamp(s)**

Briefpapier nt **writing paper**

Brieftasche f **wallet**

Briefträger(in) m/f **postman/woman**

Briefumschlag m **envelope**

Brille f **glasses** *(spectacles)*

Brillenetui nt **glasses case**

bringen **to bring**

britisch **British**

Brombeeren pl **blackberries**

Bronchitis f **bronchitis**

Bronze f **bronze**

Brosche f **brooch**

Broschüre f **brochure**

Brot nt bread ; loaf
Brötchen nt bread roll
Bruch m fracture
Brücke f bridge
Bruder(Brüder) m brother(s)
Brühe f stock (for soup, etc)
Brühwürfel pl stock cubes
Brunnen m well (for water) ; fountain
Brust f breast ; chest
Buch nt book
buchen to book
Buchhandlung f bookshop
Büchsen- canned
Büchsenöffner m can-opener
Buchstabe m letter (of alphabet)
Bucht f bay (along coast)
Buchung f booking
Bügel m coat hanger
   Bügel drücken! press down!
Bügelbrett nt ironing board
Bügeleisen nt iron (for clothes)
bügeln to iron
Bundes- federal
Bundesrepublik Deutschland f
   Federal Republic of Germany
Bungee-Springen nt bungee
   jumping
bunt coloured
Burg f castle ; fortress (medieval)
Bürger(in) m/f citizen
bürgerlich middle-class
Bürgermeister(in) m/f mayor(-ess)
Bürgersteig m pavement ; sidewalk
Büro nt agency ; office
Bürogebäude nt office block
Bürste f brush
Bus(se) m bus(es) ; coach(es)
Busbahnhof m bus/coach station
Busfahrschein m bus ticket
Busfahrt f bus tour
Bushaltestelle f bus stop
Buslinie f bus route
Busreise f coach trip
Busverbindung f bus service
Büstenhalter m bra
Butangas nt Calor gas®
Butter f butter

C

campen to camp
Campingführer m camping
   guide(book)
Campingkocher m camping stove
Campingplatz m campsite
Campingtisch m picnic table
CD-Spieler m CD player
Cent m cent (euro)
Champignon(s) m mushroom(s)
Charterflug m charter flight
Check-in m check-in
Chef(in) m/f boss
chemische Toilette f chemical loo
Chinarestaurant nt Chinese
   restaurant
Chips pl crisps ; chips (gambling)
Chor m choir
Cola f Coke®
Computer m computer
Computerprogramm nt computer
   program
Computerspiel nt computer game
Conditioner m conditioner (hair)
Cousin(e) m/f cousin
Creme f cream (lotion)
Creme(speise) f mousse

D

da there
   nicht da out (not at home)
Dach nt roof
Dachboden m attic
Dachgepäckträger m roof-rack
daheim at home
Damen ladies
Damenbinde(n) f sanitary towel(s)
Dampfer m steamer (boat)
danach after (afterwards)
Dänemark nt Denmark
danke thank you
danken to thank
Darmgrippe f gastric flu
das the ; that ; this ; which
Datei f file (computer)
Datum nt date (day)

Dauer f length ; duration
Dauerwelle f perm
Daumen m thumb
Decke f blanket ; ceiling
Deckel m top ; lid
dein your (singular familiar)
denken to think
Denkmal(-mäler) nt monument(s)
Deo nt deodorant
der the ; who(m) ; that ; this ;
  which
Desinfektionsmittel nt disinfectant
desinfizieren to disinfect
destilliertes Wasser nt distilled
  water
Details pl details
deutsch adj German
Deutsch nt German (language)
Deutsche(r) m/f German
Deutschland nt Germany
Devisen pl foreign currency
Dezember m December
Dia(s) nt slide(s)
Diabetes m diabetes
Diabetiker(in) m/f diabetic person
Diamant m diamond
Diät f diet (special)
dick fat
die the ; who(m) ; that ; this ; which
Dieb(in) m/f thief
Diebstahl m theft
Dienst m service
  im Dienst on duty
Dienstag m Tuesday
dienstbereit open (pharmacy) ; on
  duty (doctor)
Dienstreise f business trip
Dienstzeit f office hours
dies this
diese these
diese(r/s) this (one)
Diesel m diesel
Dieselöl nt diesel oil
Digitalkamera f digital camera
Digitalradio nt digital radio
Ding(e) nt thing(s)

Diplomat(in) m/f diplomat
direkt direct (route, train)
Direktflug m direct flight
Direktor(in) m/f managing director
Diskette f computer disk (floppy)
Disko f disco
Dokumente pl documents
Dollar m dollar
Dolmetscher(in) m/f interpreter
Dom m cathedral
Donner m thunder
Donnerstag m Thursday
Doppel- double
Doppelbett nt double bed
doppelt double
Doppelzimmer nt double room
Dorf(Dörfer) nt village(s)
Dorn m thorn
dort there (over there) ; that one
Dose f box ; tin ; can
Dosenöffner m tin-opener
Dozent(in) m/f teacher (university)
Drachenfliegen nt hang gliding
Draht m wire
Drahtseilbahn f cable railway
draußen outdoors ; outside
drehen to turn ; to twist
Dreibettabteil nt three-berth
  compartment
Dreieck nt triangle
Dreikönigstag m Epiphany
dringend urgent
drinnen indoors
Droge f drug
Drogerie f chemist's (not for
  prescriptions)
drücken push
Druckschrift f block letters
du you (familiar form)
dumm stupid
dunkel dark
dunkelblau dark blue
dünn thin ; weak (tea)
dunstig misty
durch through ; well-done (steak)
Durchfahrt verboten no through
  traffic

Durchfall *m* **diarrhoea**
Durchgang *m* **way ; passage**
Durchgangsverkehr *m* **through traffic**
durchgehend **direct** *(train, bus)* ; **24 hour**
Durchsage *f* **announcement**
durchwählen **to dial direct**
Durchzug *m* **draught** *(of air)*
dürfen **to be allowed**
Dürre *f* **drought**
Durst haben **to be thirsty**
durstig **thirsty**
Dusche *f* **shower**
Duschhaube *f* **shower cap**
Duschvorhang *m* **shower curtain**
Dutzend *nt* **dozen**

E

Ebbe *f* **low tide**
echt **real ; genuine**
Ecke *f* **corner**
Edelstein *m* **jewel ; gem**
ehemalig **ex-**
ehrlich **honest**
Ei(er) *nt* **egg(s)**
Eiche *f* **oak**
eifersüchtig **jealous**
Eigelb *nt* **egg yolk**
Eigentum *nt* **property**
Eigentümer(in) *m/f* **owner**
Eil- **urgent**
Eilbrief *m* **express letter**
Eilzustellung *f* **special delivery**
Eimer *m* **bucket**
ein *(with 'das'/'der' words)* **a ; one**
ein(geschaltet) **on** *(machine)*
Einbahnstraße *f* **one-way street**
Einbrecher(in) *m/f* **burglar**
einchecken **to check in**
eine *(with 'die' words)* **a ; one**
einfach **simple ; single ticket ; plain** *(unflavoured)*
Einfuhr *f* **import**
einführen **to insert ; to import**
Eingang *m* **entrance**

Eingangstür *f* **front door**
eingeschlossen **included** *(in price)*
eingeschneit **snowed up**
Eingeweidebruch *m* **hernia**
eingießen **to pour**
einige(r/s) **some ; a few**
einkaufen **to shop**
Einkaufswagen *m* **shopping trolley**
Einkaufszentrum *nt* **shopping centre**
einladen **to invite**
Einladung *f* **invitation**
Einlass ab 18 **no entry for under 18s**
einlaufen **to shrink**
einlösen **to cash** *(cheque)*
einmal **once**
einnehmen **to take** *(medicine)*
einordnen **to get in lane**
Einrichtungen *pl* **facilities**
eins **one**
einschalten **to switch on** *(light, TV)*
einschieben **to insert**
einschließlich **including**
Einschreiben *nt* **registered letter**
  per Einschreiben **by recorded delivery**
einsteigen **to get in(to)** *(bus, etc)*
einstellen **to adjust ; to appoint ; to stop**
Eintopfgericht *nt* **stew**
eintreten **to enter**
Eintritt *m* **entry ; admission** *(fee)*
Eintritt frei **free entry**
Eintrittskarte(n) *f* **ticket(s)**
Eintrittspreis *m* **admission charge/fee**
einwerfen **to post ; to insert**
einwickeln **to wrap up** *(parcel)*
Einwurf *m* **slot ; slit**
  Einwurf 2 Euro **insert 2 euros**
Einzahlung *f* **deposit**
Einzel- *(not double)*
Einzelbett *nt* **single bed**
Einzelfahrschein *m* **single ticket**
einzeln **single ; individual**
Einzelzimmer *nt* **single room**
Eis *nt* **ice cream ; ice**

Eisbahn f **skating rink**
Eisbecher m **knickerbocker glory**
Eisdiele f **ice-cream parlour**
Eisen nt **iron** *(metal)*
Eisenbahn f **railway**
Eisenwarenhandlung f **hardware shop**
Eiskaffee m **iced coffee**
Eistee m **iced tea**
Eiswürfel pl **ice cubes**
Eiweiß nt **egg white**
Elastikbinde f **elastic bandage**
elastisch **elastic**
Elektriker(in) m/f **electrician**
elektrisch **electric(al)**
elektrischer Schlag m **electric shock**
Elektrizität f **electricity**
Elektrorasierer m **electric razor**
Ellbogen m **elbow**
Eltern pl **parents**
E-Mail f **e-mail**
E-Mail-Adresse f **e-mail address**
Empfang m **reception**
empfangen **to receive** *(guest)* ; **to greet**
Empfangschef m **receptionist**
Empfangsdame f **receptionist**
Empfangsschein m **receipt**
empfehlen **to recommend**
Ende nt **end** ; **bottom** *(of page, etc)*
Endstand m **final score** *(of match)*
Endstation f **terminal**
Endsumme f **total** *(amount)*
eng **narrow** ; **tight** *(clothes)*
England nt **England**
Engländer(in) m/f **Englishman/woman**
Englisch nt **English** *(language)*
Enkel m **grandson**
Enkelin f **granddaughter**
entdecken **to discover**
Ente f **duck**
enteisen **to de-ice**
entfernt **distant**
　2 Kilometer entfernt **2 km away**

Entfernung f **distance**
entfrosten **to defrost**
Enthaarungscreme f **depilatory cream**
enthalten **to hold** *(to contain)*
entkoffeinierter Kaffee m **decaffeinated coffee**
entkommen **to escape**
entrahmte Milch f **skimmed milk**
entschädigen **to reimburse**
Entschuldigung f **pardon ; excuse me**
entweder ... oder **either ... or**
entwickeln **to develop** *(photos)*
Entzündung f **inflammation**
Epileptiker(in) m/f **epileptic**
epileptischer Anfall m **epileptic fit**
er **he ; it**
erbrechen **to vomit**
Erbsen pl **peas**
Erdbeben nt **earthquake**
Erdbeeren pl **strawberries**
Erde f **earth**
Erdgeschoss nt **ground floor**
Erdnuss(-nüsse) f **peanut(s)**
Erdrutsch m **landslide**
erfreut **pleased**
Erfrischungen pl **refreshments**
erhalten **to obtain ; to receive**
erhältlich **available**
Erkältung f **cold** *(illness)*
erkennen **to realize ; to recognize**
erklären **to explain**
Erklärung f **explanation**
erlauben **to permit** *(something)* ; **to allow**
Ermäßigung f **reduction**
Ernte f **harvest**
Ersatz m **substitute ; replacement**
Ersatzrad nt **spare wheel**
Ersatzteile pl **car parts**
erste(r/s) **first**
　erste Hilfe **first aid**
　erste Klasse **first class**
ertrinken **to drown**
Erwachsene(r) m/f **adult**

erzählen to tell
es it
essbar edible
essen to eat
Essen nt food ; meal
Essen zum Mitnehmen take-away food
Essig m vinegar
Esslöffel m tablespoon
Esszimmer nt dining room
Etage f floor ; storey
Etagenbetten pl bunk beds
etwas something
Eule f owl
Euro m Euro (currency)
Eurocent m euro cent
Europa nt Europe
europäisch European
Europäische Union (EU) f European Union (EU)
Euroscheck m Eurocheque
Exemplar nt copy
Experte (Expertin) m/f expert
exportieren to export

F

Fabrik f works ; factory
Facharzt (Fachärztin) m/f specialist (medical)
Fächer m fan (hand-held)
Faden m thread
Fahne f flag
Fahrbahn f carriageway
Fähre f ferry
fahren to drive ; to go
Fahrer(in) m/f driver (of car)
Fahrgast m passenger
Fahrkarte f ticket (train, bus, etc)
Fahrkartenschalter m ticket office
Fahrplan m timetable (trains, etc)
Fahrplanhinweise pl travel information
Fahrpreis(e) m fare(s)
Fahrrad(-räder) nt bicycle(s)
Fahrradflickzeug nt bicycle repair kit
Fahrradschloss nt bicycle lock

Fahrradvermietung f bike hire
Fahrschein(e) m ticket(s)
Fahrscheinentwerter m ticket stamping machine
Fahrscheinheft nt book of tickets
Fahrspur(en) f lane(s)
Fahrstuhl m lift ; elevator
Fahrt f journey ; drive ; ride (in vehicle)
gute Fahrt! safe journey!
Fahrzeug nt vehicle
Fall m instance
im Falle von in case of
fallen to fall
fällig due (owing)
falsch false (name, etc) ; wrong
Falten pl wrinkles
Familie f family
Familienname m surname
Familienstand m marital status
Familienzimmer nt family room
Fan m fan (football)
Farbe f colour ; paint ; suit (cards)
färben dye
farbenblind colour-blind
Farbfilm m colour film
farbig coloured
Farbstoff m dye
Fasching m carnival
Fass nt barrel
vom Fass on tap ; on draught
Fassbier nt draught beer
Fastnachtsdienstag m Shrove Tuesday
faul lazy
Fax nt fax
faxen to fax
Faxnummer f fax number
Februar m February
Feder f spring (coil) ; feather
Federball m badminton
Federung f suspension (in car)
fehlen to be missing
Fehler m fault ; mistake
Fehlgeburt f miscarriage
feiern to celebrate

Feiertag m **holiday**
Feige f **fig**
Feile f **file** (nail)
Feinkostgeschäft nt **delicatessen**
Feld nt **field**
Felsen m **cliff** (in mountains)
Fenster nt **window**
Fensterladen m **shutter** (on window)
Fensterplatz m **window seat**
Ferien pl **holiday(s)**
Ferienhaus nt **chalet** (holiday)
Ferienwohnung f **holiday flat**
Fern- **long-distance**
Fernbedienung f **remote control**
Ferngespräch nt **long-distance call**
Fernglas nt **binoculars**
Fernlicht nt **full beam** (headlights)
Fernsehen nt **television**
Fernseher m **TV set**
Fernsprecher m **public phone**
fertig **ready ; finished**
Fest nt **celebration ; party ; festival**
Festplatte f **hard disk**
Fett nt **fat ; grease**
fettarm **low-fat**
fettarme Milch f **low-fat milk**
fettig **greasy**
feucht **damp**
Feuchtigkeitscreme f **moisturizer**
Feuer nt **fire**
feuerfeste Form f **ovenproof dish**
feuergefährlich **inflammable**
Feuerlöscher m **fire extinguisher**
Feuermelder m **fire/smoke alarm**
Feuertreppe f **fire escape**
Feuerwehr f **fire brigade**
Feuerwehrauto nt **fire engine**
Feuerwerk nt **fireworks**
Feuerzeug nt **cigarette lighter**
Fieber nt **fever**
  Fieber haben **to have temperature**
Filet nt **sirloin ; fillet** (of meat, fish)
Filiale f **branch** (of store, bank, etc)
Film m **film** (at cinema, for camera)
filmen **to film**
Filter m **filter**

Filzstift m **felt-tip pen**
finden **to find**
Finger m **finger**
Fingernagel m **fingernail**
Firma f **company** (firm)
Fisch m **fish**
Fischladen m **fishmonger's**
FKK-Strand m **nudist beach**
flach **flat** (level) ; **shallow** (water)
Flamme f **flame**
Flasche f **bottle**
Flaschenbier nt **bottled beer**
Flaschenöffner m **bottle opener**
Fleck m **mark** (stain)
Fleckenmittel nt **stain-remover**
Fleisch nt **meat ; flesh**
Fleischerei f **butcher's**
Flickzeug nt **puncture repair kit**
Fliege f **bow tie ; fly**
fliegen **to fly**
Flitterwochen **honeymoon**
Flöhe pl **fleas**
Flohmarkt m **flea market**
Flug(Flüge) m **flight(s)**
Fluggast m **passenger**
Fluggesellschaft f **airline**
Flughafen m **airport**
Flughafenbus m **airport bus**
Flugplan m **flight schedule**
Flugauskunft f **flight information**
Flugschein(e) m **plane ticket(s)**
Flugsteig m **gate**
Flugstrecke f **route ; flying distance**
Flugticket(s) nt **plane ticket(s)**
Flugzeug nt **plane, aircraft**
Flur m **corridor**
Fluss(Flüsse) m **river(s)**
Flussfahrt f **river trip**
Flüssigkeit f **liquid**
Flut f **flood ; high tide**
Föhn m **hairdryer**
föhnen **to blow-dry**
folgen **to follow**
Forelle f **trout**
Form f **shape ; form**
Formular nt **form** (document)

Fortsetzung f sequel (book, film)
Foto nt photo
Fotoapparat m camera
Fotogeschäft nt photo shop
Fotografie f photography
fotografieren to take a photo
Fotokopie f photocopy
fotokopieren to photocopy
Fracht f cargo ; freight
Frage f question
fragen to ask
frankieren to stamp (letter)
Frankreich nt France
Franzose (Französin) m/f
   Frenchman/woman
französisch adj French
Frau f wife ; Mrs ; Ms ; woman
Fräulein nt Miss
frei free / vacant
   im Freien outdoor
Freibad nt open-air pool
freiberuflich freelance ; self-
   employed
Freigepäck nt baggage allowance
freimachen to stamp
Freitag m Friday
Freizeichen nt ringing tone
Freizeit f spare time ; leisure
Freizeitzentrum nt leisure centre
fremd foreign ; strange (unknown)
Fremde(r) m/f stranger
Fremdenführer(in) m/f tourist guide
Fremdenverkehrsbüro nt tourist
   office
Freude f joy
Freund m friend ; boyfriend
Freundin f friend ; girlfriend
freundlich friendly
Frieden m peace
Friedhof m cemetery
frisch fresh ; wet (paint)
Frischhaltefolie f cling film
Frischkäse m cream cheese
Friseur (Friseuse) m/f hairdresser
Frosch m frog
Frost m frost

Frostschutzmittel nt antifreeze
Früchte pl fruit
Früchtetee m fruit tea
Fruchtsaft m fruit juice
früh early
früher earlier
Frühling m spring (season)
Frühstück nt breakfast
Fuchs m fox
fühlen to feel
führen to lead
Führer(in) m/f guide
Führerschein m driving licence
Führung(en) f guided tour(s)
füllen to fill
Füller m pen
Fundbüro nt lost property office
Fundsachen pl lost property
funktionieren to work (machine)
für for
   Benzin für 30 Euro 30 euros worth
   of petrol
   für immer forever
Fuß(Füße) m foot(feet)
   zu Fuß gehen to walk
Fußball m football ; soccer
Fußballer(in) m/f football player
Fußballplatz m football pitch
Fußballspiel nt football match
Fußgänger(in) m/f pedestrian
Fußgängerüberweg m pedestrian
   crossing
Fußgängerzone f pedestrian
   precinct
Fußweg m footpath
füttern to feed

G

Gabel f fork (for eating)
Gabelung f fork (in road)
Galerie f gallery
Gang m course (of meal) ; aisle
   (theatre, plane)
Gangschaltung f gears
Gans f goose
ganz whole ; quite

ganztägig **full-time**
Garage f **garage** (private)
Garantie f **guarantee ; warrant(y)**
Garderobe f **cloakroom**
Garten m **garden**
Gartenlokal nt **garden café**
Gärtner(in) m/f **gardener**
Gas nt **gas**
Gasflasche f **gas cylinder**
Gasherd m **gas cooker**
Gaspedal nt **accelerator**
Gasse f **alley ; lane** (in town)
Gast m **guest**
   nur für Gäste **patrons only**
Gästezimmer nt **guest-room**
Gasthaus nt **inn**
Gasthof m **inn ; guesthouse**
Gastritis f **gastritis**
Gaststätte f **restaurant**
Gaststube f **lounge**
Gate nt **gate** (airport)
Gebäck nt **pastry (cake)**
gebacken **baked**
Gebäude nt **building**
gebeizt **cured ; marinated**
geben **to give**
Gebiet nt **region ; area**
Gebiss nt **dentures**
geboren **born**
   geborene Schnorr **née Schnorr**
gebraten **fried**
gebrauchen **to use**
Gebraucht- **used** (car, etc)
gebrochen **broken**
Gebühr f **fee**
gebührenpflichtig **subject to fee**
Geburt f **birth**
Geburtsdatum nt **date of birth**
Geburtsort m **place of birth**
Geburtstag m **birthday**
Geburtstagsgeschenk nt **birthday present**
Geburtstagskarte f **birthday card**
Geburtsurkunde f **birth certificate**
Gedeckkosten pl **cover charge** (in restaurant)

gedünstet **steamed**
Gefahr f **danger**
gefährlich **dangerous**
Gefälle nt **gradient**
Gefängnis nt **prison**
Geflügel nt **poultry ; fowl**
gefroren **frozen** (food)
gefüllt **stuffed**
gegen **versus ; against ; toward(s)**
Gegend f **district ; region**
gegenüber **opposite ; facing**
Gegenverkehr m **two-way traffic**
gegrillt **grilled**
Geheimzahl f **PIN number**
gehen **to go ; to walk**
   wie geht es Ihnen? **how are you?**
Gehirnerschütterung f **concussion**
gehören **to belong to**
gekocht **boiled ; cooked**
gelb **yellow ; amber** (traffic lights)
Gelbe Seiten pl **Yellow Pages**
Gelbsucht f **jaundice**
Geld nt **money**
   Geld abheben **withdraw cash**
   Geld einwerfen **insert money**
Geldautomat m **cash dispenser ; ATM**
Geldbeutel m **purse**
Geldrückgabe f **coin return**
Geldschein m **banknote**
Geldstrafe f **fine** (to be paid)
Geldstück nt **coin**
gelegentlich **occasionally**
Gelenk nt **joint** (of body)
Geltungsdauer f **period of validity**
gemischt **mixed ; assorted**
Gemüse nt **vegetables**
Gemüseladen m **greengrocer's**
genau **accurate ; precise ; exact**
Genehmigung f **approval ; permit**
genug **enough**
Genuss m **enjoyment**
geöffnet **open**
Gepäck nt **luggage**
Gepäckablage f **luggage rack**
Gepäckaufbewahrung f **left-luggage office**

Gepäckausgabe f **baggage reclaim**

Gepäckermittlung f **luggage desk** (for queries)

Gepäcknetz nt **luggage rack** (in train)

Gepäckschließfach nt **left-luggage locker**

Gepäckträger m **luggage rack** (on car) ; **porter**

Gepäckversicherung f **luggage insurance**

Gepäckwagen m **luggage trolley**

gerade **even** (number)

geradeaus **straight ahead**

Gerät nt **appliance** ; **gadget**

geräuchert **smoked** (food)

Gericht nt **court** (law) ; **dish** (food)

gerieben **grated** (cheese)

geröstet **sauté** ; **fried** ; **toasted**

Geruch m **smell**

Gesamtsumme f **total amount**

Geschäft(e) nt **business** ; **shop(s)**

Geschäftsadresse f **business address**

Geschäftsführer(in) m/f **manager**

Geschäftspartner(in) m/f **partner** (business)

Geschäftsstunden pl **business hours**

geschehen **to happen**

Geschenk(e) nt **gift(s)**

Geschenkladen m **gift shop**

Geschenkpapier nt **wrapping paper**

Geschichte f **history**

geschieden **divorced**

Geschirrspülmaschine f **dishwasher**

Geschirrspülmittel nt **washing-up liquid**

Geschirrtuch nt **tea/dish towel**

Geschlecht nt **gender** ; **sex**

Geschlechtskrankheit f **venereal disease**

geschlossen **closed/shut**

Geschmack m **taste** ; **flavour**

geschmort **braised**

geschnittenes Brot nt **sliced bread**

Geschoss nt **storey**

geschützt **sheltered**

Geschwindigkeit f **speed**

geschwollen **swollen**

Geschwür nt **ulcer**

Gesellschaft f **company**

Gesetz nt **law**

gesetzlicher Feiertag m **public holiday**

Gesicht nt **face**

Gesichtswasser f **cleanser** (for face)

Gesichtspflege f **facial** (beauty treatment)

gesperrt **closed**

Gespräch nt **talk** ; **phone call**

Gestank m **smell** (unpleasant)

gestattet **permitted**

gestern **yesterday**

gestochen **stung** ; **bitten** (by insect)

gestreift **striped**

gesund **healthy**

Gesundheit f **health** ; **bless you!**

Getränk(e) nt **drink(s)**

Getränkekarte f **list of beverages**

getrennt **separated** (couple)
  getrennt bezahlen **to pay separately**

Getriebe nt **gearbox** ; **gears**

Gewehr nt **gun**

Gewicht nt **weight**

gewinnen **to win**

Gewitter nt **thunderstorm**

gewöhnlich **usual(ly)**

Gewürz nt **spice** ; **seasoning**

Gezeiten pl **tide**

gibt es...? **is/are there...?**

Gift nt **poison**

giftig **poisonous**

Gipfel m **summit** ; **mountain top**

Gips m **plaster** (for broken limb)

Gitarre f **guitar**

Glas nt **glass** ; **jar**

Glatteis nt **black ice**

Glatteisgefahr f **danger – black ice**

glatzköpfig **bald** (person)

glauben **to believe** ; **to think** (be of opinion)

gleich **same**

Gleise pl **platforms** ; **tracks**

Gletscher m glacier
Glocke f bell
Glück nt happiness ; luck
glücklich happy ; lucky
Glühbirne f light bulb
Gold nt gold
Golf nt golf
Golfplatz m golf course
Golfschläger m golf club
gotisch Gothic
Gott m God
Gottesdienst m church service
Grad m degree (of heat, cold)
Gramm nt gram(me)
Grapefruit f grapefruit
Gras nt grass
Gräte f fish bone
grau grey
Grenze f frontier ; border (of country)
Grenzpolizei f border police
Griff m handle ; knob
Grill m barbecue ; grill
grillen to grill
Grillstube f steak house ; grillroom
Grillteller m mixed grill
Grippe f flu
groß tall ; great ; big ; high (number, speed)
Großbritannien nt Great Britain
Großbuchstabe m capital letter
Größe f size (of clothes, shoes) ; height
Großeltern pl grandparents
Großmutter f grandmother
Großraumwagen m (in train) open plan carriage
Großvater m grandfather
großzügig generous
grün green ; fresh (fish)
Grünanlage f park
Grundstücksmakler m estate agent's
grüne Versicherungskarte f green card (car insurance)
grüner Salat m green salad
Gruppe f group
Gruß m greeting

Grußkarte f greetings card
Gulasch nt goulash
gültig valid
Gummi m rubber ; elastic
Gummiband nt rubber band
Gummihandschuhe pl rubber gloves
Gummistiefel pl wellington boots
günstig convenient
Gurke(n) f cucumber(s) ; gherkin(s)
Gürtel m belt
Gürtelrose f shingles
Gürteltasche f bumbag ; moneybelt
gut good ; well ; all right (yes)
    alles Gute all the best ; with best wishes
guten Abend good evening
guten Appetit enjoy your meal
guten Morgen good morning
gute Nacht good night
guten Tag hello ; good day/afternoon
Güter pl goods
Gutschein m voucher ; coupon

H

H-Milch f long-life milk
Haar nt hair
Haarbürste f hairbrush
Haare pl hair
Haargel nt hair gel
Haarklemme f hairgrip
Haarschnitt m haircut
Haarspray nt hair spray
haben to have
Hackfleisch nt mince meat
Hacksteak nt hamburger (usually without the bread)
Hafen m harbour ; port
Hafer m oats
Haftung f liability
Hagel m hail
Hahn m tap (for water) ; cockerel
Hähnchen nt chicken
halb half
    zum halben Preis half-price
halb durch medium rare (meat)

halber Fahrpreis m half fare
Halbfettmilch f semi-skimmed milk
Halbinsel f peninsula
Halbpension f half board
Hälfte f half
hallo hello
Hals m neck ; throat
Halskette f necklace
Halspastillen pl throat lozenges
Halsschmerzen pl sore throat
Halstuch nt scarf (round neck)
Halt m stop
Haltbarkeitsdatum nt sell-by date
Haltebucht f layby
halten to hold ; to stop
Halten verboten no stopping
Haltestelle f bus stop
Hammer m hammer
Hämorrhoiden pl haemorrhoids
Hand f hand
Handbremse f handbrake (car)
Handel m trade ; commerce
Handgelenk nt wrist
handgemacht handmade
Handgepäck nt hand-luggage
Handschuhe pl gloves
Handtasche f handbag
Handtuch nt towel
Handwerker(in) m/f craftsperson
Harke f rake
hart hard (not soft)
hart gekochtes Ei nt hard-boiled
  egg
Hase m hare
Haselnuss(-nüsse) f hazelnut(s)
hässlich ugly
häufig frequent ; common
Haupt- major ; main
Hauptbahnhof m main station
Hauptgericht nt main course
Hauptstadt f capital (city)
Hauptstraße f major road
Hauptverkehrszeit f peak hours
Haus nt house ; home
  zu Hause at home
Hausarbeit f housework

Hausfrau (Hausmann) f/m
  housewife/househusband
Haushaltswaren pl household goods
Hausschuhe pl slippers
Haustier nt pet
Hauswein m house wine
Haut f hide (leather) ; skin
Hecht m pike
Hefe f yeast
Heft nt exercise book
Hefter m stapler
Heftklammern pl staples
Heftpflaster nt sticking plaster
Heidelbeeren pl blueberries
heilig holy
Heiligabend m Christmas Eve
Heim nt home (institution) ; hostel
Heimweh haben to be homesick
heiraten to marry
heiß hot
  heiße Schokolade f hot chocolate
heißen to be called
  wie heißen Sie? what's your name?
Heißwassergerät nt water heater
Heizgerät nt heater
Heizkörper m radiator
Heizung f heating
helfen to help
Helikopter m helicopter
hell light (pale) ; bright
hellblau light blue
helles Bier nt lager
helles Fleisch nt white meat
Helm m helmet
Hemd(en) nt shirt(s)
Hepatitis f hepatitis
Herbst m autumn
Herd m cooker ; oven
herein in ; come in
hereinkommen to come in
Hering m herring ; tent peg
Herr m gentleman ; Mr
Herren gents (toilet)
heruntergehen to go down
Herz nt heart
Herzanfall m heart attack

herzliche Glückwünsche! congratulations!
Herzschrittmacher m pacemaker
Heuschnupfen m hay fever
heute today
heute Abend tonight
hier here
hiesig local (wine, speciality)
Hilfe f help
Himbeeren pl raspberries
Himmel m heaven ; sky
hin there
Hin- und Rückfahrt f round trip
hineingehen to go in
hinten behind
hinten einsteigen enter at rear
hinter behind
Hinweis m notice ; information
Hirnhautentzündung f meningitis
historisch historic
hoch high
Hochsaison f high season
Höchstgeschwindigkeit f maximum speed
Höchsttarif m peak rate
Hochzeit f wedding
Hochzeitsgeschenk nt wedding present
Hochzeitskleid nt wedding dress
Hochzeitstag m wedding anniversary
Hochzeitstorte f wedding cake
Hoden pl testicles
Hof m court
hoffen to hope
höflich polite
Höhe f altitude ; height
hoher Blutdruck m high blood pressure
höher higher
    höher stellen to turn up (heat, volume)
Höhle f cave
holen to fetch
holländisch Dutch
Holz nt wood (material)

Holzkohle f charcoal
Homepage f homepage
Homöopathie f homeopathy
homosexuell homosexual
Honig m honey
hören to hear
Hörer m receiver (phone)
Hörgerät nt hearing aid
Hörnchen nt croissant
Hose f trousers
Hotel nt hotel
Hotel garni nt bed and breakfast hotel
hübsch pretty
Hubschrauber m helicopter
Hüfte f hip
Hügel m hill
Huhn nt hen
Hühnchen nt chicken
Hummer m lobster
Hund m dog
Hundeleine f dog lead
hundert hundred
Hunger haben to be hungry
Hupe f horn (of car)
husten to cough
Husten m cough
Hustenbonbons pl cough sweets
Hustensaft m cough mixture
Hut m hat
Hütte f mountain hut

I

ich I
Idiotenhügel m nursery slope
ihm him
ihnen them
ihr(e) her ; their
Imbiss m snack
Imbissstube f snack bar
immer always
Immunisierung f immunisation
Impfung f vaccination
in in (place, position) ; inside ; into
    in Ordnung all right (agreed)
Infektion f infection

Informationsbüro nt **information office**

Ingenieur(in) m/f **engineer**

Inhalationsapparat m **inhaler** (medication)

Inhalt m **contents**

inklusive **inclusive**

Inland nt **domestic** (flight, etc)

Inlandsgespräch(e) nt **national call(s)**

innen **inside**

Innenkabine f (on ship/ferry) **inside cabin**

Innenstadt f **city centre**

innerlich **for internal use** (medicine)

Insekt nt **insect**

Insektenschutzmittel nt **insect repellent**

Insel f **island**

Insulin nt **insulin**

intelligent **intelligent**

interessant **interesting**

Internet nt **internet**

Internet-Café nt **internet café**

Internet-Seite f **website**

Internetadresse f **website address**

Ire (Irin) m/f **Irishman/woman**

irgend jemand **someone**

irgendwo **somewhere**

irisch adj **Irish**

Irland nt **Ireland**

Irrtum m **mistake**

Isomatte f **camping mat**

Italien nt **Italy**

Italiener(in) m/f **Italian**

italienisch adj **Italian**

J

ja **yes**

Jacht f **yacht**

Jachthafen m **marina**

Jacke f **jacket ; cardigan**

Jagderlaubnis f **hunting permit**

jagen **to hunt**

Jahr nt **year**

Jahrestag m **anniversary**

Jahreszeit f **season**

Jahrgang m **vintage**

Jahrhundert nt **century**

jährlich **annual ; yearly**

Jahrmarkt m (fun) **fair**

Januar m **January**

jeder **everyone**

Jeans pl **jeans**

jede(r/s) **each**

jemand **somebody ; someone**

jene **those**

jetzt **now**

Jod nt **iodine**

joggen **to jog**

Jogginganzug m **tracksuit**

Joghurt m **yoghurt**

Johannisbeere(n) f **currant(s)**

Journalist(in) m/f **journalist**

jucken **to itch**

Jude/Jüdin m/f **Jew**

Jugendherberge f **youth hostel**

Jugendliche(r) m/f **teenager**

Juli m **July**

jung **young**

Junge m **boy**

Junggeselle m **bachelor**

Juni m **June**

Juwelier m **jeweller's**

K

Kabel nt **cable ; lead** (electrical)

Kabelfernsehen nt **cable TV**

Kabine f **cabin ; berth** (train, ship)

Kaffee m **coffee**

Kaffeehaus nt **café**

Kaffeemaschine f **percolator**

Kai m **quayside**

Kakao m **cocoa**

Kakerlake f **cockroach**

Kalb nt **calf** (young cow)

Kalbfleisch nt **veal**

kalt **cold**

Kamera f **camera**

Kameratasche f **camera case**

Kamillentee m **camomile tea**

Kamin m **fireplace**
Kamm m **comb ; ridge**
kämpfen **to fight**
Kanada nt **Canada**
Kanadier(in) m/f **Canadian**
kanadisch adj **Canadian**
Kanal m **canal ;** (English) **Channel**
kandiert **glacé**
Kaninchen nt **rabbit**
Kanister m (petrol) **can**
Kanu nt **canoe**
Kapelle f **chapel ; orchestra**
kaputt **broken ; out of order**
kaputtmachen **to break** (object)
Kapuze f **hood** (of jacket)
Karaffe f **decanter ; carafe**
Karfreitag m **Good Friday**
Karotten pl **carrots**
Karte f **card ; ticket ; map ; menu**
Kartentelefon nt **cardphone**
Kartoffel(n) f **potato(es)**
Kartoffelpüree nt **mashed potato**
Kartoffelsalat m **potato salad**
Karton m **box** (cardboard) **; carton**
Käse m **cheese**
Kasino nt **casino**
Kasse f **cash desk**
Kasserolle f **casserole**
Kassette f **cassette ; cartridge ; tape**
Kassettenrecorder m **cassette player
; tape recorder**
Kassierer(in) m/f **cashier**
Kastanie f **chestnut**
Katalog m **catalogue**
Katalysator m **catalytic convertor**
(car)
Kater m **hangover**
katholisch **Catholic**
Katze f **cat**
kaufen **to buy**
Kaufhaus nt **department store**
Kaugummi m **chewing gum**
Kaution f **deposit**
Kehle f **throat**
Keilriemen m **fan belt**
kein... **no...**

keine(r/s) **no ; none**
Keks(e) m **biscuit(s)** (sweet)
Keller m **cellar**
Kellner(in) m/f **waiter/waitress**
kennen **to be acquainted with**
Keramik f **pottery**
Kern m **pip**
Kerze f **candle**
Kette f **chain**
Kfz-Versicherung f **car insurance**
Kiefer f **pine**
Kiefer m **jaw**
Kilo(gramm) nt **kilo(gram)**
Kilometer m **kilometre**
Kind(er) nt **child(ren)**
Kinderbett nt **cot**
Kindermädchen nt **nanny**
Kindersitz m **child seat** (car)
Kinderstuhl m **high chair**
Kinderteller m **child's helping**
Kinderwagen m **pram**
Kinn nt **chin**
Kino nt **cinema**
Kiosk m **kiosk**
Kirche f **church**
Kirmes f **funfair**
Kirsche(n) f **cherry (cherries)**
Kissen nt **cushion ; pillow**
Kiste f **box** (wooden)
Klage f **complaint**
klar **clear**
Klarer m **schnapps**
Klärgrube f **septic tank**
Klasse f **class ; grade**
Klavier nt **piano**
Klebeband f **adhesive tape**
kleben **to stick** (with glue)
Klebstoff m **glue**
Kleid nt **dress**
Kleider pl **clothes**
Kleiderbügel m **coat hanger**
Kleiderschrank m **wardrobe**
klein **little** (small) **; short**
Kleingeld nt **change** (money)
Klempner(in) m/f **plumber**
Klettband nt **Velcro®**

klettern **to climb** (mountains)
Klimaanlage f **air-conditioning**
klimatisiert **air-conditioned**
Klingel f **doorbell**
klingeln **to ring** (bell, phone)
Klinik f **clinic**
Klippe f **cliff** (along coast)
klopfen **to knock** (on door)
Kloß m **dumpling**
Kloster nt **monastery ; convent**
Kneipe f **pub**
Knie nt **knee**
Kniestrümpfe pl **pop socks**
Knoblauch m **garlic**
Knöchel m **ankle**
Knochen m **bone**
Knödel m **dumpling**
Knopf m **button ; knob** (radio, etc)
Knoten m **knot**
Koch m **chef**
kochen **to boil ; to cook**
Kocher m **cooker ; stove**
Köchin f **cook**
Kochschinken m **cooked ham**
Kochtopf m **saucepan**
Kode m **code**
Köder m **bait** (for fishing)
koffeinfreier Kaffee m **decaffeinated coffee**
Koffer m **suitcase ; trunk**
Kofferanhänger m **luggage tag**
Kofferraum m **carboot**
Kognak m **brandy**
Kohl m **cabbage**
Kohle f **coal**
Kohlrübe f **swede**
Koje f **berth** (in ship) ; **bunk**
Kollege (Kollegin) m/f **colleague**
Köln **Cologne**
Kölnischwasser nt **eau de cologne**
komisch **funny** (amusing)
kommen **to come**
Kommode f **chest of drawers**
Komödie f **comedy**
Kompass m **compass**
Komponist(in) m/f **composer**

Kondensmilch f **condensed milk**
Konditorei f **cake shop ; café**
Kondom nt **condom**
Konfektions- **ready-made** (clothes)
Konferenz f **conference**
Konfitüre f **jam**
König m **king**
Königin f **queen**
königlich **royal**
können **to be able to ; to know how to**
Konsulat nt **consulate**
Kontaktlinsen pl **contact lenses**
Kontaktlinsenreiniger m **contact lens cleaner**
Konto nt **bank account**
Kontrolle f **check ; control**
kontrollieren **to check** (passports, tickets)
Konzert nt **concert**
Konzertsaal m **concert hall**
Kopf m **head**
Kopfhörer pl **headphones**
Kopfkissen nt **pillow**
Kopfsalat m **lettuce**
Kopfschmerzen pl **headache**
Kopftuch nt **scarf** (headscarf)
Kopie f **copy** (duplicate)
kopieren **to copy**
Korb m **basket**
Korinthe f **currant**
Korken m **cork** (of bottle)
Korkenzieher m **corkscrew**
Körper m **body**
Körperpuder m **talc**
Kortison nt **cortisone**
Kosmetiksalon m **beauty salon**
Kosmetiktücher pl **paper tissues**
kosten **to cost**
Kosten pl **cost** (price)
kostenlos **free of charge**
köstlich **delicious**
Kostüm nt **suit** (woman's)
Krabbe f **crab**
Kräcker m **cracker**
Kraftstoff m **fuel**

Kragen m collar
Krämpfe pl cramps
krank ill ; sick
Krankenhaus nt hospital
Krankenkasse f medical insurance
Krankenwagen m ambulance
Krankheit f disease
Kräuter pl herbs
Kräutertee m herbal tea
Krawatte f tie
Krebs m crab (animal) ; cancer (illness)
Kreditkarte f credit card
Kreisverkehr m roundabout
Kreuz nt cross (also crucifix)
Kreuzfahrt f cruise
Kreuzschlitzschraubenzieher m
  Phillips screwdriver®
Kreuzung f junction ; crossroads
Kreuzworträtsel nt crossword
Krieg m war
Kristall nt crystal
Krone f crown
Krücken pl crutches
Krug m jug
Küche f kitchen ; cuisine
Kuchen m flan ; cake
Küchenbrett nt chopping board
Küchenpapier nt kitchen paper
Kugel f ball ; scoop (of ice cream)
Kugelschreiber m pen ; biro
Kuh f cow
kühl cool
Kühlbox f cool-box (for picnic)
kühlen to chill (wine, food)
Kühler m radiator (of car)
Kühlschrank m fridge
Kümmel m caraway seed ; cumin ;
  schnapps
Kunde (Kundin) m/f client ; customer
Kunst f art
Kunstfaser f man-made fibre
Kunstgewerbearbeiten pl crafts
Kunsthalle f art gallery
Künstler(in) m/f artist
künstlich artificial ; man-made
künstliche Hüfte f hip replacement

Kupfer nt copper
Kupplung f clutch (of car)
Kurierdienst m courier service
Kurort m spa
Kurs m course ; exchange rate
Kurve f curve ; corner ; bend
kurz short ; brief
Kurz(zeit)parkplatz m short-stay car
  park
kurzsichtig short-sighted
Kurzwarengeschäft nt haberdasher's
Kuss m kiss
küssen to kiss
Küste f coast ; seaside
Küstenwache f coastguard

L

lächeln to smile
Lächeln nt smile
lachen to laugh
Lachs m salmon
Lack m varnish
Laden m shop ; store
Lagerhalle f warehouse
Lakritze f liquorice
Lamm nt lamb
Lampe f lamp
Land nt country (Italy, France, etc) ;
  land
landen to land
Landkarte f map (of country)
Landschaft f countryside
Landung f landing (of plane)
Landwein m table wine
lang long
Länge f length
Langlauf m cross-country skiing
langsam slow(ly)
langsamer werden to slow down
langweilig boring
Langzeitparkplatz m long-stay car
  park
Lappen m cloth (rag)
Laptop m laptop
Lärm m noise
lassen to let (allow)

163

Last f **load**
Laster m **truck**
Lastwagen m **truck ; lorry**
Lätzchen nt **bib** (baby's)
Lauch m **leek**
laufen **to run**
Laugenbrezel f **soft pretzel**
laut **noisy ; loud(ly) ; aloud**
läuten **to ring** (doorbell)
Lautsprecher m **loudspeaker**
Lautstärke f **volume** (of sound)
Lawine f **avalanche**
Lawinengefahr f **danger of avalanches**
leben **to live** (exist)
Lebensgefahr f **danger to life**
Lebensmittel pl **groceries**
Lebensmittelvergiftung f **food poisoning**
Lebensversicherung f **life insurance**
Leber f **liver**
Lebkuchen m **gingerbread**
Leck nt **leak** (of gas, liquid)
Lederwaren pl **leather goods**
ledig **single** (not married)
leer **empty ; flat** (battery) ; **blank**
Leerlauf m **neutral** (gear)
legen **to lay**
Lehrer(in) m/f **teacher** (school) ; **instructor**
leicht **light** (not heavy) ; **easy**
Leid nt **grief**
  es tut mir Leid **(I'm) sorry**
leider **unfortunately**
leihen **to rent** (car) ; **to lend**
Leihgebühr f **rental**
Leinen nt **linen** (cloth)
leise **quietly ; soft ; faint**
  leiser stellen **to turn down** (volume)
Leiter f **ladder**
Leitung f **telephone line**
Lenker m **handlebars**
Lenkrad nt **steering wheel**
lernen **to learn**
lesbisch **lesbian**
lesen **to read**

letzte(r/s) **last ; final**
Leuchtturm m **lighthouse**
Leute pl **people**
Licht nt **light**
  das Licht anschalten **to switch on lights**
Lichtmaschine f **alternator**
Lichtschalter m **light switch**
Lidschatten m **eye shadow**
liebe(r) **dear** (in letter)
Liebe f **love**
lieben **to love**
liebenswürdig **kind**
lieber **rather**
Lieblings- **favourite**
Lied nt **song**
Lieferwagen m **van**
Liegestuhl m **deckchair**
Liegewagen m **couchette**
Lift m **elevator ; lift**
Liftpass m **lift pass** (on ski slopes)
Likör m **liqueur**
Limonade f **lemonade**
Limone f **lime** (fruit)
Lineal nt **ruler**
Linie f **line** (row, of railway)
Linienflug m **scheduled flight**
linke(r/s) **left(-hand)**
links **to the left ; on the left**
Linkshänder(in) m/f **left-handed person**
Linse f **lens**
Linsen pl **lentils**
Lippen pl **lips**
Lippenpflegestift m **lip salve**
Lippenstift m **lipstick**
Liste f **list**
Liter m **litre**
Loch nt **hole**
lochen **to punch** (ticket, etc)
locker **loose** (screw, tooth)
Löffel m **spoon**
Loge f **box** (in theatre)
Lohn m **wage**
Loipe f **cross-country ski run**
Lokal nt **pub**

Lorbeerblatt *nt* **bayleaf**
los **loose**
  was ist los? **what's wrong?**
Los *m* **lot** *(at auction)* ; **ticket** *(lottery)*
lösen **to buy** *(ticket)*
löslich **soluble**
Lounge *f* **lounge**
Löwe *m* **lion**
Luft *f* **air**
Luftfilter *m* **air filter**
Luftfracht *f* **air freight**
Luftkissenboot *nt* **hovercraft**
Luftmatratze *f* **air bed/mattress**
Luftpost *f* **air mail**
Luftpumpe *f* **pump** *(bike/airmattress)*
Lüge *f* **lie** *(untruth)*
Lunge *f* **lung**
Lupe *f* **magnifying glass**
Lutscher *m* **lollipop**
Luxus *m* **luxury**

M

machen **to make** ; **to do**
Mädchen *nt* **girl**
Mädchenname *m* **maiden name**
Made *f* **maggot**
Magen *m* **stomach**
Magenschmerzen *pl* **stomachache**
Magentabletten *pl* **indigestion tablets**
Magenverstimmung *f* **indigestion**
Magermilch *f* **skimmed milk**
Magnet *m* **magnet**
Mai *m* **May**
Mais *m* **sweetcorn**
Make-up *nt* **make-up**
malen **to paint**
Malzbier *nt* **malt beer**
man **one**
managen **to manage** *(be in charge)*
manchmal **sometimes**
Mandarine *f* **tangerine**
Mandel *f* **almond ; tonsil**
Mandelentzündung *f* **tonsillitis**
Mangel *m* **flaw**
Mann *m* **man ; husband**

Männer *pl* **men**
männlich **masculine ; male**
Manschettenknöpfe *pl* **cufflinks**
Mantel *m* **coat**
Margarine *f* **margarine**
marineblau **navy blue**
mariniert **marinated**
Marke *f* **brand** *(of product)* ; **token** *(for phone)*
Markt *m* **market**
Marktplatz *m* **market place**
Marmelade *f* **jam**
Marmor *m* **marble**
März *m* **March**
Maschine *f* **machine**
Maschine schreiben **to type**
Masern *pl* **measles**
Maßband *nt* **tape measure**
Maße *pl* **measurements**
Mast *m* **mast**
Material *nt* **material**
Matratze *f* **mattress**
Mauer *f* **wall**
Maus *f* **mouse** *(animal/computer)*
Maut *f* **toll** *(motorway)*
Mayonnaise *f* **mayonnaise**
Mechaniker(in) *m/f* **mechanic**
Medikament *nt* **drug ; medicine**
Medizin *f* **medicine**
Meer *nt* **sea**
Meeresfrüchte *pl* **seafood**
Mehl *nt* **flour**
mehr **more**
Mehrwertsteuer (MWST) *f* **value-added tax (VAT)**
meiden **to avoid** *(person)*
Meile *f* **mile**
mein **my**
meiste(n) **most**
Meisterwerk *nt* **masterpiece**
melden **to report** *(tell about)*
Melone *f* **melon ; bowler hat**
Menge *f* **crowd**
Messe *f* **fair** *(commercial)* ; **mass** *(church)*
Messegelände *nt* **exhibition centre**

messen to measure
Messer nt knife
Messing nt brass
Metall nt metal
Meter m metre
Metro f metro (underground)
Metzgerei f butcher's
mich me (direct object)
Mietauto nt hire car
Miete f rent
mieten to hire ; to rent (house, etc)
Mietgebühr f rental charge
Mietvertrag m lease (rental)
Migräne f migraine
Mikrowelle f microwave oven
Milch f milk
Milchprodukte pl dairy produce
Milchpulver nt powdered milk
Millimeter m millimetre
Million f million
minderwertig low-quality
Mindest- minimum
Mineralwasser nt mineral water
Minimum nt minimum
Minister(in) m/f minister (politics)
Minute(n) f minute(s)
Minze f mint (herb)
mir me (indirect object)
mischen to mix
Missverständnis nt
    misunderstanding
mit with
Mitfahrgelegenheit f lift (in car)
Mitglied nt member (of club, etc)
mitnehmen to give a lift to
    zum Mitnehmen take-away (food)
Mittag m midday
Mittagessen nt lunch
Mitte f middle
Mitteilung f message
Mittel nt means
    ein Mittel gegen a remedy for
mittelalterlich medieval
Mittelmeer- Mediterranean
Mitternacht f midnight
Mittwoch m Wednesday

Mixer m blender ; mixer
Möbel pl furniture
Möbelpolitur f furniture polish
Mobiltelefon nt mobile phone
möbliert furnished
Modem nt modem
modern fashionable ; modern
mögen to enjoy (to like)
möglich possible
Mohn m poppy
Möhre(n) f carrot(s)
Mole f jetty
Monat m month
monatlich monthly
Mond m moon
Montag m Monday
Moped nt moped
Morgen m morning ; tomorrow
morgen tomorrow
Morgendämmerung f dawn
Morgenmantel m dressing gown
Moschee f mosque
Moskitonetz nt mosquito net
Motor m motor ; engine
Motorboot nt motor boat
Motorhaube f bonnet (car)
Motorrad nt motorbike
Motte f moth (clothes)
Mountainbike nt mountain bike
Mücke f midge
müde tired
Müll m rubbish
Müllbeutel m bin liner
Mülleimer m bin (dustbin)
Mülltrennung f waste separation
    (for recycling)
Mumps m mumps
München Munich
Mund m mouth
Mundwasser nt mouthwash
Münster nt cathedral
Münze(n) f coin(s)
Münzfernsprecher m payphone
Münztelefon nt payphone (with coins)
Muscheln pl mussels
Museum nt museum

Musik f music
Muskat m nutmeg
Muskel m muscle
müssen to have to ; to must
mutig brave
Mutter f mother
Mütze f cap *(hat)*
MWST f VAT

N

nach after ; according to ; to *(with names of places)*
Nachbar(in) m/f neighbour
Nachmittag m afternoon
nachmittags pm ; in the afternoon
Nachname m surname
Nachricht f note *(letter)* ; message
Nachrichten pl news
Nachspeise f dessert ; pudding
nächste(r/s) next
Nacht f night
  über Nacht overnight
Nachtdienst m night duty *(chemist)*
Nachthemd nt nightdress
Nachtisch m dessert
Nachtklub m night club
nachzahlen to pay extra
nackt nude ; naked ; bare
Nadel f needle
Nagel m nail *(metal)*
Nagelbürste f nailbrush
Nagelfeile f nail file
Nagellack m nail polish/varnish
Nagellackentferner m nail polish remover
Nagelschere f nail scissors
Nähe f proximity
  in der Nähe nearby
nähen to sew
Name m name ; surname
Narkose f anaesthetic
Nase f nose
nass wet
national national
Nationalität f nationality
Natur- natural

Naturlehrpfad m nature trail
Naturschutzgebiet nt nature reserve
Nebel m mist ; fog
neben by *(next to)* ; beside
Nebenstraße f minor road
Nebensaison f low season
neblig foggy
Neffe m nephew
Negativ nt negative *(photo)*
nehmen to catch *(bus, train)* ; to take *(remove)*
nein no
Nektarine f nectarine
Nelke f carnation
nennen to quote *(price)*
Nervenzusammenbruch m nervous breakdown
Nest nt nest
nett nice *(person)* ; kind
Netto- net *(income, price)*
Netz nt net ; network
neu new
neueste(r/s) newest ; latest
Neujahr(stag) m New Year's Day
Neuseeland nt New Zealand
nicht not ; non-
Nichte f niece
Nichtraucher m non-smoker
nichts nothing
nie never
Niederlande pl Netherlands
Niedersachsen nt Lower Saxony
niedrig low
Niedrigwasser nt low tide
niemand no one ; nobody
Niere(n) f kidney(s)
niesen to sneeze
nirgends nowhere
noch still *(up to this time)* ; yet
noch ein(e) extra *(more)* ; another
Norden m north
Nordirland nt Northern Ireland
nördlich north ; northern
Nordsee f North Sea
Normal(benzin) nt regular *(petrol)*
Normal- standard *(size)*

Notarzt *m* emergency doctor
Notaufnahme *f* accident & emergency
Notausgang *m* emergency exit
Notdienstapotheke *f* on-duty chemist
Notfall *m* emergency
nötig necessary
Notizblock *m* note pad
Notruf *m* emergency number
Notrufsäule *f* emergency phone *(on motorway)*
Notsignal *nt* distress signal
notwendig essential ; necessary
November *m* November
nüchtern sober
Nudeln *pl* pasta ; noodles
Null *f* nil ; zero ; nought
numerieren to number
Nummer *f* number ; act
Nummernschild *nt* numberplate
nur only
Nürnberg Nuremberg
Nuss (Nüsse) *f* nut(s)
nützlich useful

O

oben upstairs ; above ; this side up
oben auf on top of...
Oberschenkel *m* thigh
obligatorisch compulsory
Obst *nt* fruit
Obstkuchen *m* fruit tart
oder or
offen open
  offene Weine pl wine served by the glass
öffentlich public
öffnen to open ; to undo
Öffnungszeiten *pl* business hours
oft often
ohne without
ohnmächtig fainted
ohnmächtig werden to faint
Ohr(en) *nt* ear(s)
Ohrenschmerzen *pl* earache

Ohrringe *pl* earrings
okay OK
ökonomisch economic
Oktober *m* October
Öl *nt* oil
Ölfilter *m* oil filter
Olive *f* olive
Olivenöl *nt* olive oil
Ölstandsanzeiger *m* oil gauge
Ölwechsel *m* oil change
Omelett *nt* omelette
Onkel *m* uncle
Oper *f* opera
Operation *f* operation *(surgical)*
Optiker *m* optician's
orange orange *(colour)*
Orange *f* orange *(fruit)*
Orangensaft *m* orange juice
Orchester *nt* orchestra
Ordner *m* file *(for papers)*
Oregano *m* oregano
organisch organic
organisieren to organize
Organspenderausweis *m* donor card
Ort *m* place
  an Ort und Stelle on the spot
örtlich local
örtliche Betäubung *f* local anaesthetic
Ortschaft *f* village ; town
Ortsgespräch *nt* local call
Ortszeit *f* local time
Osten *m* east
Osterei *nt* Easter egg
Ostermontag *m* Easter Monday
Ostern *nt* Easter
Österreich *nt* Austria
Österreicher(in) *m/f* Austrian
österreichisch *adj* Austrian
Ostersonntag *m* Easter Sunday
östlich eastern
Ozean *m* ocean

P

Paar *nt* pair ; couple
  ein paar a couple of

packen to pack *(luggage)*
Paket nt parcel ; packet
Palast m palace
Pampelmuse(n) f grapefruit(s)
Panne f breakdown *(of car)*
Papier(e) nt paper(s)
Papiertaschentücher pl tissues
Pappe f cardboard
Paprikaschote f pepper *(vegetable)*
Parfüm nt perfume
Parfümerie f perfumery
Park m park
parken to park
  Parken verboten no parking
Parkett nt stalls *(in theatre)*
Parkhaus nt multi-storey car park
Parkkralle f wheel clamp
Parkplatz m car park
Parkscheibe f parking disk
Parkschein m parking ticket
  (to display)
Parkuhr f parking meter
Parkverbot nt no parking zone
Partei f political party
Partner(in) m/f partner *(boy/girlfriend)*
Party f party *(celebration)*
Pass m passport ; pass *(in mountains)*
  Pass geschlossen pass closed
Passagier m passenger
passen to fit
passieren to happen
Passkontrolle f passport control
Passnummer f passport number
Passwort nt password
 Patient(in) m/f patient *(in hospital)*
Pauschalreise f package tour
Pauschaltarif m flat-rate tariff
Pause f pause ; interval
  keine Pausen no intervals
Pelz m fur
Pelzmantel m fur coat
Pendelverkehr m shuttle *(service)*
Penis m penis
Penizillin nt penicillin
Pension f boarding house
pensioniert retired

per via ; by
  per Express by express mail
  per Post by post
perfekt perfect
Periode f period *(menstruation)*
Perlen pl pearls
perlend sparkling
Person f person
Personal nt staff
Personalausweis m identity card
Personalien pl particulars
persönlich personal(ly)
Perücke f wig
Pessar nt cap *(diaphragm)*
Petersilie f parsley
Pfalz f Palatinate
Pfannkuchen m pancake
Pfarrer(in) m/f church minister
Pfeffer m pepper *(spice)*
Pfefferkuchen m gingerbread
Pfefferminzbonbon nt mint *(sweet)*
Pfefferminztee m mint tea
Pfeife f pipe *(smoker's)*
Pferd nt horse
Pferderennen nt horse-racing
Pfirsich(e) m peach(es)
Pflanze f plant *(green)*
Pflaster nt plaster *(for cut)*
Pflaume(n) f plum(s)
Pforte f gate
Pfund nt pound
Pfund Sterling nt sterling *(pound)*
Picknick nt picnic
Picknickdecke f picnic rug
Pier m jetty ; pier
pikant savoury
Pille f pill
Pilot(in) m/f pilot
Pils/Pilsner nt lager
Pilz(e) m mushroom(s)
Pilzkrankheit f thrush *(candida)*
Pinzette f tweezers
Pistazie f pistachio
Piste f runway ; ski run
Pizza f pizza
planmäßig scheduled

Planschbecken nt **paddling pool**
Plastik- **plastic** *(made of)*
Plastikbeutel m **plastic bag**
Platte f **plate ; dish ; record**
Platz m **seat ; space ; square** *(in town)*
 ; court
Plätzchen nt **biscuit(s)**
Platzkarte f **seat reservation** *(ticket)*
Plombe f **filling** *(in tooth)*
plötzlich **suddenly**
pochiert **poached** *(egg, fish)*
Polen nt **Poland**
Polizei f **police**
Polizeirevier nt **police station**
Polizeiwache f **police station**
Polizist(in) m/f **policeman/woman**
Pommes frites pl **chips** *(french fries)*
Pony nt **pony**
Ponyreiten nt **pony trekking**
Porree m **leek**
Portier m **porter** *(for door)*
Portion f **portion**
Portrait nt **portrait**
Portugal nt **Portugal**
Portugiese/Portugiesin m/f
 Portuguese
portugiesisch adj **Portuguese**
Post f **post ; post office**
Post- **postal**
Postamt nt **post office**
Postanweisung f **money order**
Poster nt **poster**
Postkarte f **postcard**
postlagernd **poste restante**
Postleitzahl f **postcode**
praktisch **handy ; practical**
Pralinen pl **chocolates**
Präservativ nt **condom**
Praxis f **doctor's surgery**
Preis m **prize ; price**
Preisliste f **price list**
Priester m **priest**
Prinz m **prince**
Prinzessin f **princess**
privat **private**
Privatstrand m **private beach**

Privatweg m **private road**
pro **per**
 pro Stunde **per hour**
 pro Kopf **per person**
 pro Jahr **per annum**
probieren **to taste ; to sample**
Problem nt **problem**
Programm nt **programme**
Programmierer(in) m/f **computer
 programmer**
prost! **cheers!**
protestantisch **Protestant**
provisorisch **temporary**
Prozent nt **per cent**
prüfen **to check** *(oil, water, etc)*
Prüfung f **exam** *(school, university)*
Publikum nt **audience**
Puderzucker m **icing sugar**
Pullover m **sweater ; jumper**
Pulver nt **powder**
pulverförmig **in powder form**
Pulverkaffee m **instant coffee**
pünktlich **on schedule ; punctual**
Puppe f **doll ; puppet**
Puppenspiel nt **puppet show**
pur **straight** *(drink)*
Pute f **turkey**
Pyjama m **pyjamas**

Q

Qualität f **quality**
Qualitätswein m **good quality wine**
Qualle f **jellyfish**
Quantität f **quantity**
Quarantäne f **quarantine**
Quelle f **spring** *(of water)* **; source**
quetschen **to squeeze**
Quetschung f **bruise**
Quittung f **receipt**
Quiz nt **quiz show**

R

Rabatt m **discount**
Rad nt **wheel ; bicycle**
Rad fahren **to cycle**
Radfahrer(in) m/f **cyclist**

Radiergummi m **rubber** *(eraser)*
Radieschen pl **radishes**
Radio nt **radio**
Radweg m **cycle track**
Rahmen m **frame** *(picture)*
Rand m **verge** ; **border** ; **edge**
Randstein m **kerb**
Rang m **circle** *(in theatre)* ; **rank**
Rasen m **lawn**
Rasierapparat m **shaver** ; **razor**
Rasiercreme f **shaving cream**
rasieren **to shave**
Rasierklinge f **razor blade**
Rasierschaum m **shaving foam**
Rasierwasser nt **aftershave lotion**
Rasthof m **service area** ; **travel inn**
Rastplatz m **picnic area**
Raststätte f **service area**
raten **to advise**
Rathaus nt **town hall**
rau **rough**
Rauch m **smoke**
rauchen **to smoke**
 Rauchen verboten **no smoking**
Raucher(in) m/f **smoker**
Raum m **space** *(room)*
rechnen **to calculate**
Rechnung f **bill** *(account)* ; **invoice**
rechte(r/s) **right** *(not left)*
rechts **to the right** ; **on the right**
Rechtsanwalt m **lawyer** ; **solicitor**
Rechtsanwältin f **lawyer** ; **solicitor**
reden **to speak**
reduzieren **to reduce**
Reformhaus nt **health food shop**
Regal nt **shelf**
Regen m **rain**
Regenmantel m **raincoat**
Regenschirm m **umbrella**
regnen **to rain**
Reibe f **grater**
reich **rich** *(person)*
Reich nt **empire**
reichhaltig **rich** *(food)*
reif **ripe** ; **mature** *(cheese)*
Reifen m **tyre**

Reifendruck m **tyre pressure**
Reifenpanne f **flat tyre**
Reihe f **row** *(line)* ; **tier**
rein **pure**
reinigen **to clean**
Reinigung f **dry-cleaner's**
Reis m **rice**
Reise f **trip** *(journey)*
 gute Reise! **have a good trip!**
Reisebüro nt **travel agency**
Reiseführer m **guidebook**
Reiseführer(in) m/f **tour guide**
Reisegruppe f **party** *(of tourists)*
Reisekrankheit f **travel sickness**
reisen **to travel**
Reisepapiere pl **travel documents**
Reisepass m **passport**
Reisescheck m **traveller's cheque**
Reiseveranstalter m **tour operator**
Reiseziel nt **destination**
Reißverschluss m **zip**
reiten **to ride** *(horse)*
Reiten nt **riding**
Rennbahn f **racecourse**
rennen **to run**
Rennen nt **race** *(sport)*
Rentner(in) m/f **pensioner** ; **senior citizen**
Reparatur f **repair**
Reparaturwerkstatt f **car repairs**
reparieren **to repair** ; **to mend**
reservieren **to book** ; **to reserve**
reserviert **reserved**
Reservierung f **booking** *(in hotel)*
Reservierungen pl **reservations**
Restaurant nt **restaurant**
Restgeld nt **change** *(money)*
retten **to rescue** ; **to save** *(person)*
Rettungsboot nt **lifeboat**
Rettungsinsel f **life raft**
Rettungsring m **lifebelt**
Rettungsschwimmer(in) m/f **lifeguard**
Rezept nt **prescription** ; **recipe**
Rezeption f **reception** *(front desk)*
R-Gespräch nt **reverse charge call**
Rhein m **Rhine**

Rheinfahrten pl **Rhine cruises**
Rheumatismus m **rheumatism**
Richter(in) m/f **judge**
richtig **correct ; right ; proper**
Richtung f **direction**
riechen **to smell**
Rinderbraten m **roast beef**
Rindfleisch nt **beef**
Ring m **ring**
Ringstraße f **ring road**
Riss m **tear** (in material)
Rock m **skirt**
Roggenbrot nt **rye bread**
roh **raw**
Rohr nt **pipe** (drain, etc)
Rollo nt **blind** (for window)
Rollschuhe pl **roller skates**
Rollstuhl m **wheelchair**
Rolltreppe f **escalator**
Roman m **novel**
romanisch **Romanesque**
Röntgenaufnahme f **X-ray**
rosa **pink**
Rose f **rose** (flower)
Rosenkohl m **Brussels sprouts**
Rosenmontag m **carnival** (Monday
  before Shrove Tuesday)
Roséwein m **rosé wine**
Rosine(n) f **raisin(s)**
Rost m **rust ; grill**
Rost- **roast**
Rostbraten m **roast**
rosten **to rust**
rostfreier Stahl m **stainless steel**
rostig **rusty**
Röstkartoffeln pl **sautéed potatoes**
rot **red**
Rote Bete f **beetroot**
Röteln pl **German measles ; rubella**
rote Johannisbeeren pl **redcurrants**
Rotwein m **red wine**
Rücken m **back**
Rückerstattung f **refund**
Rückfahrkarte f **return ticket**
Rückfahrt f **return journey**
Rückflugticket nt **return airticket**

Rückgrat nt **spine**
Rücklicht nt **rear light**
Rucksack m **rucksack**
Rückspiegel m **rearview mirror**
rückwärts **backwards**
rückwärts fahren **to reverse** (car)
Rückwärtsgang m **reverse gear**
Ruder nt **rudder ; oar**
Ruderboot nt **rowing boat**
rudern **to row** (boat)
rufen **to shout**
Rufnummer f **telephone number**
Ruhe f **rest** (repose) ; **peace** (calm)
  Ruhe! **be quiet!**
ruhen **to rest**
ruhig **calm ; quiet(ly) ; peaceful**
Rührei nt **scrambled egg**
Ruine f **ruin** (castle, etc)
rund **round**
Rundfahrt f **tour ; round trip**
Rundreise f **round trip**
Rundwanderweg m **circular trail**
  for ramblers
Rutschbahn f **slide** (chute)
rutschen **to slip**
rutschig **slippery**

S

Saal m **hall (room)**
Sache f **thing**
Sachen pl **stuff** (things) ; **belongings**
Sachsen nt **Saxony**
Sackgasse f **cul-de-sac**
Safe m **safe** (for valuables)
Saft m **juice**
sagen **to say ; to tell** (fact, news)
Sahne f **cream** (dairy)
  mit Sahne **with whipped cream**
Saison f **season**
Salat m **salad**
Salatsoße f **salad dressing**
Salbe f **ointment**
Salz nt **salt**
Salzkartoffeln pl **boiled potatoes**
Salzwasser nt **salt water**
Samstag m **Saturday**

Sand m sand
Sandalen pl sandals
Sandstrand m sandy beach
Satellitenfernsehen nt satellite TV
satt full
Sattel m saddle
Satteltaschen pl panniers (for bike)
Satz m set (collection) ; sentence
sauber clean
säubern to clean
sauer sour
Sauerkraut nt sauerkraut
Sauerstoff m oxygen
Sauger m teat (on bottle)
Säule f petrol pump
Saum m hem
Sauna f sauna
Säure f acid
saure Sahne f soured cream
S-Bahn f suburban railway
Schach nt chess
Schaden m damage
schädlich harmful
Schaf nt sheep
Schaffner(in) m/f conductor (bus,
  train) ; guard
Schale f shell (egg, nut) ; dish
schälen to peel (fruit)
Schallplatte f record (music)
Schalter m switch
Schaltgetriebe nt manual (gear
  change)
Schaltknüppel m gear lever ;
  gearshift
Schaltuhr f timer
scharf hot (spicy) ; sharp
Schatten m shade
schätzen to value ; to estimate
Schauer m rain shower
Schaufel und Handfeger dustpan
  and brush
Schaufenster nt shop window
Schaukel f swing (for children)
Schaum m foam
Schaumbad nt bubble bath
Schaumfestiger m hair mousse

Schaumwein m sparkling wine
Schauspiel nt play
Schauspieler(in) m/f actor/actress
Scheck m cheque
Scheckbuch nt cheque book
Scheckkarte f cheque card
Scheibe f slice
Scheibenputzmittel nt screenwash
Scheibenwischer pl windscreen
  wipers
Schein(e) m banknote(s) ;
  certificate(s)
scheinen to shine (sun, etc) ; to seem
Scheinwerfer m headlight ;
  floodlight ; spotlight
  Scheinwerfer anschalten switch
  on headlights
Schere f scissors (pair of)
scherzen to joke
Scheuerlappen m floorcloth
Scheune f barn
Schi- see Ski-
schicken to send
schießen to shoot
Schiff nt ship
Schild nt sign ; label
Schinken m ham
Schirm m umbrella ; screen
Schlachterei f butcher's
schlafen to sleep
Schlafsack m sleeping bag
Schlaftablette f sleeping pill
Schlafwagen m sleeping car (on train)
Schlafzimmer nt bedroom
Schlag m shock (electric)
Schlaganfall m stroke (medical)
schlagen to hit
Schläger m racket (tennis, etc)
Schlagloch nt pothole
Schlagsahne f whipped cream
Schlange f queue ; snake
Schlangenbiss m snake bite
Schlauch m hosepipe ; inner tube
Schlauchboot nt dinghy (rubber)
schlecht bad ; badly
Schlepplift m ski tow

schließen to shut ; to close
Schließfach nt locker
schlimm serious
Schlitten m sleigh ; sledge
Schlittschuh laufen to ice skate
Schlittschuh(e) m ice skate(s)
Schlittschuhbahn f ice rink
Schloss nt castle ; lock (on door, etc)
Schluss m end
Schlüssel m key
Schlüsselbein nt collar bone
Schlüsselkarte f cardkey (for hotel)
Schlüsselring m keyring
Schlusslichter pl rear lights
Schlussverkauf m sale
schmecken to taste
schmelzen to melt
Schmerz m pain ; ache
schmerzhaft painful
Schmerzmittel nt painkiller
Schmerztablette f painkiller
Schmuck m jewellery ; decorations
schmutzig dirty
Schnaps m schnapps ; spirit
schnarchen to snore
Schnee m snow
Schneebrille f snow goggles
Schneeketten pl snow chains
Schneepflug m snowplough
schneiden to cut
schnell fast ; quick
Schnellboot nt speedboat
Schnellimbiss m snack bar
Schnellzug m express train
Schnittbohnen pl green beans
Schnittlauch m chives
Schnittwunde f cut
Schnorchel m snorkel
Schnuller m dummy (for baby)
Schnur f string
Schnurrbart m moustache
Schnürschuhe pl boots (ankle)
Schnürsenkel pl shoelaces
Schokolade f chocolate
schön lovely ; fine ; beautiful ; good
  (pleasant)

Schornstein m chimney
Schotte (Schottin) m/f Scot
schottisch Scottish
Schottland nt Scotland
Schrank m cupboard
Schraube f screw
Schraubenmutter f nut (for bolt)
Schraubenschlüssel m spanner
Schraubenzieher m screwdriver
schrecklich awful
schreiben to write
Schreibmaschine f typewriter
Schreibtisch m desk
Schreibwarenhandlung f stationer's
schriftlich in writing
Schritt m pace ; step
  Schritt fahren! dead slow
Schublade f drawer
Schuh(e) m shoe(s)
Schuhcreme f shoe polish
Schuhgeschäft nt shoe shop
Schuhputzmittel nt shoe polish
schulden to owe
Schulden pl debts
Schule f school
Schulter f shoulder
Schuppen pl scales (of fish) ; dandruff
Schürze f apron
Schüssel f bowl (for soup, etc)
Schuster m shoe mender's
Schutzhelm m helmet (for bike)
Schutzimpfung f vaccination
schwach weak
Schwager m brother-in-law
Schwägerin f sister-in-law
Schwamm m sponge
schwanger pregnant
schwarz black
Schwarzbrot nt brown bread
schwarze Johannisbeeren pl black-
currants
Schwarzweißfilm m black and white
  film
Schwein nt pig
Schweinefleisch nt pork
Schweiß m sweat

Schweiz f Switzerland
Schweizer(in) m/f Swiss
schweizerisch adj Swiss
Schwellung f swelling
schwer heavy
Schwester f sister ; nurse ; nun
Schwiegermutter f mother-in-law
Schwiegersohn m son-in-law
Schwiegertochter f daughter-in-law
Schwiegervater m father-in-law
schwierig hard (difficult)
Schwimmbad nt swimming pool
schwimmen to swim
Schwimmflossen pl flippers
Schwimmweste f life jacket
schwindelig dizzy
schwitzen to sweat
See f sea
See m lake
seekrank seasick
Segel nt sail
Segelboot nt sailing boat
segeln to sail
sehen to see
Sehenswürdigkeit f sight
Sehne f tendon
sehr very
seicht shallow (water)
Seide f silk
Seife f soap
Seil nt rope
Seilbahn f cable railway ; funicular
sein(e) his
sein to be
seit since
Seite f page ; side
Seitenspiegel m wing mirror
Seitenstraße f side street
Seitenstreifen m hard shoulder
Sekretär(in) m/f secretary
Sekt m sparkling wine
Sekunde f second (time)
Selbstbedienung f self-service
Sellerie m celery
selten rare (unique)
seltsam strange (odd)

Senf m mustard
September m September
servieren to serve (food)
Serviette f napkin
Servolenkung f power steering
Sessel m armchair
Sessellift m chairlift
setzen to place ; to put
    sich setzen to sit down
    setzen Sie sich bitte please take
    a seat
Sex m sex (intercourse)
Shampoo nt shampoo
Shorts pl shorts
sicher sure ; safe ; definite
Sicherheit f safety
Sicherheitsgurt m seatbelt ; safety
    belt
Sicherheitsnadel f safety pin
Sicherung f fuse
Sicherungskasten m fuse box
sie she ; they
Sie you (polite singular and plural)
Sieb nt sieve ; colander
Silber nt silver
Silvester m New Year's Eve
singen to sing
Sitz m seat
sitzen to sit
Ski(er) m ski(s)
    Ski fahren to ski
Skianzug m ski suit
Skihose f ski pants
Skijacke f ski jacket
Skilanglauf m cross-country skiing
Skilaufen nt skiing
Skilehrer(in) m/f ski instructor
Skilift m ski lift
Skipass m ski pass
Skipiste f ski run
Skistiefel pl ski boots
Skistock m ski stick/pole
Skiverleih m ski hire
Slip m knickers ; underpants
Slipeinlage f panty liner
SMS f text message

175

Snack *m* snack
Snowboard *nt* snow board
Socken *pl* socks
Soda *nt* soda water
Sodbrennen *nt* heartburn
Sofa *nt* sofa
Sofabett *nt* sofa bed
sofort at once ; immediately
Software *f* computer software
Sohle *f* sole (of shoe)
Sohn *m* son
Sojabohnen *pl* soya beans
Sojamilch *f* soya milk
Sommer *m* summer
Sommerfahrplan *m* summer railway timetable
Sommerferien *pl* summer holidays
Sonder- special
Sonderangebot *n* special offer
sonn- und feiertags Sundays and public holidays
Sonnabend *m* Saturday
Sonne *f* sun
Sonnenaufgang *m* sunrise
sonnenbaden to sunbathe
Sonnenbrand *m* sunburn
Sonnenbräune *f* suntan
Sonnenbrille *f* sunglasses
Sonnencreme *f* sunblock
Sonnendach *nt* sunroof
Sonnenöl *nt* suntan oil
Sonnenschirm *m* sun umbrella ; sunshade
Sonnenstich *m* sunstroke
Sonnenuntergang *m* sunset
sonnig sunny
Sonntag *m* Sunday
Sonntagsdienst *m* Sunday duty (chemist, doctor, etc)
sorgen für to look after ; to take care of
Soße *f* dressing ; sauce
Souterrain *nt* basement
Souvenir *nt* souvenir
Spanien *nt* Spain
Spanier(in) *m/f* Spaniard

spanisch *adj* Spanish
Spannung *f* voltage
sparen to save (money)
Spargel *m* asparagus
Sparpreis *m* economy fare
Spaß *m* fun ; joke
spät late
Spaten *m* spade
Spätvorstellung *f* late show
Spaziergang *m* stroll ; walk
Speck *m* bacon
Speicherkarte *f* memory card
Speise *f* dish ; food
Speiseeis *nt* ice cream
Speisekarte *f* menu
Speisesaal *m* dining hall
Speisewagen *m* dining car
Spesen *pl* expenses
Spezialität *f* speciality
Spiegel *m* mirror
Spiegelei *nt* fried egg
Spiel *nt* game ; pack (of cards)
Spielbank *f* casino
spielen to gamble ; to play
Spielkarte *f* card (playing)
Spielplatz *m* playground
Spielzeug *nt* toy
Spielzeugladen *m* toy shop
Spielzimmer *nt* playroom
Spinat *m* spinach
Spirale *f* coil (IUD) ; spiral
Spirituosen *pl* spirits (alcohol)
Spitze *f* lace ; point (tip)
Splitter *m* splinter
Sportartikel *pl* sports equipment
Sportgeschäft *nt* sports shop
Sporttauchen *nt* scuba diving
Sprache *f* speech ; language
Sprachführer *m* phrase book
Spraydose *f* aerosol
sprechen to speak
    sprechen mit to talk to
Sprechstunde *f* surgery (hours of opening)
springen to jump

Spritze f injection ; hypodermic needle
sprudelnd fizzy
Sprudelwasser nt sparkling water
Sprungschanze f ski jump
Spucktüte f sick bag
Spülbecken nt sink (kitchen)
spülen to flush toilet ; to rinse
Spülkasten m cistern (of toilet)
Spülmittel nt washing-up liquid
Spur f lane (of motorway/main road)
Staatsangehörigkeit f nationality
Stachel m sting
Stadion nt stadium
Stadt f town ; city
Stadtführung f guided tour of the town
Stadtmitte f city centre
Stadtplan m map (of town)
Stadtzentrum nt town/city centre
Stahl m steel
Stand m stall ; taxi rank
ständig permanent(ly) ; continuous(ly)
Standlicht nt sidelight
stark strong
Starthilfekabel nt jump leads
Station f station ; stop ; hospital ward
statt instead of
stattfinden to take place
Statue f statue
Stau m traffic jam
Staub m dust
Staubsauger m vacuum cleaner
Staubtuch nt duster
stechen to bite (insect)
Stechmücke f mosquito ; gnat
Steckdose f socket (electrical)
Stecker m plug (electric)
Steckrübe f turnip
stehen to stand
stehlen to steal
steil steep
Stein m stone
Stelle f job ; place ; point (in space)

stellen to set (alarm) ; to put
stempeln to stamp (visa)
Steppdecke f quilt
sterben to die
Stereoanlage f stereo
Stern m star
Steuer f tax
Steuerung f controls
Steward (Stewardess) m/f steward/stewardess
Stich m bite (by insect) ; stitch (sewing) ; sting
Stiefel pl boots (long)
Stiefmutter f stepmother
Stiefvater m stepfather
Stil m style
still still (motionless)
stilles Wasser nt still water
Stimme f voice
stimmt so! keep the change!
Stirn f forehead
Stock m cane (walking stick) ; stick ; floor
Stockwerk nt storey
Stoff m cloth (fabric)
Stoppschild nt stop (sign)
Stöpsel m plug (in sink)
stören to disturb (interrupt)
    bitte nicht stören do not disturb
stornieren to cancel
Stornierung f cancellation
Störung f hold-up ; fault ; medical disorder
Stoßdämpfer m shock absorber
stoßen to knock ; to push
Stoßstange f bumper (car)
Stoßzeit f rush hour
Strafe f punishment ; fine
Strafzettel m parking ticket (fine)
Strand m beach
Strandkorb m wicker beach chair with a hood ; beach hut
Straße f road ; street
    Straße gesperrt road closed
Straßenarbeiten pl roadworks
Straßenbahn f tram

Straßenkarte f road map
Streichhölzer pl matches
Streifenkarte f multiple journey travelcard
Streik m strike (industrial)
streiten to quarrel
Stress m stress
stricken to knit
Strickjacke f cardigan
Stricknadel f knitting needle
Strohhalm m straw (for drinking)
Strom m current ; electricity
Stromanschluss m electric point
Strömung f current (water)
Stromzähler m electricity meter
Strümpfe pl stockings
Strumpfhose f tights
Stück nt bit ; piece ; cut of meat ; play (theatre)
Student(in) m/f student
Studentenermäßigung f student discount
Stufe f step (stair)
Stuhl m chair
stumpf blunt (knife, blade)
Stunde f hour ; lesson
Sturm m storm
Sturzhelm m crash helmet
suchen to look for
Suchmaschine f search engine
Süden m south
südlich southern
Summe f sum (total amount)
Sumpf m marsh
Super(benzin) nt four-star petrol
Supermarkt m supermarket
Suppe f soup
Surfbrett nt surfboard
surfen to surf
süß sweet
Süßigkeiten pl sweets
Süßstoff m sweetener ; saccharin
Süßwaren pl confectionery
Synagoge f synagogue
Szene f scene

T

Tabak m tobacco
Tabakwarenhandlung f tobacconist's
Tablett nt tray
Tablette(n) f tablet(s) ; pill(s)
Tachometer nt speedometer
Tafel f table ; board ; bar of chocolate
Tafelwein m table wine
Tag m day
    jeden Tag every day
Tageskarte f day ticket ; menu of the day
Tagespauschale f daily unlimited rate
Tagessuppe f soup of the day
täglich daily
Taille f waist
Tal nt valley
Tampons pl tampons
Tank m fuel/petrol tank
Tankanzeige f fuel gauge
Tankdeckel m petrol cap
Tanksäule f petrol pump
Tankstelle f petrol station
Tanne f fir
Tante f aunt
Tanz m dance
tanzen to dance
Tarif m rate ; tariff
Tasche f pocket ; bag
Taschenbuch nt paperback
Taschendieb m pickpocket
Taschenlampe f torch ; flashlight
Taschenmesser nt penknife
Taschenrechner m calculator
Taschentuch nt handkerchief
Tasse f cup
Taste f button ; key (on keyboard)
    Taste drücken push button
taub deaf
Taube f pigeon
tauchen to dive
Tauchen nt diving
Taucheranzug m wetsuit
Taucherbrille f goggles (swimming)

tauschen to exchange
tausend thousand
Taxi nt taxi ; cab
Taxifahrer(in) m/f taxi driver
Taxistand m taxi rank
Tee m tea
Teebeutel m tea bag
Teekanne f teapot
Teelöffel m teaspoon
Teig m pastry
Teil nt part
teilen to divide ; to share
Teilkaskoversicherung f third party,
  fire and theft insurance
Telefon nt telephone
Telefonauskunft f directory
  enquiries
Telefonbuch nt phone directory
telefonieren to telephone
Telefonkarte f phonecard
Telefonnummer f phone number
Telefonzelle f phonebox
Telegramm nt telegram
Teller m plate
Tempel m temple
Temperatur f temperature
Tennis nt tennis
Tennisplatz m tennis court
Tennisschläger m tennis racket
Teppich m rug
Teppichboden m fitted carpet
Termin m date ; deadline ;
  appointment
Terminal m terminal (airport)
Terminkalender m diary ; Filofax®
Terminplaner m personal organizer
Terrasse f patio ; terrace (of café)
Terrorist(in) m/f terrorist
Tesafilm® m Sellotape®
teuer dear (expensive)
Theater nt theatre
Theke f counter (in shop, bar, etc)
Thermometer nt thermometer
Thermosflasche f flask (thermos)
Thunfisch m tuna
Thüringen nt Thuringia

Thymian m thyme
tief deep ; low (in pitch)
Tiefkühltruhe f deep freeze ; freezer
Tier nt animal
Tierarzt (Tierärztin) m/f vet
Tinte f ink
Tintenfisch m octopus ; squid
Tisch m table
Tischdecke f tablecloth
Tischler(in) m/f carpenter
Tischtennis nt table tennis
Tischwein m table wine
Toastbrot nt sliced white bread
  for toasting
Tochter f daughter
Tochtergesellschaft f subsidiary
Toilette f toilet ; lavatory
Toilettenartikel pl toiletries
Toilettenbürste f toilet brush
Toilettenpapier nt toilet paper
Tollwut f rabies
Tomate f tomato
Tomatenpüree nt tomato purée
Tomatensaft m tomato juice
Tomatensoße f tomato sauce
Ton m sound ; tone ; clay
Tönung f hair dye
Töpferwaren pl pottery
Tor nt gate ; goal (sport)
Törtchen nt cake (small)
Torte f gâteau ; tart
tot dead
töten to kill
Tourist(in) m/f tourist
Touristeninformation f tourist
  information
Touristenkarte f tourist ticket
Touristenklasse f economy class
Touristenroute f tourist route
Touristticket nt tourist ticket
tragbar portable
tragen to carry ; to wear
Tragflügelboot nt hydrofoil
Trainingsschuhe pl trainers
trampen to hitchhike
Trauben pl grapes

traurig **sad**
Treffen nt **meeting**
treffen to **meet** (by chance)
Treppe f **stairs**
Tresor m **safe**
Tretboot nt **pedalo**
trinken to **drink**
Trinkgeld nt **tip** (for waiter, etc)
Trinkwasser nt **drinking water**
trocken **dry** ; **stale** (bread)
Trockenmilch f **powdered milk**
Trockenobst nt **dried fruit**
trocknen to **dry**
Truthahn m **turkey**
Tschechien nt **Czech Republic**
tschüs **cheerio** ; **bye**
T-shirt nt **T-shirt**
Tuch nt **cloth** ; **scarf** ; **towel** ; **shawl**
tun to **do** ; to **put**
　　das macht nichts **that doesn't
　　matter**
Tunfisch m **tuna**
Tunnel m **tunnel**
Tür f **door**
türkis **turquoise** (colour)
Turm m **tower**
Turnschuhe pl **gym shoes**
typisch **typical**

U
u.A.w.g. **RSVP**
U-Bahn f **metro** ; **underground**
übel **sick** (nauseous) ; **bad**
über **over** ; **above** ; **about** ; **via**
überall **everywhere**
überbuchen to **overbook**
Überfahrt f **crossing** (sea)
Überfall m **mugging**
überfällig **overdue**
überfüllt **crowded** (train, shop, etc)
übergeben to **hand over** ; to
　present (give)
　　sich übergeben to **vomit**
Übergewicht nt **excess baggage** ;
　overweight
überhitzen to **overheat**

überholen to **overtake**
Überholverbot nt **no overtaking**
Übernachtung mit Frühstück **bed
　and breakfast**
überprüfen to **check** (to examine)
Überschwemmung f **flash flood**
übersetzen to **translate**
Übersetzung f **translation**
überweisen to **transfer** (money)
Überzelt nt **fly sheet**
Überzieher m **overcoat**
übrig **left over** ; **extra** (spare)
Ufer nt **bank** (of river) ; **shore**
Uhr f **clock** ; **watch**
Uhrarmband nt **watch strap**
Uhrmacher m **watchmaker's**
um **around**
　　um 4 Uhr **at 4 o'clock**
umdrehen to **turn around**
umgeben von **surrounded by**
Umgehungsstraße f **ring road** ;
　bypass (road)
Umkleidekabine f **changing room**
　(at swimming pool, in shop)
Umleitung f **diversion**
Umschlag m **envelope**
umsonst **free** (costing nothing)
umsteigen to **change**
umstoßen to **knock over** (object)
Umweg m **detour**
Umwelt f **environment**
unbefugt **unauthorized**
　　Unbefugten Zutritt verboten **no
　　entry to unauthorized persons**
unbegrenzt **unlimited**
und **and**
Unfall m **accident**
Unfallstation nt **casualty department**
ungefähr **approximately**
ungefährlich **safe** (not dangerous)
ungerade **odd** (number)
ungewöhnlich **unusual**
Unglück nt **accident**
ungültig **invalid**
ungültig werden to **expire** (ticket,
　passport)

Universität f university
unmöglich impossible ; unsafe
uns us
unser(e) our
unsicher uncertain (fact)
unten downstairs ; below
  nach unten downward(s) ;
  downstairs
unter under(neath)
unter Wasser underwater
unterbrechen to interrupt
Unterbrecher m circuit breaker
Unterbrecherkontakte pl points
  (in car)
untere(r/s) lower ; bottom
Unterführung f subway ; underpass
  (for pedestrians)
Unterhemd nt vest
Unterhose f underpants
Unterkunft f accommodation
unterrichten to teach
Unterrichtsstunde f lesson
unterschreiben to sign
Unterschrift f signature
Untersuchung f test ; medical
  examination
Untertasse f saucer
Untertitel pl subtitles
Unterwäsche f underwear ; lingerie
unwohl unwell
Urin m urine
Urlaub m leave ; holiday
  auf Urlaub on holiday ; on leave
Urlaubsgebiet nt resort (holiday)
Ursprungsland nt country of origin
USA pl USA

V

Vagina f vagina
Vanille f vanilla
Vanilleeis nt vanilla ice cream
Vanillesoße f custard
Vase f vase
Vater m father
Vegetarier(in) m/f vegetarian
vegetarisch vegetarian

Veilchen nt violet (flower)
Ventil nt valve
Ventilator m fan (electric) ; ventilator
Verband m bandage
Verbandskasten m first aid kit
verbinden to connect (join)
Verbindung f connection (train, etc) ;
  service (bus, etc) ; line (phone)
verbleit leaded
verboten forbidden
Verbrechen nt crime
verbrennen to burn
Verbrennung f burn
verbringen to spend (time)
verderben to go bad (food) ; to spoil
verdienen to deserve ; to earn
verdorben bad (fruit, vegetables)
Verein m society (club)
vereinbaren to agree upon ; to
  arrange
Vereinbarung f agreement
Vereinigtes Königreich nt United
  Kingdom
Vereinigte Staaten (von Amerika) pl
  United States (of America)
Verfallsdatum nt expiry date ;
  eat-by date
verfault rotten (fruit, etc)
Vergangenheit f past
Vergaser m carburettor
vergeben to forgive
vergessen to forget
vergewaltigen to rape
Vergewaltigung f rape
Vergnügen nt enjoyment ; pleasure
  viel Vergnügen! have a good time!
Vergnügungspark m amusement
  park
vergoldet gold-plated
Vergrößerung f enlargement
verhaften to arrest
verheiratet married
verhindern to prevent
Verhütungsmittel nt contraceptive
Verkauf m sale
verkaufen to sell

Verkäufer(in) m/f **salesman/woman**
Verkehr m **traffic**
Verkehrspolizist(in) m/f **traffic warden**
Verkehrszeichen nt **road sign**
verkehrt **wrong**
verkehrt herum **upside down**
verlängern **extend** (stay) ; **renew** (visa)
Verlängerungskabel nt **extension cable**
Verleih m **rental company** ; **hire company**
verletzen **to injure**
verletzt **injured** (person)
Verletzung f **injury**
verlieren **to lose**
verlobt **engaged** (to be married)
Verlobte(r) m/f **fiancé(e)**
verloren **lost** (object)
vermeiden **to avoid**
vermieten **to rent** ; **to let** (room, house)
Vermieter(in) m/f **landlord/lady**
Vermietung f **hire**
vermisst **missing** (person)
Vermittlung f **telephone exchange** ; **operator**
verpassen **to miss** (plane, train, etc)
Verrenkung f **sprain**
verschieben **to postpone**
verschieden **different**
verschiedene **several** ; **different**
verschlucken **to swallow**
verschmutzt **polluted**
verschreiben **to prescribe**
verschwinden **to disappear**
verschwunden **missing**
versichern **to insure**
versichert sein **to be insured**
Versicherung f **insurance**
Versicherungsbescheinigung f **insurance certificate**
versilbert **silver-plated**
verspätet **delayed**
Verspätung f **delay**
versprechen **to promise**

Verstauchung f **sprain**
verstecken **to hide**
verstehen **to understand**
verstopft **blocked** (pipe) ; **blocked** (road) ; **constipated**
versuchen **to try**
Vertrag m **contract**
Vertreter(in) m/f **sales rep**
Verwandte(r) m/f **relative**
verwenden **to use**
verwirrt **confused**
Verzeihung! **sorry** ; **excuse me**
verzollen **to declare goods** (customs)
Video nt **video**
Videokamera f **video camera**
Videokassette f **video cassette/tape**
viel **much**
viele **many**
vielleicht **perhaps**
Viertel nt **quarter**
Viertelstunde f **quarter of an hour**
vierzehn Tage **fortnight**
Villa f **villa**
violett **purple**
Virus nt **virus**
Visitenkarte f **business card**
Visum nt **visa**
Vitamin nt **vitamin**
Vogel m **bird**
Volkslied nt **folk song**
Volkstanz m **folk dance**
voll **full**
Volleyball m **volleyball**
Vollkornbrot nt **dark rye bread; wholemeal bread**
Vollmilchschokolade f **milk chocolate**
Vollnarkose f **general anaesthetic**
Vollpension f **full board**
vollständig **whole**
voll tanken **to fill tank** (petrol)
von **from** ; **of**
vor **before** ; **in front of**
  vor 4 Jahren **4 years ago**
voraus **ahead**
  im Voraus **in advance**

vorbei **past**
vorbereiten **to prepare**
Vorbestellung f **reservation**
Vorder- **front**
Vorderradantrieb m **front-wheel drive**
Vorfahrt f **right of way** (on road)
  Vorfahrt beachten **give way**
vorgekocht **ready-cooked**
Vorhang m **curtain**
Vorhängeschloss nt **padlock**
Vorname m **first name**
vorne einsteigen **enter by front door**
Vorschrift f **regulation** (rule)
Vorsicht f **caution**
Vorspeise f **starter** (in meal) ; **hors d'œuvre**
Vorstellung f **performance**
Vor- und Zuname m **first name and surname**
Vorverkauf m **advance booking**
Vorwahl(nummer) f **dialling code**
vorziehen **to prefer**
Vulkan m **volcano**

W

Waage f **scales** (weighing)
wach **awake**
Wache f **security guard**
Wachsbehandlung f **waxing**
Waffe f **gun**
Wagen m **car** ; **carriage** (railway)
Wagenheber m **jack** (for car)
Wahl f **choice** ; **election**
wählen **to dial** (number) ; **to choose**
Wählton m **dialling tone**
während **while** ; **during**
Währung f **currency**
Wald m **wood** ; **forest**
Waldlehrpfad m **nature trail**
Wales nt **Wales**
Waliser(in) m/f **Welshman/woman**
walisisch **Welsh**
Walnuss(-nüsse) f **walnut(s)**
wandern **to hike**

Wanderschuhe pl **walking boots**
Wanderstock m **walking stick**
Wanderung f **hike**
Wanderweg m **trail for ramblers**
Wange f **cheek**
wann? **when?**
Waren pl **goods**
warm **warm**
Wärmflasche f **hot-water bottle**
Warmwasser nt **hot water**
Warnblinkanlage f **hazard warning lights**
Warndreieck nt **warning triangle**
Warnung f **warning**
Wartehalle f **lounge** (at airport)
warten (auf) **to wait** (for)
Wartesaal m **waiting room**
warum? **why?**
was? **what?**
waschbar **washable**
Waschbecken nt **washbasin**
Wäsche f **linen** ; **washing** (clothes)
Wäscheklammer f **clothes peg**
Wäscheleine f **clothes line**
waschen **to wash**
Waschen und Föhnen **wash and blow dry**
Wäscheraum m **laundry room**
Wäscherei f **laundry**
Wäschereiservice m **laundry service**
Wäschetrockner m **tumble dryer**
Waschmaschine f **washing machine**
Waschmittel nt **detergent**
Waschpulver nt **washing powder**
Waschsalon m **launderette**
Wasser nt **water**
wasserdicht **waterproof**
Wasserfall m **waterfall**
Wasserhahn m **tap**
Wassermelone f **water melon**
Wassermotorrad nt **jet ski**
Wasserski fahren **to water ski**
Wassertreter m **pedal boat/pedalo**
Watte f **cotton wool**
Wattebausch m **cotton bud**

Wechsel *m* change
Wechselgeld *nt* change *(small coins)*
Wechselkurs *m* exchange rate
wechseln to change *(money)* ; to give change
Wechselstube *f* bureau de change
Weckdienst *m* early morning call
Wecker *m* alarm clock
Weckruf *m* alarm call
weder ... noch neither ... nor
Weg *m* path ; way ; country lane
wegfahren to leave in vehicle
weggehen to leave on foot
Wegweiser *m* signpost
Wegwerfwindeln *pl* disposable nappies
weh tun to ache ; to hurt *(be painful)*
weiblich female ; feminine
weich soft
weich gekochtes Ei *nt* soft-boiled egg
Weihnachten *nt* Christmas
Weihnachtsgeschenk *nt* Christmas present
Weihnachtskarte *f* Christmas card
weil because
Wein *m* wine
Weinberg *m* vineyard
Weinbrand *m* brandy
weinen to cry *(weep)*
Weinhandlung *f* wine shop
Weinkarte *f* wine list
Weinkeller *m* wine cellar
Weinprobe *f* wine-tasting
Weinstube *f* wine bar
Weintrauben *pl* grapes
weiß white
Weißbrot *nt* white bread
Weißwein *m* white wine
weit far ; loose *(clothing)*
weiter farther ; further on
weitermachen to continue
weitsichtig long sighted
Weizen *m* wheat
welche(r/s) which ; what ; which one

Wellen *pl* waves *(on sea)*
Welt *f* world
Wende *f* U-turn *(in car)*
wenden to turn
wenig little
weniger less
wenn if ; when *(with present tense)*
wer? who?
Werbespot *m* advert *(on TV)*
werden to become
Werk *nt* plant *(factory)* ; work *(of art)*
Werkstatt *f* garage *(for repairs)*
Werktag *m* weekday
Werkzeug *nt* tool
Werkzeugkasten *m* toolkit
Wert *m* value
Wertbrief *m* registered letter
Wertsachen *pl* valuables
wertvoll valuable
wesentlich essential
Wespe *f* wasp
wessen? whose?
Weste *f* waistcoat
Westen *m* west
westlich western
Wetter *nt* weather
Wetterbericht *m* weather forecast
Wettervorhersage *f* weather forecast
Wettkampf *m* match *(sport)*
Whirlpool *m* jacuzzi
wichtig important
wie like ; how
  wie viel? how much?
  wie viele? how many?
wieder again
wiederaufladen to recharge *(battery)*
wiederholen to repeat
wiegen to weigh
Wien Vienna
Wiese *f* lawn ; meadow
Wild *nt* game *(hunting, meat)*
Wildleder *nt* suede
Wildschwein *nt* boar
willkommen welcome

Wimpern *pl* **eyelashes**
Wimperntusche *f* **mascara**
Wind *m* **wind**
Windeln *pl* **nappies ; diapers**
windig **windy**
Windmühle *f* **windmill**
Windpocken *pl* **chickenpox**
Windschutz *m* **windbreak** *(camping)*
Windschutzscheibe *f* **windscreen**
windstill **calm** *(weather)*
Winter *m* **winter**
Winterreifen *pl* **snow tyres**
wir **we**
wirksam **effective** *(remedy, etc)*
Wirt(in) *m(f)* **landlord (landlady)**
Wirtschaft *f* **pub ; inn ; economy**
wissen **to know** *(facts)*
Witwe(r) *f(m)* **widow(er)**
Witz *m* **joke**
wo? **where?**
Woche *f* **week**
Wochenende *nt* **weekend**
Wochentag *m* **weekday**
wöchentlich **weekly**
woher? **where from?**
wohin? **where to?**
Wohnadresse *f* **home address**
wohnen **to stay ; to live** *(reside)*
Wohnheim *nt* **hostel**
Wohnmobil *nt* **dormobile**
Wohnort *m* **home address**
Wohnung *f* **flat** *(apartment)*
Wohnwagen *m* **caravan**
Wohnzimmer *nt* **living room ;**
  lounge *(in house)*
wolkig **cloudy**
Woll- **woollen**
Wolldecke *f* **blanket**
Wolle *f* **wool**
wollen **to want** *(wish for)*
Wort *nt* **word**
  in Worten **in words** *(on cheques)*
Wörterbuch *nt* **dictionary**
Wunde *f* **wound** *(injury)*
Würfel *m* **dice**

Wurst *f* **sausage**
Würstchenbude *f* **hot-dog stand**
würzig **spicy**
Würzmischung *f* **seasoning**

Y

Yachthafen *m* **marina**

Z

zäh **tough** *(meat)*
Zahl *f* **number** *(figure)*
zahlen **to pay**
Zähler *m* **meter**
Zahn *m* **tooth**
Zahnarzt (Zahnärztin) *m/f* **dentist**
Zahnbürste *f* **toothbrush**
Zahncreme *f* **toothpaste**
Zähne *pl* **teeth**
Zahnpasta *f* **toothpaste**
Zahnschmerzen *pl* **toothache**
Zahnseide *f* **dental floss**
Zahnstocher *m* **toothpick**
Zange *f* **pliers**
Zäpfchen *nt* **suppository**
z.B. **e.g.**
Zebrastreifen *m* **zebra crossing**
Zehe *f* **toe**
Zeichentrickfilm *m* **cartoon**
Zeichnung *f* **drawing**
zeigen **to show**
Zeit *f* **time** *(of day)*
Zeitkarte *f* **season ticket**
Zeitschrift *f* **magazine**
Zeitung *f* **newspaper**
Zeitungskiosk *m* **newsstand**
Zelt *nt* **tent**
Zeltboden *m* **groundsheet**
zelten **to camp**
Zentimeter *m* **centimetre**
zentral **central**
Zentralheizung *f* **central heating**
Zentralverriegelung *f* **central locking**
  (car)
Zentrum *nt* **centre**
zerbrechlich **fragile ; breakable**

zerrissen **torn**
Ziege f **goat**
Ziegel m **brick**
ziehen **pull**
Ziel nt **destination ; goal ; target**
ziemlich **quite** *(rather)*
Zigarette(n) f **cigarette(s)**
Zigarettenpapier nt **cigarette papers**
Zigarre(n) f **cigar(s)**
Zimmer nt **room** *(in house, hotel)*
  Zimmer frei **vacancies**
Zimmermädchen nt **chambermaid**
Zimmernummer f **room number**
Zimmerservice m **room service**
Zirkus m **circus**
Zitrone f **lemon**
Zitronentee m **lemon tea**
Zoll m **customs/toll**
zollfrei **duty-free**
Zone f **zone**
Zoo m **zoo**
Zopf m **plait**
zornig **angry**
zu **to ; off ; too ; at**
  zu Hause **at home**
  zu mieten **for hire**
  zu verkaufen **for sale**
  zu viel **too much**
  zu viel berechnen **to overcharge**
zubereiten **to prepare**
Zucchini pl **courgettes**
Zucker m **sugar**
zuckerfrei **sugar-free**
Zuckerkrankheit f **diabetes**
zudrehen **to turn off** *(tap)*
Zug m **train**
Zuhause nt **home**
zuhören **to listen**
Zukunft f **future**

Zulassung f **log book** *(car)*
zum Beispiel f **for example**
Zuname m **surname**
Zündkerzen pl **spark plugs**
Zündschlüssel m **ignition key**
Zündung f **ignition**
Zunge f **tongue**
zurück **back**
zurückfahren **to go back** *(by car)*
zurückgeben **to give back**
zurückgehen **to go back** *(on foot)*
zurückkommen **to come back**
zurücklassen **to leave behind**
zusammen **together**
Zusammenstoß m **crash** *(collision)*
zusätzlich **extra ; additional**
zuschauen **to watch**
Zuschlag m **surcharge ; supplement**
zuschließen **to lock**
Zustellung f **delivery** *(of mail)*
Zutaten pl **ingredients**
Zutritt m **entry ; admission**
  Zutritt verboten **no entry**
zu viel **too much**
  zu viel berechnen **to overcharge**
zuzüglich **extra**
zwanglose Kleidung f **informal dress**
zwei **two**
Zweigstelle f **branch** *(office)*
zweimal **twice**
zweite(r/s) **second**
zweite Klasse f **second class**
Zwiebel f **bulb ; onion**
Zwillinge pl **twins**
zwischen **between**
Zwischenlandung f **stopover** *(plane)*
Zwischenstecker m **adaptor**
Zyste f **cyst**

GRAMMAR

Grammar

NOUNS

In German all nouns begin with a capital letter. The plural forms vary from noun to noun – there is no universal plural as in English (cat – cats, dog – dogs):

singular	plural
Mann	Männer
Frau	Frauen
Tisch	Tische

(In the dictionary, plural forms appear where they may be useful.)

German nouns are *masculine (m)*, *feminine (f)* or *neuter (nt)*, and this is shown by the words for **the** and **a(n)** used before them:

	masculine	feminine	neuter
the	der Mann	die Frau	das Licht
a, an	ein Mann	eine Frau	ein Licht

The plural for **the** for all forms is **die**:

die Männer	die Frauen	die Lichter

There is no plural for the **ein** form. The plural noun is used on its own.

From the phrases in this book you will see that the endings for the word for **the** vary according to what part the noun plays in the sentence:

If the noun is the subject of the sentence, i.e. carrying out the action, then it is in the *nominative* case (the one found in dictionaries), e.g. **der Mann steht auf (the man stands up)**. The subject **der Mann** comes before the verb.

If the noun is the direct object of the sentence, i.e. the action of the verb is being carried out on the noun, then the noun is in the *accusative* case, e.g. **ich sehe den Mann (I see the man)**. Note how the ending of **der** has changed to **den**. The same applies to **ein**, e.g. **ich sehe einen Mann (I see a man)**.

If you see in front of the English noun of, or after it, **'s**, or **s'**, then the noun is in the *genitive* case (i.e. it belongs to someone or something), e.g. **das Haus der Frau (the woman's house)**. Note how the ending of **die** (Frau) has changed to **der**. The same applies to **ein**, e.g. **das Haus einer Frau (a woman's house)**.

If you see **to the** or **to a** in front of the English noun, then the noun is in the *dative* case, e.g. **ich gebe es der Frau (I give it to the woman)**. Note how the ending of **die** (Frau) has changed to **der**. The same applies to **ein**, e.g. **ich gebe es einer Frau (I give it to a woman)**.

Several other words used before nouns have similar endings to **der** and **ein**. Those like **der** are:

dieser this ; **jener that** ; **jeder each** ; **welcher which**

Those like **ein** are:

mein my ; **dein your** (familiar sing.) ; **Ihr your** (polite sing. and plural) ; **sein his** ; **ihr her** ; **unser our** ; **euer your** (familiar plural); **ihr their**

Here are the cases for **der**:

	masculine	feminine	neuter	plural
Nominative	der Mann	die Frau	das Licht	die Frauen
Accusative	den Mann	die Frau	das Licht	die Frauen
Genitive	des Mannes	der Frau	des Lichtes	der Frauen
Dative	dem Mann	der Frau	dem Licht	den Frauen

Here are the cases for **ein**:

	masculine	feminine	neuter
Nominative	ein Mann	eine Frau	ein Licht
Accusative	einen Mann	eine Frau	ein Licht
Genitive	eines Mannes	einer Frau	eines Lichtes
Dative	einem Mann	einer Frau	einem Licht

The word **kein** (**no**, **not any**) also has the same endings as for **ein**, except that it can be used in the plural:

Nominative	keine Männer
Accusative	keine Männer
Genitive	keiner Männer
Dative	keinen Männern

ADJECTIVES

When adjectives are used before a noun, their endings vary like the words for **der** and **ein**, depending on the gender (*masculine, feminine* or *neuter*) and whether the noun is plural, and how the noun is used in the sentence (whether it is the subject, object, etc.). Here are examples using the adjective **klug – clever**

	masculine	feminine
Nominative	der kluge Mann	die kluge Frau
	ein kluger Mann	eine kluge Frau
Accusative	den klugen Mann	die kluge Frau
	einen klugen Mann	eine kluge Frau
Genitive	des klugen Mannes	der klugen Frau
	eines klugen Mannes	einer klugen Frau

189

Dative	dem klugen Mann	der klugen Frau
	einem klugen Mann	einer klugen Frau

	neuter	*plural*
Nominative	das kluge Kind	die klugen Männer
	ein kluges Kind	kluge Frauen
Accusative	das kluge Kind	die klugen Männer
	ein kluges Kind	kluge Frauen
Genitive	des klugen Kindes	der klugen Männer
	eines klugen Kindes	kluger Frauen
Dative	dem klugen Kind	den klugen Männern
	einem klugen Kind	klugen Frauen

When the adjective follows the verb, then there is no agreement:

der Mann ist klug
die Frau ist klug
das Kind ist klug

MY, YOUR, HIS, HER

These words all take the same endings as for **ein** and they agree with the noun they accompany, i.e. whether *masculine, feminine, neuter, plural* and according to the function of the noun (*nominative, accusative,* etc.):

mein Mann kommt my husband is coming (*nom.*)
ich liebe meinen Mann I love my husband (*acc.*)
das Auto meines Mannes my husband's car (*gen.*)
ich gebe es meinem Mann I give it to my husband (*dat.*)
meine Kinder kommen my children are coming (*nom. pl.*)
ich liebe meine Kinder I love my children (*acc. pl.*)
die Spielsachen meiner Kinder my children's toys (*gen. pl.*)
ich gebe es meinen Kindern I give it to my children (*dat. pl.*)

Other words which take these endings are:
dein your (*familiar sing.*) ; **sein his** ; **ihr her** ; **unser our** ;
euer your (*familiar plural*) ; **Ihr your** (*polite sing. and plural*) ; **ihr their**

PRONOUNS

subject		direct object	
I	ich	**me**	mich
you *(familiar sing.)*	du	**you** *(familiar sing.)*	dich
he/it	er	**him/it**	ihn
she/it	sie	**her/it**	sie
it *(neuter)*	es	**it** *(neuter)*	es
we	wir	**us**	uns
you *(familiar plural)*	ihr	**you** *(familiar plural)*	euch
you *(polite sing. & pl.)*	Sie	**you** *(polite sing. & pl.)*	Sie
they *(all genders)*	sie	**them** *(all genders)*	sie

Indirect object pronouns are:

to me mir ; **to you** *(familiar sing.)* dir ; **to him/it** ihm ; **to her/it** ihr ; **to it** *(neuter)* ihm ; **to us** uns ; **to you** *(familiar plural)* euch ; **to you** *(polite sing. and plural)* Ihnen ; **to them** ihnen

YOU

There are two ways of addressing people in German: the familiar form – du (when talking to just one person you know well), ihr (when talking to more than one person you know well), and the polite form – **Sie** (always written with a capital letter), which can be used for one or more people.

VERBS

There are two main types of verb in German – **weak** verbs (which are regular) and **strong** verbs (which are irregular).

	weak **SPIELEN** to play	*strong* **HELFEN** to help
ich	spiele	helfe
du	spielst	hilfst
er/sie/es	spielt	hilft
wir	spielen	helfen
ihr	spielt	helft
Sie	spielen	helfen
sie	spielen	helfen

Other examples of **strong** verbs are:

	SEIN	**HABEN**
	to be	**to have**
ich	bin	habe
du	bist	hast
er/sie/es	ist	hat
wir	sind	haben
ihr	seid	habt
Sie	sind	haben
sie	sind	haben

To make a verb negative, add nicht:

ich verstehe nicht	**I don't understand**
das funktioniert nicht	**it doesn't work**

PAST TENSE

Here are a number of useful past tenses:

ich war	**I was**
wir waren	**we were**
Sie waren	**you were** *(polite)*
ich hatte	**I had**
wir hatten	**we had**
Sie hatten	**you had** *(polite)*
ich/er/sie/es spielte	**I/he/she/it played**
Sie/wir/sie spielten	**you/we/they played**
ich/er/sie/es half	**I/he/she/it helped**
Sie/wir/sie halfen	**you/we/they helped**

Another past form corresponds to the English **have ...ed** and uses the verb haben **to have**:

ich habe gespielt	**I have played**
wir haben geholfen	**we have helped**

In German the present tense is very often used where we would use the future tense in English:

ich schicke ein Fax	**I will send a fax**
ich schreibe einen Brief	**I will write a letter**